TOMMY GEMMELL

ALL THE BEST

TOMMY GEMMELL

ALL THE BEST

Tommy Gemmell and Alex Gordon

CQN BOOKS

www.celticquicknews.co.uk

TOMMY GEMMELL

ALL THE BEST

Published by CQN Books, Quick News Media Limited, Glasgow
Copyright © Quick News Media, 2014.
All rights reserved.

First published in the United Kingdom in 2014 by CQN Books
ISBN 978-0-9928828-0-8

A catalogue for this book is available from the British Library

Design and typeset by Suzanne Waters (CQN Magazine)
Printed in the UK – Print and logistics by Tony Warrington

Edited by Alex Gordon.
Special thanks to the contributors to the Celtic blog
www.celticquicknews.co.uk for asking Tommy a wide
range of questions after he wrote a guest blog posting on
the the CQN site in February 2014.

CONTENTS

CONTENTS 7

DEDICATION 9

ACKNOWLEDGEMENTS.. 11

FOREWORD: BERTIE AULD.. 13

PROLOGUE..17

Chapter 1: THE TRUTH? THE WHOLE TRUTH?
AND NOTHING LIKE THE TRUTH! 23

Chapter 2: A SOUTH AMERICAN LIBERTY! 39

Chapter 3: THE BEST ACTOR IN THE UNTOUCHABLES 53

Chapter 4: SCOT (TAX) FREE 79

Chapter 5: THE RUDE, THE FAB AND THE BUBBLY...........................105

Chapter 6: BEST BAR NONE..127

Chapter 7: HOORAY HENRIK! LAUDABLE LUBO!...............................155

Chapter 8: NOTTINGHAM FOREST B.C. (BEFORE CLOUGH)...........171

Chapter 9: DARK BLUES' BOOZE BROTHERS 195

Chapter 10: VODKA VIC AND THE WILD ROVERS 229

Chapter 11: ALL THE BEST..241

Chapter 12: CELTIC QUICK NEWS: QUESTIONS AND ANSWERS 245

DEDICATION

This is for my wife Mary who has been a source of inspiration throughout. She is my rock and will always be my best friend.

Tommy Gemmell, Dunblane, March 2014

ACKNOWLEDGEMENTS

To all the people I have met on my football travels, from chairmen to managers to players to supporters to tea ladies, who have enriched my life on and off the field.

A special 'Thank you', obviously, to my fellow-Lisbon Lions who made a day in the Portuguese capital on 25 May 1967 so very, very special.

Thanks, also, to co-author Alex Gordon who came up with the idea for this book in the first place. We had a lot of fun putting it together. His lovely wife, Gerda, too. We spent a few months in some fine dining establishments getting my thoughts into print.

So, a pat on the back for Gary, David and staff at the Birds And Bees, in Stirling, Michael and Jamie who used to run the Old Bridge Inn at Bridge of Allan, Darren at the Inn at Torbrex and Big Joe and Jack at The Ferry on Glasgow's Broomielaw.

Also, thanks to the Celtic Quick News guys – David Faulds, Jim McGinley, Paul Brennan, Tony Warrington – a pleasure to work with such devoted Celtic supporters.

Brian and Tommy – you know who you are!

There are so many to mention, so if I have overlooked you, please forgive me.

It's been great fun getting to this stage – and I couldn't have done it with any of you!

FOREWORD

I used to disagree vehemently with people who insisted Tommy Gemmell was the best left-back in Europe.

'You don't know what you're talking about,' I would say. 'Tommy Gemmell is the best left-back in the WORLD!'

Forget the fact that he is a nice big bloke, disregard that we were the best of mates, on and off the park, and dismiss the notion I give out praise lightly.

When I stress my old mucker was the absolute top man on the planet in his chosen position I genuinely mean it. This is not part of an old pal's act. Tommy and I, thankfully, are still very friendly to this day and, yes, we do go for a wee walk down memory lane every now and again when we get together. It's sheer nostalgia and we've both got a lot to reminisce about. I can tell you this, too - we're better players now than we were back then!

So what was so special about Tommy Gemmell? Set aside his mesmerising ability for a moment and look at his other qualities. Tommy was a leader and would probably have captained any other team in the game. Billy McNeill, of course, was our skipper supreme, but Tommy wouldn't have felt uncomfortable wearing the armband. Jock Stein insisted on all his players taking responsibility and others embraced the task more willingly than others. Tommy Gemmell was always one of the first to step up to the plate.

You need a strong character to volunteer to take penalty-kicks. Tommy stood in when Big Jock was looking for a regular taker. I had taken a few and so, too, had the likes of Bobby Murdoch, John Hughes, Charlie Gallagher and Joe McBride. Some we scored and some we missed before Jock decided we needed a man to accept the obligation on a match-by-match basis whenever we were awarded a spot-kick. Tommy didn't hesitate. 'I'm your man, Boss,' he said and that's the way it remained until he left the club.

You need courage to take a penalty-kick. Think of the onus that was on Tommy when we were awarded a spot-kick against Racing Club in the World Club Championship Final in Buenos Aires. We were a goal ahead from the first leg after Caesar's wonderful headed goal at Hampden. Jimmy Johnstone was hauled down by their keeper in the second confrontation and no referee could have dismissed our claim. It was a stonewaller and their fans were going crazy. They were hissing, booing and jeering in their thousands as Tommy centred the ball and took a couple of paces back. A lot of players might have gone weak-kneed at the prospect. Not Tommy. He took off on his run, made perfect contact and sent the ball hurtling straight and true past their keeper. Trust me, that took a lot of bottle. But that's exactly what I mean when I say he was a leader. He never shirked from being accountable.

Of course, he also revolutionised the left-back position when he first came into the team in the early sixties. Until then, Celtic had fielded players in that position who rarely strayed into the other team's half of the field. Jim Kennedy, known to everyone as Pres, had played in that role for years before Tommy came on the scene. Absolutely no disrespect to Pres, but I don't recall him ever hurtling down the wing and sending over crosses. I have no memory of him peppering the opponents' goal with long-range shots. The Pres actually admitted he got a nosebleed when he crossed the halfway line. The record books show he scored two goals in his ten years at Celtic. Tommy could score two in ten minutes! He came in and simply became a pioneer in our team.

Assistant manager Sean Fallon abhorred defenders charging into enemy territory and I know he threatened to drop Tommy if he went against orders. Fortunately for Celtic, Tommy didn't listen. he had a natural urge to surge forward into attack and, by and large, ignored Sean. We can all be thankful for that. There might not be a European Cup triumph in Celtic's illustrious history if Tommy had curbed his instincts right at the start of his career. Perish the thought!

It's clear, though, that Tommy Gemmell was something special on the football pitch. He was a cavalier who brought colour to the game. You always knew you were going to get something extra from my chum. I have to admit he was an absolute dream to play alongside. You may believe I am praising him just for the sake of it. If that's the case, you don't know Bertie Auld. I was more likely to give someone a bit of a tongue-lashing when we were playing and I didn't think they were pulling their weight.

That never happened with Tommy. Not once. In fact, it might have been the other way around with Tommy giving me a rollicking on occasion! The marvelous thing about that great Celtic team was the fact that EVERYONE wanted the ball. I was always spoiled for choice when I was looking to pick out a team-mate. Bobby Murdoch would want it over in his right-sided midfield area, Wee Jinky would be screaming for it out on the right, Stevie Chalmers, Bobby Lennox, Willie Wallace and Joe McBride would be signaling for a through ball. There was John Hughes on the left, too, and then Tommy would race into the picture. 'Stick it here,' he would shout as he stormed forward, galloping into space on the left wing. He was a refreshing, flamboyant sight in that team and became synonymous in our carefree up-and-at 'em outlook.

A goalscoring full-back? It was totally unheard of. Through his own ambition, Tommy took on the exhausting role on behalf of Celtic. When Big Jock arrived he told my mate that it was okay to be adventurous, but his main job in the team was to defend. If Tommy was caught upfield and out of position when our opponents broke forward he knew he would have to carry the can. However, that never stopped him charging into attack and, once again, we can all be grateful for that.

Best in Europe? No way. Tommy Gemmell was the best in the world.

Bertie Auld

23 February 2014

PROLOGUE

Bestie to Beckenbauer. Di Stefano to Dalglish. Cruyff to Caesar. Eusebio to O'Neill. Law to Larsson. Mazzola to Moravcik. Big Jock Stein to Old Big 'Ead Cloughie.

Wee Jinky to the towering Facchetti. The magnificent Moore to the strolling Baxter. The gifted Masopust to the wonderful Rivera. The impeccable Banks to the timeless Simpson. The outstanding Charlton to the industrious Jansen. The mighty Muller to the excellent Van Himst. The deadly Seeler to the masterful Coluna. The legendary Yashin to the colourful Maier.

I've played against them, I've played with them and I've watched them from the stand. Believe it or not, I have also faced Stanley Matthews on a football field. Okay, he was about sixty years old at the time and performing in a Charity Game in Grangemouth, but I was still impressed by the English legend.

One big name that got away, I'm sad to say, was Pele and I only have myself to blame for that one. The Brazilian great was at Hampden in June 1966 as the-then world champions prepared for the defence of their trophy in England later that year. I was named in the Scotland international squad, but there was one snag - I had already booked my holidays in the Spanish resort of Lloret de Mar. The prospect of performing against the world's greatest player was appealing, but so, too, was the opportunity of putting my feet up on a sun-kissed beach and doing nothing more strenuous than lifting an exotic cocktail or two to my lips for a fortnight. I went on holiday. I was twenty-two years old at the time. Oh, the folly of youth.

However, as I have done my research while putting this book together, even I have to admit I have been mightily impressed with the parade of talent I have encountered during my wonderful footballing adventure. Sitting down to select the best players from such a glittering array of sheer, irresistible genius was thoroughly enjoyable, if a little exhausting and daunting. The glorious memories flooded back, the recollections bringing smiles and some scowls, the reminiscences of unforgettable experiences with extraordinary characters making me pinch myself that I was actually involved in all these magical moments.

It's been a fair old journey, believe me. I can look back at fabulous games for club and country. I can mix in memoirs of truly remarkable occasions at Wembley with the delights of Recreation Park. There was the splendour of Celtic Park compared to the ramshackle Cliftonhill, home of Albion Rovers, where I had two spells as a manager. The San Siro Stadium in Milan was a wee bit different from Station Park in Forfar. The electric atmosphere of a sell-out international or Cup Final at Hampden slightly dwarfs the flavour of a largely meaningless league encounter against Montrose at Links Park where two men and a dog might turn out.

I've been in the company of the exquisite and the x-certificate, the great and the grim, the awesome and the ordinary. Aye, it's been a fairly varied sortie through the beautiful game. One thing it hasn't been is dull. There was never any chance of that with a cast list containing Jinky, Bestie, Cloughie and Co.

It would have been difficult enough compiling one Dream Team, but somehow I managed to lumber myself with NINE! When my co-author Alex Gordon originally mooted the idea, I thought it would be a stroll in the park. I believed I was merely being asked to put together my Celtic Dream Team. Then Alex told me the working title was 'ALL THE BEST' and it was to be taken quite literally. That would mean exploring everything and everyone I have encountered over the many, many years in the sport, on and off the field.

It was a Herculean task from the outset. First up, of course, was the Lisbon Lions line-up, Celtic's 1967 European Cup-winning team. Those colleagues are the untouchables, as far as I am concerned. I couldn't possibly leave any of them on the sidelines in putting together my all-time special outfit. So, I've formed another unique side with other players with whom I have enjoyed some great times in the green and white hoops. I'm talking about the likes of Kenny Dalglish, Davie Hay, Lou Macari and Danny McGrain. Still with Celtic, I started to stitch together a team of players I have watched from the Parkhead stand. I have to admit that compilation just about overwhelmed me. It just wasn't possible to fit all of those charismatic, colourful individuals into one side. So, I've selected a Team A and also a Team B and, hopefully, you'll agree they are both attractive outfits who would play in the expected Celtic manner.

Then I looked at Scotland and my international team-mates. Suddenly, names such as Denis Law, Jim Baxter and Alan Gilzean came into sharp focus bringing vivid memories with them. So, that was another task in naming my country's kingpins. After that, there was the rest of the world to scrutinise. Georgie Best, Alfredo di Stefano and Eusebio were characters that sprung to mind. I put my manager's hat on again to pull that squad together. And, after playing for Nottingham Forest and Dundee and managing Albion Rovers, I thought the book had to really live up to its title, so I've named my top teams from those three outfits, too.

And, just to keep the pressure on, I looked at the team bosses who had been in the dug-outs during my playing career. I made up my mind to nominate my managerial mastermind. I wonder who won that particular honour?

Football, of course, is all about opinion and I've given an honest summing-up on all the excellent players I have encountered on my travels. No doubt there will be more than a few who won't agree with my selections and I think that's healthy. Inevitably, someone's particular favourites won't have got the nod, but, remember, I could only choose eleven for each team and that is a mere fraction of the galaxy of stars I have played with and against. I also realise I will probably get it in the neck from some of my former Celtic and Scotland colleagues who have been omitted. But it would be a boring old world if everyone agreed with each other. Debate is good and should be encouraged.

Well, I hope you have as much fun in reading this book as I had in writing it during my walk down football's memory lane. Enjoy yourselves while I enjoy my dreams. All the best

CHAPTER ONE
THE TRUTH?
THE WHOLE TRUTH?
AND NOTHING LIKE
THE TRUTH!

Jock Stein lied to me almost every day for over two years. He ditched me from the first team on the day of a Cup Final. He dropped me into the reserves without warning. He thought nothing of berating me in front of my colleagues. He booted me out of the club I adored. He deprived me of the opportunity of saying a last farewell to the supporters I rated – and still rate - the best in the world.

I loved that man.

I played under the guidance of eight managers during my career - five at club level and three on the international stage. Big Jock was undoubtedly the best of the bunch by a country mile. Jock and Jimmy McGrory were my bosses at Celtic, Matt Gillies and then Dave Mackay were in charge at Nottingham Forest during my thirteen-month stint in England and Davie White was my gaffer at Dundee. John Prentice gave my first Scotland cap in a Home International against England at Hampden in 1966. Malcolm MacDonald was the caretaker boss shortly afterwards who selected me twice and then Bobby Brown took over. Coincidentally, all eight are Scots. But there was on Englishman who would have been delighted to have become my manager if he had got his way.

Vic Buckingham was appointed manager of Barcelona in 1970 and was more than a little interested in yours truly after I had asked Big Jock for a transfer in October 1969. I was raging when I was dropped from the team to face St.Johnstone in the League Cup Final that year. I am not so precious that I ever believed a place in the top side was guaranteed. That would have been a dangerous assumption with a bloke like Big Jock around. But I was disgusted at the way I had been treated before that Final against the Saints. Even all these years later, I still can't quite get my head round why the Celtic manager acted the way he did. I'll never know.

I had played in all the League Cup-ties leading up to the Hampden game. I even scored the only goal of a must-win encounter against Rangers at Parkhead that helped us get through the qualifying section. I thought I was playing fairly well at the time and I had absolutely no reason to think I might be axed. The problem came three days earlier when I was playing for Scotland in a World Cup-tie against West Germany in Hamburg. We lost 3-2, despite Jimmy Johnstone giving us a third-minute lead. We were drawing 2-2 with only nine minutes to go and we were still in with a shout of reaching the World Cup Finals in Mexico the following summer. Then Reinhard Libuda netted to put our opponents ahead.

It had been a frustrating night, but we still believed there was a third goal in us. With one minute remaining on the clock, I managed to get through into one of my favourite shooting positions just outside the penalty box. I had scored a few screamers from that range and angle and I had Sepp Maier's goal in my sights. I had picked up momentum as I charged through and I pulled back my right boot in preparation of giving that ball a mighty whack. The next thing I recall is hobbling on one leg. Helmut Haller, an ordinary player in a very good team, had clipped my heels from behind. I was furious and my mood didn't change when the referee, an Austrian by the name of Alfred Droz, didn't even give us a foul. He was only yards from the incident and couldn't have missed Haller's sneaky trip on me. I couldn't believe it when he waved play on.

I'm not proud of what I did next. I turned round immediately and saw Haller smirking. He had got away with a blatant foul and he was well pleased with himself. His expression changed, though, when he saw me going straight for him. I booted him up the backside and, if I hadn't been pulled away by a posse of my team-mates, God only knows what a state he would have been in by the time I had finished with him. It was wrong, of course. So very wrong. My patience had snapped and all I could see was red. The referee didn't miss that one. To be fair, he couldn't. No-one in the 72,000 crowd at the Volkspark Stadion that fateful evening could have overlooked that incident. Off I went and, sixty seconds later, the game ended with the West Germans holding on for an ill-deserved victory.

I like to think of myself as a reasonable bloke, but I found it difficult to control my emotions for a helluva long time afterwards. Manager Bobby Brown and my colleagues consoled me and told me they would have done the exact same thing in an identical situation. I appreciated their support, but that was as angry as I can ever remember being during and after a football game. The newspaper reports absolved me of blame, too, because everyone had witnessed Haller's foul on me. Everyone, that is, except the referee from neighbouring Austria. Why on earth FIFA appointed a German-speaking match official from just across the border to take charge of an international involving West Germany beggars belief. Would they have put in an Englishman to officiate in an important Scotland match? Highly unlikely, I would have thought.

I was still simmering when Scotland flew home. Jock Stein was with the official SFA party on that flight and he didn't say a word to me. And that was the same situation when we prepared at our Troon HQ for the League Cup Final against St.Johnstone. I had absolutely no inkling that I wouldn't be playing. There wasn't the merest suggestion that I would be left out. We travelled on the coach to Hampden and I was looking forward to the game. The Saints had a wee nippy outside-right by the name of Kenny Aird and we had had some memorable jousts in the past. I was prepared for him. What I wasn't prepared for was the action of my manager just before kick-off. I often mingled with relatives, friends and fans at the front door at the national stadium, passing out tickets and the like. I then joined my team-mates in the dressing room. I was just going through the door when Jim Kennedy, a former player who did some backroom work for the club, stopped me and handed me two complimentary tickets. 'Who are these for?' I asked. Jim actually looked embarrassed. 'They're for you, Tommy,' he answered. It took awhile for the penny to drop. I looked over to the No.3 peg and I saw Davie Hay getting prepared in the left-back position. That was the first time I realised I would not be playing that afternoon. Big Jock hadn't even hinted that I would be dumped. I was well and truly humiliated.

My head was in a whirl, but I still had the presence of mind to go over to Davie, shake his hand and wish him all the best. I wasn't going to create a fuss so close to kick-off. I went up to take my seat in the stand, passing Celtic fans I knew and, to a man, they asked me if I was injured. I told them the truth. 'I've been dropped,' I said. Their jaws hit the floor at my reply. I watched the game, Celtic won 1-0 with a second minute goal from my wee mate Bertie Auld and I was heading home before the trophy presentation. Davie Hay played very well, I'm happy to say.

The following day I demanded to talk to Big Jock. I knew he would be at Parkhead on the Sunday morning because he normally had a press conference with the newspaper guys twenty-four hours after a game. The manager didn't want to speak to me. I continually asked, 'Why was I dropped?' He answered, 'I'm not discussing it over the phone.' 'Right, then, I'll be there in half-an-hour and you can tell me then.' I lived in Kirkintilloch at the time and I got into my car and raced through to Celtic Park. Naturally, I was still upset and couldn't quite work out why my manager would treat me in such a shoddy manner. I burst through the front doors just as the pressmen were coming out. Amazingly, no-one thought to ask me what I was doing at Parkhead on a Sunday. I met Jock in his office and asked for the umpteenth time that day, 'Why was I dropped?' 'I don't have to give you reasons,' replied the manager with whom I thought I had some sort of bond although he rarely let anyone in. He never did explain himself which I thought was the least I could expect. Had the Celtic directors stepped in to express their displeasure over a Celtic player being sent off while playing for his country? They might have made some noises to that effect, but Big Jock never let them dictate team matters to him. It was his decision, I was sure of that.

When I realised we were going round in circles and I wasn't going to get any kind of answer, I said, 'You better put me on the transfer list, then.' Jock stared at me. He actually looked a little surprised because he knew only too well what playing for Celtic in front of those wonderful supporters meant to me. 'Okay,' he said and I turned on my heel, walked out of Celtic Park, got into my car and drove home. 'What have I done?' I asked myself over and over on the journey back. But I could be as stubborn and obstinate as Big Jock and I was fuming at my treatment. Frankly, I still don't think it was fair.

Absolutely no disrespect to Davie Hay, but does anyone think Big Jock would have left me out if we had been playing Rangers? I don't think so. In fact, neither does Davie Hay. Thankfully, we're friends to this day, but we rarely discuss that afternoon at Hampden. I've said to him on more than a few occasions, 'Ach, Davie, I had enough medals, anyway. I wasn't going to miss another one!' In later years I could make a joke about the matter, but, believe me, I was deadly serious when I told Big Jock I wanted out of the club that were always in my heart. Still are, as a matter of fact.

And that's when my manager took to telling me porkies on a regular basis. Secretly, I had been informed Barcelona wanted me. Vic Buckingham had been put in charge of the Spanish giants and told to restore them to their former glories. He wanted to piece together an attractive, attacking unit and he wanted Tommy Gemmell to be part of the revolution. A newspaper reporter got in touch with me to see if I would be interested. I told him I would. The notion of playing in Spain hadn't been one that I had ever given any thought to before, but it had a certain appeal. So, I waited for the next instalment. I was informed Barcelona had got in touch with Celtic about the possibility of a deal. The position between clubs and players back then was heavily tilted in favour of the club. They held your registration and you were their property. If they didn't want you to leave, there was nothing you could do. It's a bit different today, of course, with the Bosman Ruling and players now have total say in their futures. They can leave at the end of their contracts and the clubs simply have to accept it.

I had been tapped by Barcelona. They had made an illegal approach through a third party and I would have been in serious trouble if Big Jock had ever discovered the truth. So, I had to act dumb. I would knock on Big Jock's door, look in and ask, 'Anyone interested in me, boss?' He rarely even looked in my direction. He would sit at his desk and wave his big left paw at me and say, 'Naw, I'll keep you informed.' And that was that. A couple of days later, I would go through the same routine. Again, it was 'Naw, I'll keep you informed.'

At the same time, I'm being told by the pressman that Buckingham has made contact and is asking for a price. Obviously, the Barcelona manager couldn't tell Jock he had already been in touch with me. It was a wee bit frustrating. Eventually, Buckingham couldn't wait any longer and looked elsewhere for a new left-back. Then I was told Spurs and Leicester City, both in the top division, were interested. 'Any bids, boss?' 'Naw, I'll keep you informed.' I was on that bloody transfer list for just over two years and, according to my manager, no-one was interested. I was a European Cup winner, a regular international and, according to some, even Big Jock, was the finest left-back in the world. But still I wasn't of any interest to any other club on the planet.

I could never be churlish enough to dismiss the true merits of Jock Stein as a manager. I thought he was brilliant and years ahead of his time. It's all on record what he achieved at Celtic. When he arrived in March 1965 he literally changed everything at the club. He looked at things in the most minute detail. Before he took over, the players used to assemble in the snooker room before a match. We would have a game or two, but Jock noticed that too many players were wondering around with their hands in their pockets doing nothing while waiting for their chance to get on the table. Out went snooker and in came table tennis. The manager reckoned that would keep more of the players active and he believed table tennis would actually sharpen our reflexes. A small point, perhaps, but it underlined Big Jock's thought process. By the way, our manager was the unofficial table tennis champion of the world. He hated to lose at anything and used to play a game or two with us. God help you if you ever beat him.

Big Jock looked at the grubby old training gear we used to wear. We would be out pounding round the track at Parkhead in the sunshine of July wearing the sort of big heavy woollen jerseys you would expect a fisherman to wear out on the high seas. I think the training stuff used to get washed once a week - if it was ever washed, at all! If you weren't quick, you would be saddled with some smelly gear that had seen better days. Within a week or so of Jock being around, we were all provided with brand new top-quality stuff. Lightweight T-shirts, fresh shorts and socks and training shoes that weren't falling apart. The gear was laundered on a daily basis, pressed and laid out in the dressing room. Beforehand, it had all been left in a heap in the middle of the room and it was a free-for-all among the players to try to get something half-decent to wear.

Jock didn't like his players wearing tracksuit bottoms, no matter the weather. It could be a freezing cold January morning at bleak Barrowfield and Jock would insist his players wore shorts. Some days your nether regions felt as though they were encased in ice, but Big Jock never wavered. I asked him once why we had to wear shorts when he, in fact, was allowed to wear tracksuit trousers. 'It's to make sure you lot keep on the move in training,' he answered logically. 'I don't want you all standing about. If you want to keep warm, you'll have to keep on the go.'

Jock was always a stickler for detail. He never actually told you to get your hair cut if you had allowed it to grow a wee bit. But he liked his players to look like professional sportsmen and that meant well-clipped locks. George Best would never have earned the tag 'The Fifth Beatle' if Jock had been his manager! He wasn't a big fan of facial hair, either. At one stage, I decided to grow a moustache as I was curious just to see what it would look like. 'What's that thing under your nose?' he would ask. 'What are you doing with that on your face?' I have to say

29

my moustache was fairly intriguing because it was growing in with what seemed all the colours of the rainbow. I started to tire of trimming it, but, as a little bit of devilment, I kept it for longer than I really wanted just to see Jock's reaction. 'That thing still there?' he would enquire. Eventually, the offending strip of hair was shaved off and I was greeted with, 'That's better. You never suited that bloody thing.' Look at all the Celtic players who were around when Big Jock was in charge and you won't see too many moustaches or beards. There wasn't a law against them, but he let you know he didn't like them. Danny McGrain must have got special dispensation to grow his trademark beard that earned him the Biblical nickname of Barabus.

Jock, as we all know, was a gambling man. Our trainer Neilly Mochan used to telephone a bookie in Glasgow and put on some bets for himself, the backroom staff and the manager. 'That's a £1 each way from me on such-and-such a horse,' Neilly would say. 'There's £1 each way from someone else.' And then would come, 'There's £20 from Jock.' He was a big punter, but I never knew if he was a winner or a loser. His good friend was Tony Queen. Surprise, surprise he was a bookmaker. In fact, he was in Jock's Mercedes, along with their wives, when they were returning from a summer holiday in Menorca in 1975 that was involved in a collision near Lockerbie. It was a head-on smash with a car driving in the wrong direction on the motorway. I was a player with Dundee at the time when I was told the news. I may have had my run-ins with Big Jock, but, in moments like that, you realise how close you have come to losing a special friend. Thankfully, he was out of hospital after a week or so and made a full recovery, but it couldn't have been mere coincidence that Celtic endured their worst season in eleven years while he was ordered by the doctors to take complete rest and stay away from the dug-out throughout a dreadful campaign.

I'm often asked if the manager had a sense of humour. He was no Billy Connolly, that's for sure, but he did have his moments. He liked to wind up players. He would look at us in training and target a specific individual. 'Aren't you happy that you've got so many good players around you during a match? They'll make sure you get a win bonus.

You are so lucky.' And the individual would then work even harder to prove to the boss he was in that first team on merit. He tried it on with everyone, me included. Celtic had a midweek match against Aberdeen at Pittodrie immediately after the 1969 League Cup Final. I wasn't even on the substitutes' bench as we won 3-2. I was left out again as the team travelled to Somerset Park to take on Ayr United on the Saturday. I was picked to play for the reserves against our Ayr counterparts at Parkhead. I scored an absolute belter that day. You'll have to take my word for it, but it was as perfect a strike as I have ever delivered. I connected from about thirty yards and the ball zoomed high into the old postage stamp corner. That game was on 1 November and I was well aware that Celtic had a forthcoming European Cup-tie against Benfica at Parkhead only eleven days later.

Jock knew I was a big game player. The bigger the occasion, the more I seemed to rise to the task. That left my manager with a problem. He couldn't just pitch me in against the Portuguese champions, depending on me to come up with all the answers on a crucial occasion. That wouldn't look too clever. Again, he could leave me out for the games he expected us to win, but a meeting with Eusebio and Co was a bit different. I got the nod to play in a league encounter against Hearts on the Saturday before the midweek European match. That denied the headline writers the opportunity to come up with 'GEMMELL BACK AGAINST BENFICA'. Big Jock wouldn't have liked that. So, quietly and without any drama, I played against Hearts and then against Benfica. Apart from three games, I played in every other league match that season and I was an ever-present in every European Cup and Scottish Cup-tie.

Big Jock was a great psychologist. I played against Benfica that night and you might say I was right up for the challenge. It was a packed night at Parkhead and I was back in the spotlight. I scored in the second minute with a long-range drive that almost took the net away. I ran to The Jungle to receive their rapturous applause and then, as our stunned opponents prepared to kick off, I sneaked a wee look over at Big Jock in the Celtic dug-out. I had proved my point and I am sure I detected a smile on his lips. He probably expected me to come up with such an answer. Points even, I think.

There is no doubt Jock had an aura about him. He possessed a certain presence and you were always aware when he was around. He was the manager and you were a player. We weren't allowed to forget that fact. Wee Jinky used to drive him round the bend sometimes with his antics, but I also thought the manager had a genuine soft spot for the player. I recall a story back in 1972 when Tommy Docherty was the Scotland team boss. Jinky was never the type to worry about a curfew. Deadlines were for the other players. The Doc caught him coming back to the Queen's Hotel in Largs one evening well past the designated time. 'What on earth are you playing at? You can't do that. I'm your manager,' roared The Doc. Jinky replied, 'Naw yer no' - Jock Stein's ma manager!' Even The Doc was rendered speechless.

Jock, of course, was a strict teetotaller. He couldn't abide alcohol. He detested the demon drink. The nearest I ever saw him come to touching a drop was when Billy McNeill brought in a couple of bottles of champagne to celebrate the birth of his twin daughters, Carol and Libby. 'Come on, boss, you must wet the babies' heads,' said Big Billy, coaxing the manager. Jock thought about it and then relented. 'Give us a glass, then,' he said. We watched in surprise. Was he actually going to take a swill of bubbly? He raised the glass to his lips, let it touch them and then put the glass down. 'Good luck to the weans,' was all he said as he took off before we could persuade him to drain the glass.

Like I say, Jock was light years ahead of any other manager with whom I was involved. It was Jimmy McGrory who signed me, of course, four years before Jock returned to Celtic. Jimmy was a lovely bloke, but he wasn't cut out to be a manager. Actually, he was too nice for the job. Jock made up for him!

In football parlance, I was over the moon when John Prentice told me I would be playing for Scotland against England at Hampden on 2 April 1966. Honestly, representing my country was one of the greatest achievements in my career. Like any other football-loving kid, I dreamed of turning out for my nation. In my perfect world, I would play my club football for Motherwell and turn out for Scotland in vital international games. Didn't quite work out that way. Thank God!

I was just getting used to how Big Jock handled things at club level when I took a step back into the tactics twilight zone on the international front. John Prentice, smashing lad though he was, simply wasn't in Jock's class when it came to know-how and preparation. Whereas Jock would go into detail, spell out exactly what he expected from you and how you had to perform within the team's structure, Prentice wasn't on the same wavelength. He selected the best players and, basically, we were allowed to play it largely off the cuff.

I sat in the dressing room before that game against England and I had my Celtic team-mates Bobby Murdoch and Jimmy Johnstone for company. There was also the incomparable Denis Law, a player who always excited me. Willie Wallace was with Hearts at the time, but he would join up with us later that year. It was my first game alongside that strolling minstrel Jim Baxter who had made life hell for a young Tommy Gemmell and Co before his move from Rangers to Sunderland. The Ibrox trio of John Greig, Ronnie McKinnon and Willie Johnston were also in the line-up and it was great to meet up with Billy Bremner, who would later become a wonderful personal friend. He played for Leeds United, of course, but all he ever seemed to want to talk about was Celtic. I got the impression this chirpy wee lad from Stirling would have happily walked over broken glass to get to Parkhead. Kilmarnock goalkeeper Bobby Ferguson completed the eleven.

My breath was taken away at the formalities before the game. Tartan seemed to be in evidence everywhere, the Lion Rampant flags were flying and the place was packed out with precisely 123,052 fans inside Hampden for the occasion. Could it get any better than this? I asked myself. Well, yes, as a matter of fact it could. We were two goals down after just over half-an-hour with Geoff Hurst and Roger Hunt sticking two past Ferguson, who looked a nervous wreck throughout, I thought. Denis Law netted with a trademark whiplash header from a Willie Johnston left-wing corner-kick just before the interval to put us back into the contest. What words of wisdom could we expect from the manager at half-time? Very little, really, is the quick answer. Basically we were told to keep playing the way we had and maybe the jigsaw would come together. Sadly, it doesn't work like that in football. We conceded a third goal two minutes after the turnaround - Hurst on target again - but Jinky threw us a lifeline just before the hour mark. Could we get a draw? Bobby Charlton hit a long-range effort at our goal in the 73rd minute and, sadly, our keeper stood rooted to the spot with inertia setting in once again. Jinky scored another, but it was too late to save us from a 4-3 defeat. I remember Nobby Stiles clearing a Willie Wallace effort off their line right at the death.

Astoundingly, John Prentice didn't look too downbeat at the end. 'We were unlucky, lads,' he told us, adding fairly needlessly, 'Another goal and we would have got a draw.' So, that's how football worked? I was happy to get back to club football and Big Jock. It was still a momentous occasion, though. Prentice didn't last too long before he was sacked. The SFA were furious to find he had been interviewed for a job in Canada without their knowledge. The blazers at Park Gardens were mortified. Out went Prentice and in came Malcolm MacDonald in a caretaker capacity until a full-time manager could be appointed. MacDonald, who played for Celtic in the forties and also managed Kilmarnock, was a quiet individual and, I'm afraid, no genius on the tactics board, either. He selected me twice - a 1-1 draw in Wales and a 2-1 win over Northern Ireland in Glasgow - and then Bobby Brown took over.

Brown was another genuine, affable fellow. He had played in goal for Rangers in the late forties and fifties and no-one ever saw him with a blond hair out of place. We were told he used to keep a comb in his bunnet in his goal and, when the action was up at the other end, he would tend to his locks. He was extremely dapper and when he led us out at Wembley on the Saturday afternoon of 15 April 1967 he was the image of sartorial elegance. He could have come straight out of a Saville Row tailor's front window. It was his first game in charge of his country and he couldn't have wished for a better debut. We won 3-2 and it was just one of those games where everything clicked into place.

Certainly, it wasn't down to any ground-breaking planning from our new team boss.

'You know who you are playing today,' he said before the game as if any one of us had overlooked the fact we were taking on the world champions at Wembley. 'Go out there and do your best.' That was about it. He wished us all good luck individually and then we went out and demolished our old foes. Tactics? There weren't any. Afterwards, a beaming Brown addressed his celebrating players and said, 'Tonight, gentlemen, London belongs to you. Enjoy yourselves.' And we did. I'll tell you more about that in another chapter.

I played my eighteenth and final game for my country in a 3-0 defeat against a Paul van Himst-inspired Belgium in Liege in 1971. I can think of better ways of pulling down the final curtain on an international career. Sadly, Bobby Brown lasted only another six matches before he, too, was shown the exit door and Tommy Docherty took over. It would have been interesting to have played for The Doc as manager, but the opportunity never materialised. To be fair to The Doc, he wanted to introduce youth and guys such as Partick Thistle's Alex Forsyth and John Hansen, brother of Liverpool's Alan, Hibs' Alex Cropley and John Brownlie, Aberdeen's Martin Buchan, Manchester City's Willie Donachie and a fresh-faced youngster called Kenny Dalglish were all introduced in an exciting period on the international scene. When I joined Nottingham Forest in December 1971 it appeared to be a case of out of sight and out of mind. It was Matt Gillies who signed me, of course, for the Midlands outfit and he was another who didn't dwell too much on tactics. He put a side together and, once again, it was a case of 'get out there and get on with it'.

Dave Mackay took over from Matt after we were relegated and I hardly got to meet the former Scottish international before I was on my way back to Scotland with Dundee. Mackay didn't impress me much, to be honest. Davie White, at Dens Park, was a breath of fresh air. He had some innovative ideas and was extremely ambitious. I think he was still hurt at how he had been treated by Rangers and had a point to prove. I have to admit I was surprised when he got the Ibrox job in the first place after Scot Symon was sacked. He was still in his thirties and was right up against Jock Stein. Originally, it could have been viewed as the chicken trying to outwit the fox. Trying to put one over on our manager must have been as easy a task as juggling bowling balls in the dark. He did change things around at Rangers and wasn't afraid to break the Scottish transfer record in paying out £100,000 for striker Colin Stein from Hibs. At that time, the most Jock Stein had spent was £30,000 on my wee pal Willie Wallace.

Davie White took Celtic all the way to the wire in the championship in his first season in charge. Amazingly, Rangers only lost one league game all season, the last match of the campaign against Aberdeen at Ibrox. They went down 3-2 that day and that virtually wrapped up the title for Celtic on goal average, as it was then. Just to make sure, we beat Dunfermline 2-1 at their place to take the flag by two points. However, it must be said that Davie White, after only a couple of years' worth of experience at Clyde and not even a full season at Rangers, had proved himself a worthy opponent. If he had a problem at Dundee, it was in his team talks that seemed to ramble on a bit. Players will start to lose interest if a manager spends too much time going over and over every little detail. On a personal level, I liked Davie. I had met him a few times with my wee buddy Willie Henderson and when I heard he was interested in taking me to Dundee I didn't hesitate. You can't rewrite history, of course, but if Davie White had been manager of Rangers in any other era outwith Jock Stein he might have been revered alongside someone such as Walter Smith.

Big Jock, though, was a major obstacle to anyone in football management back then. Davie White was just one of the many more than capable team bosses who hit a brick wall up against Jock. There was Eddie Turnbull at Aberdeen and then Hibs, Willie Cunningham and George Farm at Dunfermline, Bob Shankly at Hibs and a few others who just couldn't fathom out the complexities or the game plans of our gaffer.

Jock Stein may have lied to me almost every day for over two years, ditched me from the team on the day of a Cup Final, dropped me into the reserves without warning, berated me in front of my team-mates, booted me out of Celtic and deprived me of the opportunity of saying farewell to the fans I rated the best in the world.

But I still loved that man.

CHAPTER TWO
A SOUTH AMERICAN LIBERTY!

Tommy Gemmell wrote his first book, The Big Shot, when he was at the height of his career as a professional footballer. The Big Shot was a best seller when it was first published in 1968. In The Big Shot, Tommy told for the first time his side of the story regarding the notorious incidents that occurred in Montevideo in a World Club play-off match against Racing Club, of Argentina in 1967. Tommy's account in the 1968 book is remarkable when looking back in 2014 at these matches. Much has been written about these games in later years, but Tommy's account, written so close to the matches, gives a real insight into what actually happened and what drove Tommy to make that most famous of well-aimed kicks to the tender regions of the Racing No.11 Norberto Raffo, who, apparently, squealed like a pig! Here is how Tommy described these matches with Racing Club in The Big Shot...

A South American Liberty!

Ever since 1960 the European champions have met the top team in South America for a trophy called the Inter – Continental Cup. That name is hardly ever used, however, as everyone accepts that this home and away fixture is for the World Championship – the supreme status symbol in club football. So, I imagine there are lots of youngsters in many countries who dream of playing in these very special show games.

Frankly, my advice to them all is...FORGET IT! Aim as high as you like in football, but don't worry if you never get to play for that World title because then your dream might just become a nightmare – and as a Celtic player I can speak from bitter experience. We were the first British club ever to play for the Inter-Continental Cup and, naturally, it was a terrific honour. It was also a great feeling to be going forward as Europe's champions, knowing that only one team stood between you and the World title.

In 1967, we thought we could win that title. We were playing good football and we were a better side than the South Americans. But that was before we knew very much about our opponents, Racing Club of Argentina. Later, we were to discover that their plans for winning the World Crown had very little to do with football.

These Argentines were like no players I had ever encountered before. Indeed, I think it is fair to say that they were the dirtiest, most ruthless and despicable bunch of soccer hatchet-men ever gathered together under the one set of jerseys. In all grades of football you'll find the tough guy and the 'fly' man. But Racing Club were in a class of their own.

They were the masters at heel-clicking and catching you with their elbow when the ball was well away and they had long since perfected every other dirty trick known in football, including a fair amount of spitting. I'm not saying they took us by surprise. The Boss, Jock Stein, had compiled a pretty thick dossier on them before they reached Scotland and he warned us that in the first leg at Hampden they would be a certain amount of trouble, as the best way to slow any game down is to commit as many fouls as possible. We were just as determined not to let them knock us out of our stride.

The Hampden tie worked out as anticipated. They played a purely destructive game and we refused to be upset. Self-discipline was easy for us on that October evening because as far as behaviour was concerned this game was no different from any other. Every player at Parkhead knows he will get no sympathy if he is guilty of field offences.

In fact, although it was well into the second-half before Billy McNeill headed the winner I think we all gained confidence from this match because Racing did not appear to have much to offer in the finer points of football, although they gave us one or two hints that they knew a thing or two about unarmed combat.

It was not until the second leg in Buenos Aires, however, that we fully realised why Racing are known as the 'dirtiest team in South America'. The astonishing thing is that their coach, Jose Pizzuti, is a most pleasant wee man off duty and was a really skilful player in his day. You would think he would seek the same kind of reputation for his team. Instead, when he went for that coaching certificate, he must have studied under SMERSH!

Ten days after the Hampden game, we were flying in over the skyscrapers of Buenos Aires to prepare for the second leg. At that time we were an optimistic outfit because we sensed that the Boss believed we were capable of getting the draw, which would be enough to give us the World title. We moved out immediately to the luxurious Hindu Club and on that first Sunday we got off to a light-hearted start.

As it was a Day of Obligation, most of our party went off to find the nearest Catholic church. That left the Boss, Bertie Auld, Willie Wallace, Ronnie Simpson and myself. So, we headed for the golf course. And what a start the Boss made. Over the first nine holes he played as if he had been searching for that course all his life. No wonder all the wee local boys skipped around his heels and fought to pull his clubs. They knew class when they saw it and the Boss looked at us as if we were lucky to be playing with him. He was in a great mood and, like any golfer who thinks he has suddenly found the secret, he could hardly keep the smile off his face.

Then the bubble burst. After the turn, the Boss's ball began to go in all directions and the wee boys retreated to a safe distance. Even the smallest member of the gallery soon realised that old man Simpson, commonly known as 'Faither', was the real golfer in the company. By the eighteenth he had the gallery to himself and the Boss was pulling his own caddie-car.

Yet I think I remember that round of golf because it was the only time during our stay in South America that I saw him looking really relaxed. Usually, he hides his feelings well, especially in the tension before a big game, but he was obviously concerned about these matches with Racing Club.

The strain the Boss was under would show through during training sessions. Usually, as we train, a lot of crosstalk goes on and the Boss is liable to take as much a part in it as anybody, but in those days before the tie in Buenos Aires he would turn on anyone who was capering about and tell them, 'That's enough. We are here to work'…or words to that effect. So, we were all on our best behaviour while we stayed at the Hindu Club. Even if we thought we were good enough to get the draw, which would give us the title, we sensed it was going to be no picnic.

And when we reached the Avellanda Stadium, our worst fears were justified. Even before the game started, as we loosened up and hit a few shots at goal, Ronnie Simpson suddenly staggered and put his hands to his head. He had been hit. A narrow rectangular piece of iron, about two inches long, had been thrown through the fence, which is supposed to protect the players.

Boy, were we angry! It was ridiculous that a thing like that should happen to any player before such a big game. Ronnie, dazed, shocked and obviously in pain, couldn't possibly play and it meant our reserve John Fallon suddenly found himself playing in a World tie at two minutes' notice. At least, he hardly had time to get nervous, but I could not help thinking this was one time when fate wasn't working for Celtic.

Yet, despite Ronnie's injury and despite all the unfriendly Argentines in that stadium, we actually came very near to victory in Buenos Aires. In fact, we scored first. With what was virtually his last gesture of neutrality, the referee awarded us a penalty. I never took a kick with more determination and it was worth a guinea a box to see the expressions on the faces of Racing Club. The turning point came, however, when Jimmy Johnstone scored what looked like a perfectly good second goal, only to have it chalked off. Racing equalised after that, yet at the interval we still thought we had a chance. The Boss urged us, as he had done before kick-off, not to 'annoy' either Racing or their supporters. He couldn't have guessed how difficult this was going to be!

For Racing got their second goal soon after the interval and from there on they decided to take no chances. Their tackling became worse and worse and after awhile you didn't need to decide whether to pass or hold the ball, because if you did not get rid of it immediately, someone was sure to send you sprawling. Jimmy Johnstone suffered more than most of us, but we all had to remember, firstly, not to annoy the Argentines.

Well, we didn't annoy them. Instead, they hacked, tripped and pushed their way to a 2-1 victory, which earned them a third-game play-off for the title, which they were obviously determined to get at all costs. We trooped back to our dressing room, disgusted. I'll never forget it. We were so incensed at the treatment we had had to take from these South American soccer gangsters. Nobody made a dive for the bath as they would normally do. We just sat there trying to think of words bad enough to describe Racing Club who had obviously been confident the Uruguayan referee would let them away with anything.

Then we were joined in the dressing room by our own officials. Chairman Bob Kelly told us he would not allow us to play a third game against these opponents. I think that cheered most of us up because we were so fed up with the whole affair we would have like nothing better than to grab the first plane back to Glasgow.

Half-an-hour later we would have been happy to settle for a 'pass out' from that dressing room. The atmosphere had become chaotic. Argentinian and Uruguayan officials poured in when they heard we did not want to play a third game in Montevideo and they were followed by Press men, photographers, police and anyone in Buenos Aires who had nothing better to do at the time. At least, that's how it seemed because there was simply no room to move and most of us had still not changed.

As the flashbulbs went off and interpreters tried to sort out the various arguments, it was difficult to know whether our next destination would be Scotland or Uruguay. At one stage, the Boss asked us if we were prepared to play Racing Club again and we said 'Yes', mainly because we could tell from his attitude that he thought we could still win the third game if we got protection from the referee. The Uruguayans assured us the next game would be strictly controlled and, finally, Mr. Kelly took their word for it.

I didn't know then, of course, that if the Chairman had been adamant and refused to play in Montevideo I would have been spared the most embarrassing football experience of my career...but I'll tell you about that later.

We had cheered up a lot by the time we flew out to Uruguay the next day. We had heard that the fans in Montevideo didn't like Racing Club at all and were sure to be behind us. And any doubts we may have had about this story were quickly dispelled at the airport. We got a great reception; the crowds were shouting 'Celtic, Celtic' and that really gave our morale a boost. It pleased us even more when we were visited at out hotel by the Penarol players, the former World Champions who had played us in a friendly at Parkhead. They confirmed that Racing Club had a reputation for being a really nasty bunch, but they were sure we could beat them.

The Boss must have been cheered by all this, too, because there were two occasions when he showed how quick he can be with the gags. There was a phone call and one of the waiters in the hotel came up to him and asked, 'Are you Stein?' In the local accent, however, it sounded like 'Are you stayin'? – and quick as a flash the Big Man replied, 'No, I'm leaving on Sunday.'

Outside the hotel the following day he really had us rolling about. We had been invited to go to a nearby shop where we could get some bargains in clothes. The proprietor was delighted to see us. He wore a broad smile and, like me, he had the kind of nose, which leaves very little room for the rest of your face. 'This is wonderful,' he said. 'To think you come all the way from Glasgow to my shop. And you know what? I've got a cousin in Glasgow. Maybe you know him. His name is Levy.'

The rest of us, smilingly, shook our heads. Our clothier friend didn't realise how many people there are around Glasgow with a name like Levy. But the Boss had the answer. After a moment he said, 'Levy? Sure I know him. Your cousin must be Betting Levy!'

As the rest of us nearly choked trying not to laugh, the Montevideo man could hardly contain himself. 'Sure, sure,' he cried, 'that sounds like him. But is he doing well?'

Back came the deadpan reply, 'Doing well? He takes a fortune every week!'

That was the news this leading light in Montevideo Menswear had been waiting for. He could hardly serve us after that because he was obviously bursting to spread the word among his relations that their nearly-forgotten cousin in Scotland was making a fortune and seemed to be a household name.

This little bit of kidding by the Boss gave the clothier a great deal of pleasure – and it helped the Celtic camp a lot, too. It gave us something to look back and laugh about for the rest of the day and as the 'decider' approached our mood of optimism was increasing. Yet, at the same time, our preparations were deadly serious – so serious that Bertie Auld and I were nearly thrown out of the tem altogether!

It happened like this. On the afternoon before the game, Bertie and I sat in the hotel lounge chatting to some Press men. Time passed quickly and it was a long while before we realised we were the only players around. No wonder. Up in one of the rooms the Boss was holding his final tactics talk and nobody had noticed we were missing. By the time we sheepishly put our heads round the door the meeting was almost over. Later the Boss had a few things to say to both of us and he finished by telling us very frankly that if the next day's game had been anything less important than a World tie we would have been out of the team and in the grandstand.

Since we were in we were able to join the rest of the boys in a search for a Uruguayan flag. It had been decided that since the local fans were supposed to be on our side, they would back us even more if we went out with their flag. So about twenty minutes before the kick-off we all strolled on to the field, waved, acted like a most friendly bunch of fellas, then unfurled the flag. The fans seemed to like the gesture, but their response wasn't quite as enthusiastic as we had hoped. Back in the pavilion we soon found the answer. Someone told us that ten minutes earlier the Racing Club party had been waving an even bigger Uruguayan flag than ours!

Yes, one up to the Argentines – and a lesson to us all that no matter how smart you may think you are in these top international competitions you should always remember that the other fellow is thinking, too, and he may come up with an even better idea than you. It's this kind of thing, no doubt, which puts an extra strain on managers.

Before the game, the Boss warned us, as usual, of the need for self-control. He no doubt hoped, as we all did, that the assurances given about firm refereeing would keep the wild men of Racing Club in check. Yet I'm sure he sensed our mood that if the South Americans kicked, hacked and spat at us any more we would do a wee bit of Scottish 'sorting out'.

It was obvious, after hardly any time at all, that Racing had no intention of altering their tactics. Our appeals to the referee were a pure waste of time and after one particularly vicious foul on Jimmy Johnstone I think we all decided that was the last straw. I could see our blokes were no longer holding back and the game became nothing more than an exhibition of unarmed combat.

The Paraguayan referee was not slow, however, to spot crimes committed by anybody in a Celtic jersey and as the game went on John Hughes, Jimmy Johnstone and Bobby Lennox were all ordered off and Racing had the one goal lead which they no doubt felt justified all their diabolical tactics.

So, as near as I can guess, there would be about ten minutes to go when I decided that justice had to be done. After the umpteenth incident players and officials were gathered round the referee and Bertie Auld. It was all very heated and everyone was trying to see what was happening…but one player was standing apart. He was making sure he wouldn't be involved. I wasn't surprised because he had managed to stay out of all the real trouble throughout the tie. This was Raffo, wearing a No.11 jersey and looking quite pleased with himself. It made me so annoyed to think that the tie was nearly over and this man looked like finishing it unscathed, yet of all the members of the ruthless Racing team he had been the most consistently dirty. Yet he was crafty enough to do all his spitting and kicking when the referee was looking the other way. Nobody had been able to get their own back on him because he jumped high in the air every time you tried to tackle him. As I looked at him I thought, 'I bet he's thinking the Scots are a soft lot because he's "given us stick" all that time and got away with it.' All this had gone through my mind in a matter of seconds and in sheer temper I decided to hand out justice myself. I ran quickly round to where he was standing and kicked him. The swing was well-timed, the aim was good, too, and my boot landed on a very tender spot. Mr. Raffo squealed like a pig and went down in a heap. I quickly returned to my previous stance feeling very, very pleased with myself. Because of the fuss round Bertie hardly anyone had seen my little deed and it did my heart good to know that Raffo had got what was coming to him.

Now, I'm not going to defend myself. I'm not suggesting this was a nice thing to do. If another player annoys you it is no solution to kick him deliberately. But in this instance it seemed the only way to deal with him. Racing Club had set their own standards in these matches and to get down to them you had to stoop pretty low.

Mark you, I had no idea what an infamous kick that was to become. I certainly never dreamed I would have to spend days, even weeks, explaining it when I got back to Glasgow.

The trouble began when, on the Wednesday evening after we returned home from South America, the BBC showed a film taken during the game in Montevideo. I never saw it, so I was completely taken by surprise when I arrived at Parkhead on the following morning and the first people I met said,

'You're some guy, you…what a daft thing to do in front of the cameras! What a fool you are!' And I couldn't even start to print some of the other things which were said to me in the days that followed.

It seemed that the BBC had managed to get hold of a film which highlighted most of the fouls committed by Celtic and somehow missed the dirty work done by the Argentines. And I was assured that by far the most dramatic shots were of a bloke called Gemmell kicking a bloke who was standing minding his own business.

Yes, while I had been getting my revenge on Raffo, a TV camera high in the stands had followed my every move. I haven't seen that particular film yet, but I've been told often enough that my hasty retreat after delivering the blow did not look particularly dignified on the screen. I thought I was just helping the cause of justice… but I never thought justice would be seen to be done by about ten million British viewers, including my family and friends. I was widely criticised, of course, especially by English critics who had been waiting on an opportunity to knock Celtic. They had been shocked when we won the European Cup, annoyed that we had done so much more than any of their teams.

Even my mother said to me the first time I visited her after the TV film had been shown, 'Why did you have to go and kick that man?' I explained, as I've tried to explain here, and I think she understood. Many other people still think what I did to Raffo was outrageous, but I think they will understand the atmosphere in Montevideo better when I tell this story, which has never been told before.

The fact is, the most amazing thing about that game, as far as I was concerned, happened as I was walking off the field, Raffo ran over to me… and was smiling. He made signals and at first I thought he was looking for a fight! Then I realised he wanted to swap jerseys with me. Swapping jerseys is an international football custom, of course, but you tend to do more of it in a game where relations have been good. It seemed strange to me in that situation and I admit I was suspicious. I thought, ' This bloke probably wants me to pull the jersey over my head so he can belt me one when I can't see him.'

But Raffo looked so darned friendly I felt I could hardly turn him down. So, I warily got out of one sleeve first, then the other, then, stepping back quickly, I whipped my jersey over my head. His smile became even broader and as we swapped jerseys he warmly shook my hand. Indeed, as he ran towards the tunnel he had a grin on his face and, in English, he shouted a little remark about the accuracy of my kick.

In the game of football as we know it, it seems unlikely that Raffo should have anything to do with me. But at home, among my other souvenirs, I have a neatly-pressed Racing Club jersey with vertical blue and white stripes and a No.11 on the back which proves that its former owner was less upset by that kick than the millions of TV fans who saw it in Britain.

Players like him kick – and expect to be kicked. It is the way some of them play the game. Referees in most European countries would not stand for that behaviour. That's why I started off warning youngsters that playing in the World Championship is an experience they can probably do well without. I feel certain Celtic would not take part again in similar circumstances. It is a good idea that the European Champions should meet the Champions of South America each year, but these games are going to get out of control too often unless these is a neutral venue.

I would play the World final in New York. It might deprive the clubs of a financial bonanza, but if the referee was a thoroughly reliable man, carefully selected, then we could be sure the winners would be worthy champions. I certainly think no British team should ever agree to a World series in which two of the three matches could be played in South America. If the 1967 title had been decided over ninety minutes in a neutral country there is no doubt we would have been able to take it back to Parkhead.

As it was, our encounter with Racing Club brought us nothing but trouble. After we got home, and even after the TV film, another shock awaited those of us who had played in Montevideo.

One morning during training we were told the Chairman wanted to meet us at 11.30. The Boss admitted that it had to do with our behaviour in that third game in Uruguay. Celtic through the years had always had a good reputation for discipline on the field and it certainly been tarnished in Montevideo. There had to be a punishment and the Boss wanted our opinion on whether it should be spread over the entire team or merely those who had been sent off. We immediately said it should be a team affair. He had known what our answer would be, anyway.

So, there were eleven very shocked individuals in Parkhead that morning when Mr. Kelly announced that the Board had decided to fine each of us £250!

There were those who thought this was just a gesture to impress the public and that we would never really have to pay all that money. But they didn't know Bob Kelly. He doesn't do things like that – and every penny of the fine was deducted from bonuses, which we had earned previously in other matches.

Mr. Kelly was also ready, however, to accept part of the responsibility. As he announced the fines he confessed that he should have stuck to his original decision in Buenos Aires. He said he ought never to have allowed us to play in that third game and that he had no doubt in his own mind that he had made a mistake.

I think everyone would agree with him now. If we had refused to play the third game, especially after what happened to Ronnie Simpson, football people everywhere would have been on our side. Many would have regarded us as the best team in the world even if we had no official title. But it is easy to be wise after the event.

CHAPTER THREE
THE BEST ACTOR IN THE UNTOUCHABLES

Wee Jimmy Johnstone often told me that I had been decorated more often than the Queen's living room. I never thought to ask Jinky exactly how he knew of the specific arrangements for the makeovers at Buck House, but I got the drift.

What the Wee Man didn't know was that there was one honour I should have won on a weekly basis - the Best Actor's award.

No doubt my former team-mates and fans alike will be surprised by this revelation, but it's time to come clean. I was never quite as laidback as everyone thought I was. It was all an act. I wasn't a bag of nerves before every game, but I can tell you the butterflies were there. I was as much subject to normal human frailties as the next man. I just did my best to disguise it while sauntering around the dressing room looking as though I didn't have a care in the world. But, deep inside, I felt the tension. The trick was not to show it. And once you have done it a couple of times as a cocky youngster coming into the first team to mix with the big boys, then you are stuck with it for the rest of your life. It becomes unshakeable and forms your personality.

Looking back, I realise I had more front than Brighton Pier. I was never really concerned about the image. That was never a priority from someone from a housing scheme in Craigneuk, Lanarkshire. But I realised I had lumbered myself with a part to play. I read in the newspapers that I was flamboyant, cavalier, buccaneering, flashy, swashbuckling, exciting and dashing. I don't think any other Celtic full-back in the history of the club had ever been described in such graphic, praiseworthy terms. Again, that is not being big-headed. In the earlier days, they were defenders first and foremost. They were never encouraged to cross the halfway line. That was a massive no-no. However, that had always been my natural instinct, to get into enemy territory and do as much damage as possible. I knew I had a good shot in either foot, with my right being the stronger, and, with Jock Stein around, you were given every opportunity to get forward and attempt to create havoc.

I scored my first league goal for the club on 28 October 1964, but I didn't do too much celebrating as we had just been humped 5-2 by Kilmarnock at Rugby Park. At least, I had put down my marker. It was quite awhile afterwards that Big Jock handed me the penalty-taking duties. Before me, the players on the spot were Dunky MacKay, Bobby Murdoch, Bertie Auld, Ian Young, Charlie Gallagher, Joe McBride and John Hughes. So, I had to wait my turn before I was given the nod when we were awarded one in our European Cup first round second leg tie against Zurich in Switzerland on 5 October 1966 en route to conquering Europe. I had scored in the first game in Glasgow, a 2-0 win, and I had netted again in Zurich. We were 2-0 up in that game - Stevie Chalmers got the other - and I was given the ball to complete a hat-trick over the two legs. I clubbed it into the net and that was me the No.1 choice.

I have to say I was never nervous before I took a penalty. Normally the adrenalin would be pumping because you don't often get a spot-kick in the first five minutes or so unless, of course, it is an absolute stonewaller. So, I was mainly into my stride by the time we ever received an award. I felt sorry for the goalkeeper before I took a penalty. He had no idea where I was going to place it for one very good reason - I hadn't a clue myself. My secret of a good penalty-kick was simple; hammer it as hard as you can, get it on target and see what happens after that. I had a fairly good record, even if I do say so myself. I think I missed three out of thirty-seven attempts and I believe I hit the keeper on two of those occasions. They weren't quick enough to get out of the way!

Back then, my guilty pleasure was cars. Well, I had to continue to play and look the part, hadn't I? My first car was a gas-guzzling Ford Zodiac which I bought from Ian Skelly's dealership in Motherwell where my mum worked. It was a big three-litre, six-cylinder job which was Britain's version of the American Chevy. It caused a bit of a stir when I parked it outside my parents' tenement block in Craigneuk, I can tell you. It was my pride and joy. I had arrived! Ian Skelly's brother Billy was in Lisbon in 1967 when I bumped into him. 'Score a goal today, Tommy, and I'll give you fifty gallons of petrol free.' And he was as good as his word.

From the Zodiac I moved onto the Ford Zephyr. I bought all my cars from Skelly's and I paid £500 for a Ford Cortina out of my European Cup bonus of £1,500. Over the period I must have owned about twenty cars although, unlike today's players, I only had one at a time. My favourite was a white S-type Jaguar that was really sleek. I enjoyed driving up to Celtic Park on matchdays in that stylish, eye-catching vehicle with the fans waving at me. It was a world away from the days of cycling to Fir Park as a kid with my knees regularly clattering off the handlebars of a bike I had clearly outgrown. Aye, I had come a long way right enough.

I was fairly fashion conscious in those days. Well, I thought I was trendy. I can look at photographs now of me in the late sixties and early seventies and wonder what on earth I was thinking. I had shirts with collars the size of bed sheets. If you got caught in a fierce tail-wind there was a possibility you could be whisked off to another country. I wore flare-bottomed trousers that had enough surplus material to make about six suits. Shoes? Don't even go there. Dodgy colours with equally dodgy soles and heels. Most footballers sported hair styles that weren't dissimilar to blow-dried stoats perched on their napper. Thankfully, I missed the bubble-perm look. That was hilarious. All those big ba'-faced, ugly players with broken noses and hair like Shirley Temple. My only consolation was the fact everyone looked the same, so no-one pointed and laughed. Walk down the street today with that gear on and everyone would believe the circus was in town.

Being a Celtic player was simply wonderful. The public might never have believed it, but Celtic and Rangers players actually got on quite well with each other. Wee Willie Henderson was a particular friend of mine and still is to this day. Bertie Auld, Willie Wallace, myself and a couple of others used to go to Reid's Bar on Hope Street in Glasgow after a game on a Saturday. It was owned by Partick Thistle chairman and SFA President Tom Reid and a lot of footballers used to hang out there. They had an upstairs bar where you could get a bit of privacy. Normally we would be joined by the Rangers contingent of Wee Willie, Ronnie McKinnon, Davie Provan and Willie Johnston. It was all very affable, I must say.

Talking of Wee Willie reminds me of a story he told me back in the sixties when Muhammad Ali was visiting Glasgow in a worldwide publicity exercise. The heavyweight champion of the world and, in my opinion, the greatest-ever sportsman was due to pop in and see us at Celtic Park and then he was going across the city to Ibrox to do the same with the Rangers players. Willie said, 'I shook hands with Ali and this handsome specimen took a look at my flattened nose. He smiled and said, "You a footballer? Man, I'm sure glad I'm a boxer." I couldn't argue.'

Jock Stein abhorred alcohol, as we all know, so it may surprise a few that the Celtic players were allowed a drop of whisky before every game. Okay, it wasn't enough to cater for a party. In fact, it was only a quarter bottle of whisky and it was kept out of sight in the shower room. Big Jock never allowed anyone else into the dressing room apart from the players and staff, but on the off-chance someone did enter his exclusive sanctum, there would never be any booze on display. However, if the players fancied a nip before kick-off they could go and have a quick snifter with the boss's blessing. I'm not a whisky drinker, but I had a swig one day to test out its therapeutic qualities. That was a one-off. I never touched it again. A lot of the other players didn't bother, either, but that bottle was almost always empty before we left to take the field. I'm not pointing any accusing fingers, you understand, but Ronnie Simpson seemed to make more visits to the shower room than anyone else. Read into that what you will.

Ronnie was a great character. Do you know the only two members of the Lisbon Lions squad who smoked were the goalkeepers, Ronnie and John Fallon? And, before them, the only other bloke I saw smoking at Celtic Park was Frank Haffey, another goalkeeper. Bertie Auld would often be photographed with a giant cigar after a trophy triumph, but I doubt if he ever smoked it. That cigar probably followed him throughout his career and was never lit!

Our veteran keeper, known to everyone as 'Faither' for obvious reasons, was a quiet man off the field. He adored golf, of course, and probably could have made the professional circuit. Away from Parkhead, he had his own friends in Edinburgh where he lived. Mainly he would socialise with those guys. He had a droll sense of humour. Bobby Lennox remembered making a speech when he was voted by the supporters into the Greatest-Ever Celtic Team at the millennium. He went up to accept his award at a fabulous night at the Armadillo in Glasgow. He was handed his trophy, cleared his throat and addressed the packed audience. 'What an honour,' he said. 'Actually, I am very surprised to be named in the team.' From behind him came a staged whisper, 'Aye, you're not the only one!' Ronnie at his best. I have to say those Celtic supporters have impeccable taste. At the same poll, they also voted for the club's Greatest-Ever Goal. Who won? Yours truly for my effort against Inter Milan in Lisbon on a day no-one will forget.

Ronnie was only about 5ft 9in, but he had massive feet! He took a size eleven in a shoe and that was bigger than me and probably the rest of the team. Jim Craig, Billy McNeill and I were all 6ft-plus, but I don't think we even came close to Ronnie's giant peds. Coco The Clown didn't have feet that size. When you went into the dressing room on matchday all the boots were laid out on the floor under the respective peg numbers. Ronnie's stood out a mile. We would joke with him, 'When you go skiing, Ronnie, do you bother with skis?' Or 'When you walk into a room, do your feet arrive a couple of minutes before you?' He would laugh, 'At least, I've got a good grip of earth.' Actually, our goalkeeper made great use of those gigantic feet. How many times did you see him kick the ball off the line? I saw him do it on scores of occasions. Ronnie never bothered about being flashy. He would keep the ball out of the net by any means possible or by any part of his anatomy. 'Just so long as it doesn't cross the line, son,' he would say. 'That's the main thing.'

Jim Craig flummoxed Big Jock. Our manager could never understand why our right-back had a profession outside football. Jim, of course, was a dentist and combined both trades fairly well. How many dentists do you know who have a European Cup winner's medal in their possession? The man known to us as Cairney must be unique. Cairney? Back then, there was a Scottish actor called John Cairney who starred in a TV series called This Man Craig, so we simply switched names.

To be honest, I don't think Cairney ever received the praise he deserved. I'm probably to blame to a certain extent. The supporters would see me bombing up and down the left flank and, if I was lucky, walloping in a goal or two. Scoring goals wasn't Cairney's forte, though. What he provided was remarkable athleticism on the right. He didn't go on eye-catching mazy runs, but he certainly contributed to the cause. You should have seen him on the track during training. He was amazing. He could run all day and leave the rest of us in his slipstream. He had the stamina to be an Olympian. I really mean that. On top of that, he was extremely reliable.

Like myself, he rarely dived into a tackle. That would have been a last resort. He knew he had the pace to keep up with any winger, so if they nipped the ball past him there was every chance he would recover and get in a tackle. Jim was the University-type. I'm sure he thought the rest of his team-mates were half-footballer half-imbecile. He probably believed an amoeba had more brain cells than the lot of us put together. I never tired of telling him he wasn't the only one who possessed grey matter in the team. I had won the Dux medal at Wishaw High School Senior Secondary, after all.

People used to get the wrong impression about Bobby Murdoch. Obviously, he struggled with a weight problem and in Glasgow that can only mean one thing - he likes a bucket. Bobby did like a pint or two, like the rest of us, but he was no boozer. As a matter of fact, Bobby suffered from a fluid retention problem and that's what bulked him up. So, it was grossly unfair when I heard some critics talking about him not taking care of himself. It just wasn't true. Bobby trained as hard as the next guy, but could do little about his medical condition. He was no speed merchant - even when he was breaking into the team as a teenager - and that probably fuelled the speculation that he wasn't doing his bit in training. His team-mates knew where the problem lay, of course, but Bobby kept his secret to himself.

Big Jock used to send Bobby off to a health farm every now and again to see if that would help him. Bobby went to a place in Tring, Hertfordshire, where they put him on a special diet. There was one snag, though. Jock would send Jimmy Steele, our masseur, with him to keep him company and once Bobby had had his healthy breakfast, his healthy walk and his healthy dinner, they would both go to a pub nearby for a couple of pints. All the good work was probably undone in half-an-hour standing at the bar!

My old team-mate was one of the finest passers of the ball I have ever seen. 'Why run sixty yards with the ball when one pass can do it in seconds?' he would say and who could argue? His vision was extraordinary and his touch was first-class. He killed the ball in an instant before launching another inch-perfect pass forward. He could tackle, too. He didn't really require a burst of pace because his anticipation was exceptional. I'm not sure Bobby would have been any more influential if he could have run all day. For me, even without the speed, he was just perfect. Bobby may not have been a great goalscorer, but he was the scorer of great goals. He could fizz in pulverizing shots from long distance that must have frightened the life out of goalkeepers. I did my bit, too, I hope in terrorising rival No.1s.

Billy McNeill would give his team-mates dog's abuse during a game if he thought it was merited. If you gave the ball away needlessly with a slack pass you could expect to get it in the ear from Big Billy. In fact, every individual in the Celtic team would give a colleague pelters if it was deserved. That was the type of team we were. We all wanted to be winners and no-one was shy about firing out a verbal volley if we thought somebody was falling short of the required standard. It didn't do us any harm, did it? We could spend an-hour-and-a-half shouting and bawling at each other, but it never carried on into the dressing room afterwards. Not once. You hear all sort of stories about bust-ups among players in the privacy of their sanctuary away from prying eyes, but, no matter how heated it got during a game, that wasn't the case with us. Sure, there could be a word or two, but that was all.

Big Billy was Jock's general on the park, but he realised he was surrounded by players with the same positive outlook. Billy got it in the neck every now and again, too. No-one was immune. We won as a team and we lost as a team. People can look at the surviving Lisbon Lions today and see us all getting on well with each other. They may think that is merely for the public's consumption. Believe me, that affection we have for each other is genuine and has lasted well over four decades. My wee pal Willie Wallace may now be living on the other side of the world in Queensland, Australia, but we still keep in touch. That wee bugger will telephone me in the dead of winter to tell me he is enjoying a barbeque in his back garden. Now that's what I call a friend.

It was a minor source of irritation to some players that Big Billy was getting a tenner a week more than the rest of us. Jock's secretary revealed this to me once and I took it up with the manager. At first, Jock, who was always very careful with Celtic's cash, denied the claim. I couldn't drop the secretary in it, so I wouldn't disclose my source of information. Jock then twigged that I knew something I shouldn't. He dropped the charade. He said, 'Billy gets more because he is the captain.' I hasten to add that no-one at Celtic was thinking of walking out, taking strike action or anything as drastic as that over the issue. However, I pressed the matter with Jock, in the nicest possible way, of course. Remarkably, he relented and said, 'Ach, I'll have a word with the board about it. Away you go now.' He waved his big left paw at me once more.

About a week later, Big Jock called a team meeting at Parkhead. Our crafty manager didn't mention that he had a wee wage 'negotiation' with yours truly. 'I've got some good news for you,' he said. 'I think you are well due a pay rise and I have presented the case to the chairman and the board of directors. They have agreed to give you all an extra fiver a week starting immediately. I think you're worth it.' My team-mates were delighted at their unexpected windfall - £5 was a reasonable bit of money in those days - and I was pleased, too. So was Big Billy, who was still getting a tenner a week more than the rest of us!

John Clark could have starred in the lead role of one of my favourite movies, The Quiet Man. He doesn't look a bit like John Wayne, of course, but he could certainly do the silent bit. You could sit with Luggy in the dressing room and forget he was there. On the park, he was the perfect foil for Billy McNeill in the middle of the Celtic defence. They both complemented each other perfectly. Billy did his best work in the air where I never saw anyone master him. He may not have been as flawless on the deck, but that was where Luggy came into his own. He read play brilliantly and was outstanding at covering behind Billy and cleaning things up. The Celtic support christened him 'The Brush' and he took that as a huge compliment. Not the most exciting of nicknames, but one that meant a lot to Luggy.

He was never one to blow his own trumpet and that's probably why he has never put his thoughts into an autobiography. The things he could reveal would be highly interesting, but he insists he will never tell all about his days as a player or assistant manager to Big Billy. I'm not surprised because he is a genuine tranquil sort of guy who has never sought out the spotlight. He was a very effective player for us, but rarely hit the headlines. That didn't bother him one jot. In fact, if anything, it suited him down to the ground. It was Big Jock who converted him from the old-fashioned wing-half role to sweeper and it was a magnificent piece of manoeuvring from our manager. I think it would be fair to say most of us were going through the motions on matchday before Big Jock appeared on the scene. He arrived from Hibs in March 1965 and held a meeting with all the players before we went on our summer holidays that year. We had just won the Scottish Cup - our first piece of silverware in eight years - and were on a high. Jock, though, wasn't satisfied.

We had been playing in the time-honoured 2-3-5 formation with two full-backs, a centre-half, two half-backs on either side of him, two wingers and three forwards who helped out in midfield and attack with the centre-forward staying up front. Big Jock told us there would be massive changes in the way we played. It was the start of the Stein revolution as he introduced a more fluid 4-2-4 system. Luggy was one of the guys who was told his position would be changing. And for the better, I'm happy to add. He was a workmanlike wing-half - and I'm sure he won't mind me making that observation - but he was outstanding as a sweeper. He made his Scotland debut in the summer of 1966 when he was up against Brazil legend Pele. Stevie Chalmers scored in the first minute in a 1-1 draw with the-then world champions at Hampden, but the main thing was that the great Pele hardly got a kick of the ball. Luggy saw to that.

Another reason I liked our defender was the fact he owned a wee bar in Chapelhall that had a hotel licence. Back in the sixties, public bars didn't open on a Sunday. If you fancied a quick snifter you had to go to a hotel. Chapelhall wasn't too far from my house in Kirkintilloch, so every now and again, Luggy would be joined at the bar by yours truly. Aye, he was a handy man to know!

Jimmy Johnstone was always one of my favourite guys. Obviously, he was much, much more than a mere team-mate. He was great company and I always thoroughly enjoyed our time together, whether it was on a football field, sitting by a loch doing a spot of fishing, taking in a movie, having a quiet drink in a bar, oh, anywhere and everything. His courage in his gallant battle against motor neurone disease was humbling. I used to pop into his home in Uddingston to say a quick hello almost on a daily basis. His wife Agnes had rigged up a room that was custom-built for the Wee Man. He had a big comfortable armchair and a massive TV screen that was normally tuned into one of the sports programmes. I would go there to try to cheer up my little chum, but, more often than not, it was he who had me in gales of laughter by the time I got back to my car.

I remember a day Bertie Auld and I arranged to visit him. We were sitting in his room simply shooting the breeze. There were just the three of us as Agnes had taken the opportunity to do a bit of shopping in Glasgow. We were nattering away when the doorbell sounded. 'Are you expecting anyone, Jinky?' I asked. 'Aye, Rod Stewart said he might drop in,' replied my wee mate, who was one of the best wind-up merchants in the business. 'I'll see who it is,' I said as I made my way to the front door. I opened it and standing there right in front of me was...Rod Stewart. 'Hiya, Tommy,' said Rod. 'How's it hanging?' Before I could think of an answer, he said, 'Is Jinky coming out to play?' We both fell about laughing. Rod was completely on his own, no minders, no entourage, just a chauffeur who remained in the Bentley which was parked in Jinky's driveway. Of course, it didn't take long for half of Uddingston to turn up on Jinky's doorstep to get a glimpse of the celebrity Hoops fan. I showed Rod to Jinky's room and all four of us, three Lisbon Lions and one of the world's biggest rock stars, were sitting there talking about the good old days. Amazing, really.

One the saddest aspects of Jinky was the fact he could never quite comprehend or take in the fact that he had been allowed to leave Celtic. He was only thirty years old when Big Jock gave him a free transfer. I don't think he could ever quite accept that he was no longer a Celtic player. The club and the fans became his world. He was a true working class hero and the supporters identified with him. He was easily one of the best footballers in the world during his prime. I will never forget his impeccable display against Real Madrid in the Alfredo di Stefano Testimonial Match at a sell-out Bernabeu Stadium, with 130,000 cramming in to say farewell to their legendary striker. Wee Jinky went onto steal the show after Alfredo, who had been a boyhood idol of his, left the field after fifteen minutes. The forty year old looked as though he could have lasted the entire game, but he decided to take his seat in the stand. And from that vantage point he viewed my mate at his virtuoso best. That was as near to perfection I have ever witnessed from an individual on a football pitch. I am not saying that out of misplaced sentiment, I really mean it.

That memorable evening was in June 1967 only a week or so after Celtic had won the European Cup. Celtic could have named their price for Jinky after that awesome showing and teams throughout the world would have been queuing up to throw money at the club. Jinky wouldn't have wanted to know. He wouldn't even have explored any possibilities even out of curiosity. Celtic were his club. He never wanted to kick a ball for anyone else. In fact, as his manager of Dundee for an all-too-brief spell in 1977, I can inform you he never wanted to kick a ball against Celtic, either. Honestly, that thought haunted him. When he signed for us, Jinky told me, 'Ye know, TG, Ah cannae play against Celtic. Honestly, Ah'll no' play.' I reminded him Celtic were in the Premier League and we were in the First Division. 'Aye, but whit if we draw them in the Cup? Whit happens then? Ah'm no' playing. Pick me if ye want, but Ah'll no' turn up. Ah'll be injured or something. Ah'm no' playing against Celtic. Ah never will, nae chance.' The Wee Man meant it, too.

Another thing Jinky found difficulty in understanding was that once he had left Celtic there would be no way back as a player. Big Jock wouldn't have made the decision lightly to release such a favourite of the support. And, at thirty, Jinky could still have contributed something, even if it was only coming off the substitutes' bench late in a game. His mere presence would have lifted the entire place. So, Jock would have thought long and hard before letting him go. I can tell you Jinky, in fact, persisted with the thought that there might have been an opportunity of playing again in those green and white hoops.

Unfortunately, he only lasted three months with us at Dundee, but I'll cover that in another chapter. Clearly, though, his heart wasn't in it at Dens Park. It seemed it was Celtic or nothing. Jock allowed him to train with the first team and it was like the good old days for my wee pal.

Then Irish club Shelbourne got in touch to see if he would be interested in playing for them. With Jinky in the team, they must have realised they would have sell-out crowds wherever they played. They made him a good offer and Jinky phoned me to relay the news. He actually seemed fairly excited. 'Tommy, Ah've had a word wi' Jock. Shelbourne have offered me a twelve-month contract, but Big Jock says I should only sign a monthly deal. Do ye think that's because he might want to sign me and he won't have to pay a fee?' I thought for a moment. It did seem highly unlikely, but Big Jock did move in mysterious ways. I couldn't break Jinky's heart and tell him what I really thought. I knew my days as a Celtic player were over when Jock had made up his mind. I realised it would have been the same in Jinky's case. However, I said, 'You never know, Wee Man. Train hard, get yourself fit, show some of that old magic and anything could happen.' Deep down, I didn't believe it, but extraordinary things happened around that wee chap and if anyone could have pulled it off it would have been him.

I wondered if the move to Shelbourne, unlikely though it would have seemed only a couple of years earlier, might just give him the sort of boost he needed. I also knew Jinky had come straight out on one occasion and asked Jock if there was any chance of a return to Celtic. That must have caught the manager on the back-foot. Jinky confided in me, 'He said Ah've to wait and see, Tommy. He didnae say naw.' I wanted to believe with all my heart that somehow Jinky could manufacture a comeback to Paradise, but I just couldn't see it. However, the Wee Man was determined to have one last kick of the ball at Parkhead. Shelbourne agreed to fly him in on the day of the game and fly him straight home again afterwards. He could spend the week with Agnes and the family and train with Celtic.

Jinky would often admit the devil would come out in him when he had too much to drink. Unfortunately, that was true. But he was so determined to attempt to get back to Celtic that he went on the wagon for a couple of months. And, then, in typical Jinky fashion, he decided to end his spell of abstinence in a hotel in a quaint little place called Balybofey on Hogmanay 1977 as Shelbourne prepared for a game against Finn Harps in Donegal the following day. It had all the makings of a disaster. The script had already been written. Jinky got involved and, sadly, there were reports that he had overdone the celebrations. Possibly he believed 1978 might be the year to signal his emotional return to his first love. His new club weren't impressed. His monthly contract wasn't renewed and he was on his way home after only nine games and two goals during his Emerald Isle adventure. The door was well and truly closed on any remote chance of going back to Celtic.

He phoned me to explain, 'Ah wisnae even looking for a drink, Big Man. Honest. One of the lads came in with a bottle of Jameson's Irish Whiskey and he shared it among a few of us. We had a couple of other drinks, but it wisnae a bevvy session.' I believed him, but Jinky's idea of a bevvy session and most other people's do not run along parallel lines. I often thought my wee pal could drink his own body weight in alcohol in one sitting. He would have had a few, that's for sure, but he would also have been certain he would be fit and ready for the game the following afternoon. In his heyday he could have managed it. He was thirty-three years old now and it was a different ball game. Once everything sunk in, he was forced to concede there was no longer any possibility of him finishing his career at Celtic. Sad, really.

I'm certainly not going to talk ill of the dead, but it was obvious Jinky had a drink problem. That's been fairly well documented. He could go over the score, but, believe me, that wee man had a heart of solid gold. Bertie Auld told me the story of the pair having a quiet beer in a bar in Uddingston a day or so after Celtic had beaten Blackburn Rovers at Ewood Park on their way to the 2003 UEFA Cup Final. Jinky would hardly have been flush at the time, but he looked through the window and saw a couple of unfortunates sitting in an alleyway across the road. Jinky immediately ordered six cans of lager and took them over to hand to the two blokes. They probably hadn't a clue as to the identity of their kind benefactor, but that little cameo was so typical of the man.

And I still laugh at the memory of what became a ritual with the Wee Man when we both lived in Uddingston. The window in my kitchen at the back of our house was actually quite high up. Anyway, one Sunday evening, around ten o'clock, I heard a noise at the back door. 'Burglars!' was my immediate thought. I tip-toed into the kitchen to investigate. And there at the back window was Jinky, standing on a dustbin, knocking gently on the pane of glass. 'Let me in, Big Man,' he said as if this was perfectly normal behaviour. Goodness only knows why he didn't come to the front door. Maybe that would have been too mundane and ordinary for my wee mate and he didn't do mundane and ordinary.

'How about a wee nip?' he asked as I let him in. We went through to the front room and had a couple of quick ones. 'How about a drive doon the road?' was the next question an hour or so later. I should have anticipated that one. Jinky could have afforded a taxi or he could even have walked the short distance between our two homes, but he much preferred yours truly to take on the chauffeur's duties. I protested, 'Jinky, I've had a couple of drinks, as well. I don't want to get done for being over the limit.' 'Ach, ye'll be fine,' came the reply. 'Ah'm only minutes away.' I said, 'Look, I'll give you the keys to my car and you can take it down the road and I'll get it in the morning.' There was an indignant reply. 'Whit? And get me done for drunk driving!'

For whatever reason, this became a Sunday night ritual. Jinky balancing on a dustbin, tapping on the kitchen window and coming in the back door for a few snifters. I realised I would be driving him home, so I went onto the soft drinks while my drinking partner put away a few nips. Then he would bounce to his feet, announce it was time for him to go and order, 'Right, Big Man, get me doon the road.'

There was another time when some of the Lisbon Lions had agreed to play in a Charity Match in Iceland. We were all aware of Jinky's fear of flying and he didn't look too impressed when we turned up at Glasgow Airport in the morning to find two modest-sized planes waiting for us. The big one was an eight-seater! The other was a six-seater. Jinky stared at them for a moment. 'Ah'm no' goin' on wan of them,' he said. I assured him we would be fine and we would only be up in the air for about half-an-hour. Jinky seemed content enough to accept that. He sat up front in the six-seater and I parked myself behind him. He was clearly nervous and his mood didn't get any better when the door to the cabin opened and out stepped the pilot.

Jinky looked at this immaculately-tailored character with the gold braid on the cuffs of his jacket. 'Are you the pilot?' he asked.

'I am,' was the response.

'Where's the other pilot?'

'There isn't one. I'm flying solo.'

Jinky looked aghast. 'That's all we fuckin' need. You're the only pilot? What happens if you have a heart attack?'

'Then you'll need this,' said the captain, handing Jinky a booklet. 'These are the flying instructions. Don't worry, they'll tell you all you need to know about flying an aircraft.' Jinky didn't bother to look at the booklet and he was very quiet for the entire journey.

Jinky was astonished to learn he had been voted Celtic's Greatest-Ever Player in the supporters' millennium poll. He was genuinely surprised. He told me, 'I thought they would give it to Henrik Larsson. Was I better than him, Big Man?' I told him it was the choice of thousands of Celtic fans worldwide and he had won by a landslide. 'The voting was unanimous, Wee Man.' (I don't know if that was strictly accurate, but it sounded convincing.) Jinky was never one for long-winded speeches. He could sing 'Dirty Old Town' all night long, but don't put a microphone in front of him and expect to be regaled by an Orson Welles-type oratory.

However, he brought the house down on the night he went up onto the stage to collect his Greatest-Ever Player honour. It was a poignant address and there couldn't have been a dry eye in the house when he said, 'There is wan guy no' here the night who should be standing here wi' this trophy,' said Jinky. 'Ah'm talkin' aboot Bobby Murdoch. He wis the best, the absolute greatest, no' me. Ah'm dedicating this award to Bobby.' The applause seemed to go on for about half-an-hour. Another gesture that was so typical of a man I was always proud to call a friend. He would have given you his last.

Indeed, Bobby Murdoch was missing that evening; physically, anyway, but certainly there in spirit. Unfortunately, he had passed away the previous year, but the supporters never overlooked his worth to Celtic. He was voted into their Greatest-Ever Celtic Team and he would have appreciated that honour. The fans had chosen Ronnie Simpson as their top goalkeeper with Danny McGrain at right-back and myself on the left. Billy McNeill - who else? - was centre-half and captain. Paul McStay, Bobby and Bertie Auld were in midfield and Jinky, Kenny Dalglish, Henrik Larsson and Bobby Lennox were the front four. Breathtaking, isn't it?

I was having a quick break with my wife Mary in Tenerife when I received the telephone call on 13 March 2006 that informed me Jinky, after a brave six-year battle, had died of that dreaded motor neurone disease. Of course, it wasn't totally unexpected, but it was still an almighty shock to the system. I had seen him the day before I flew out and it was obvious his health was in steady decline. Remarkably, he was still joking and laughing. It's impossible to be maudlin when I think about Jinky and all the fun we had together. I made arrangements to fly home immediately and I was a pall-bearer on 17 March - St.Patrick's Day - when the Wee Man made his last journey to Celtic Park. His cortege left from the front of his spiritual home to take the funeral party to St.John the Baptist Church in Uddingston and then on to Bothwell Park cemetery. Thousands lined the streets along London Road to say their last farewell to an extraordinary wee chap. To be honest, everything was a bit of a blur. I didn't get much sleep the previous evening and that, plus a heavy heart, combined to put me in my bleary-eyed state.

All of the Lisbon Lions were in attendance with the exception of Willie Wallace who didn't have time to make arrangements to fly in from Queensland. I looked around and I saw Rod Stewart, Denis Law, Martin O'Neill, Gordon Strachan, Kenny Dalglish, Danny McGrain, Davie Hay, Alex McLeish, Walter Smith, Ally McCoist, John Greig, Sandy Jardine, Davie Wilson, Peter Lorimer, Eddie Gray and so many, many others. Politicians mingled with rock stars, legends from Celtic and Rangers reached across the Great Divide and former Scotland international team-mates made the journey to pay their respects and say goodbye to a colourful little character whose courage was nothing short of awesome.

He was finally laid to rest wearing a garment he treasured most of all - his Lisbon Lions blazer. Thanks for the memories, Jinky. You made it back to Paradise, after all.

Willie Wallace may have been too small to play in goal, but that guy could operate in just about every other position on the football field. I recall a game where our right-back - I think it was Jim Craig - was sent off and Big Jock immediately dropped Wispy into the void in our defence. He performed there like that had been his position all of his career. He actually played most games as a main striker alongside Stevie Chalmers and scored 135 goals from 234 appearances since signing from Hearts in December 1966. On this occasion, he simply, slotted into the No.2 position. We were walking off the pitch at the end and I said, 'Great game, Wispy. How many times have you played at right-back?' Nonchalantly he replied, 'Just the once - today.'

He was a superb all-round performer who sacrificed personal glory for the team. He had played wing-half, outside-right, inside-forward and centre-forward with his previous clubs Stenhousemuir and Raith Rovers as well as Hearts. I recall a photograph in the newspapers the day after he completed his £30,000 signing. It showed Wispy sitting in our dressing room with five pairs of shorts hanging on the pegs behind him. They were the numbers seven, eight, nine, ten and eleven and the headline was, 'CELTIC SIGN A FORWARD LINE'. They could have added a number two, as well, a couple of months later.

Wispy must have wondered if Big Jock was pulling his leg before we took on Dukla Prague in the second leg of our European Cup semi-final in 1967. We were 3-1 ahead from the first game and Big Jock was out to make absolutely certain we wouldn't give anything away in the Czech capital. Wispy had scored two of our three goals in the first game and Dukla might have thought he would be playing up front again in the next game. In fact, Wispy hardly even crossed the halfway line that day. Our manager handed him a thankless task of shadowing Josef Masopust, the Czech side's main orchestrator in the middle of the park. The former 1962 European Footballer of the Year may have been at the veteran stage of his career, but he was still their main man, the guy who pulled the strings. Wispy had never played in that position, either, but he didn't complain.

He told me before the game, 'This is going to be interesting, Tommy. I've no idea what to expect. But Big Jock thinks it's a role I can take on board, so let's see if it works.' After our goalless draw, we were getting our photographs taken, leaping around like lunatics after cementing our place in the European Cup Final in Lisbon. I asked Wispy, 'How did you enjoy that?' He replied, 'I must have done okay because Masopust has just refused to shake my hand.'

I got on very well with Wispy, of course, and I liked him even before he joined Celtic. I remember a game against Hearts at Tynecastle in January 1966. That was a match we were ordered to play by the SFA and the Scottish League, despite just getting back from our European Cup-tie against Kiev Dinamo on the Friday night. Atrocious weather conditions delayed us from getting out of Moscow and we were grounded until the weather relented. Then we managed to get to Stockholm before returning home. Obviously, we weren't in the best of nick for a tough game in Edinburgh. Certainly, I wasn't feeling great after one of their defenders, George Miller, took me out with an over-the-top tackle. It would be a straight red card these days and slow motion TV replays would leave Miller without any hope of an appeal. He did me, alright, and he knew he had, as well. He got off with it, too.

I managed to stay on the field for the rest of the game, but I was in a fair bit of pain. When I took off my boot at the end my foot just about exploded. My ankle and my right foot both went up like balloons. However, as were coming off the field, after losing 3-2, I appreciated Wispy coming over to see me. 'That was a sore one, Tommy,' he said. 'Will you be okay?' I replied, 'I hope so, but I don't think I'll be going to the dancing tonight.' It was a nice touch from the Hearts man and one I never forgot. Mind you, I should have told him to fuck off - he scored two of their three goals that day!

Stevie Chalmers was one of those players who was always stripped and ready to go on the field about an hour before kick-off. Stevie just wanted to get out there and get involved immediately. Like Ronnie, he was another golfing bandit. On the football field, though, he was a trusted team-mate. Unselfishly, he would run all day, going in where it hurt. Normally, Stevie was quite a placid bloke. He would mix it with the big guys, but he was never dirty. However, there was one incident during a match on our five-week 1966 United States tour when I thought he had blown a gasket. We had played in places such as New York, Chicago,

Ontario, Toronto and Bermuda and we were due to play Bayern Munich, Franz Beckenbauer, Gerd Muller and Co, in San Francisco. They had just won the West German FA Cup and joined the tour late. They were in great shape when they played us and we found ourselves two goals down with only twenty minutes to play. Our opponents from Munich were putting it about a wee bit and they didn't like it when Joe McBride pulled one back. They were more than a little agitated when Bobby Lennox made it all-square.

Then came a sight I will never forget. Their right-back must have kicked Stevie in a tender place because I have never seen him react so angrily. Normally, he wouldn't say boo to a goose, but on this occasion our frontman was out to exact instant revenge. In a fury, he took after the German. The Bayern man wasn't hanging around to try to talk Stevie out of whatever he had in mind. He took to his heels. It was like the chase scenes at the end of a Benny Hill Show. The German was running round the track and there was Stevie racing after him. For a moment I wondered if Stevie had indulged in some wacky-baccy with the hippies on Haight Avenue before getting ready for the game. Stevie eventually caught up with his prey and threw him to the ground. Fists were flying everywhere. I turned to Big Billy, 'Am I seeing things or is that really our Stevie?'

'It certainly looks like him,' replied our skipper adding, 'What's got into him? Do you think we should go over and separate them?' I laughed, 'Are you joking? This is more entertaining than Ali v. Liston!'

The referee blew for time about five minutes early with the score at 2-2. The Bayern Munich players helped their stricken team-mate to the dressing room. I caught up with Stevie. 'What was that all about?' My team-mate told me, 'I told him if he kicked me again I would give him a doing.' That's fine, if the German actually understood any English and, if he did, had a clue about the old Glasgow expression 'doing'. Either way, he would undoubtedly have thought twice about kicking another opponent for the rest of his career!

Bertie Auld was always more of a rascal than a rogue in my eyes. And, of course, there is a world of a difference between the two. Bertie had a reputation as being a hard man and just let's say he often got his retaliation in first. No-one messed around with my wee pal. 'You're a fuckin' hooligan,' I would say often enough. 'Aye,' he would nod, 'and nobody better forget it!' Actually, Bertie was another superb exponent of making the ball do all the hard work. He possessed a magnificent left foot - his magic wand, as he said - and could float balls all over the place. He was also part of Big Jock's shake-up in the summer of 1965. Before Jock arrived, Bertie had played as an outside-left, going up and down the flank in front of me. Jock, though, spotted something in Bertie's play he believed would be of more benefit to the team. He moved him into midfield and he really flourished in his new role. His quick thinking, eye for a pass and devastating accuracy in his delivery made him one of the best midfielders in the game, in my opinion.

He had a wicked sense of humour and he put to a good use once in a game against Stirling Albion at their old ground at Annfield. Sammy Baird, the former Rangers player, was the Stirling boss and he had ordered one of his players to man-mark Bertie straight from the kick-off. The guy was giving Bertie some serious attention. When there was a lull in play, with one of their players receiving treatment, my mate sidled up to me. 'Hey, TG,' he winked, 'just watch this.' Without warning, Bertie suddenly took off down the wing and, would you believe, the Stirling Albion player raced after him for about forty yards! The game had stopped, but Bertie's marker was still sticking like a limpet to him. Now that's dedication.

Bertie was a shrewd wee cookie and as fly as a bag of monkeys. But he was a fabulous guy to have on your side. When we played Leeds United in the 1970 European Cup semi-final there was a lot of talk of how Bertie and Bobby Murdoch would match up against my good friend Billy Bremner and his equally tough midfield partner Johnny Giles, who had a bit of a nasty reputation. It was almost being billed as a game within a game with those four going head-to-head. How did my mates fare? We won home and away. That tells you all you need to know. Bertie was frightened of no-one. But there might have been a few who would have given my mate a wide berth.

Bertie, Wispy and I were all very good friends and we did a fair bit of socialising. Now is the time, though, to put a persistent rumour to bed. The three of us did NOT go out for a drink on the evening before the European Cup Final in Lisbon. I've read it and I've heard it, but, trust me, it is not true. If I was the litigious type I would sue. It's some people's good fortune that I am a fairly equable type. I will concede Bertie, Wispy and I did go for a couple of beers, but folk are getting their days mixed. We arrived in Portugal on the Tuesday and the game was due to take place in Lisbon on the Thursday. On Tuesday, as we settled in at our plush HQ at Estoril, we decided to do a quick bit of sightseeing. We didn't need to seek Big Jock's permission, so we just went ahead and made our own arrangements.

We jumped into a taxi and went to a quiet little spot just outside Estoril called Cascais. There was a pub called the John Bull which was, as you've guessed, an English bar. We had been travelling most of the day and had worked up a bit of a drouth, so we pulled up three chairs and sat outside in the tranquillity of this picturesque spot. There wasn't a Celtic fan in sight. They were congregating in Lisbon and this was a wonderful wee haven for us three. I've never been one to be bothered about the attendance of supporters just so long as they respect your privacy. You don't want to be halfway through your dinner in a restaurant when some bloke you've never seen before pulls up a chair to your table and wants to talk about such-and-such a game. There was little chance of that happening in Cascais. We had two or three beers before getting another taxi to drop us off at Estoril. Now that's the truth.

Where were we the night before the Final, the most important game in the club's history? Would you believe stumbling around in the dark coming back from a hilltop golfing complex owned by a top Scottish amateur golfer called Brodie Lennox, no relation to my wee team-mate. Big Jock was trying to arrange all sorts of things to prevent the players from getting bored and to keep us focused. England were due to play Spain in a friendly at Wembley on the Wednesday and Jock thought it would be a good idea to herd up the troops and take us to watch the action on Brodie's state-of-the-art big-screen TV. It also gave him the perfect excuse to keep an eye on his players, as well. The manager had no worries on that score. No-one was even thinking about misbehaving before such a momentous occasion. Not even Wee Jinky!

We had our evening meal, as usual, and then we took off up this long and winding road to Brodie's place, which was about thirty minutes' walk away. We were all fit guys, of course, so there was no problem in getting to the complex. It was a fair old hike, though. Anyway, we reached our destination, watched England win the match 2-0 and, after a few soft drinks, decided to wend our merry way back to our hotel. Neilly Mochan, who was our trainer, decided to take a short cut. He pointed to our hotel and said to Jock, 'I reckon we can cut about ten minutes off our trip, Boss. Let's go down through the fields.' Jock had wrapped us up in cotton wool in Portugal. He watched what we were eating and drinking, how long we were in the sun or in the pool. Remarkably, he agreed that it was a good idea.

We found ourselves wandering around in the dark with no lights in sight. All you could hear was an 'Ouch!' or 'Fuckin' hell!' as we tried to find our bearings. We had to climb over a couple of rickety fences and there was wild bracken everywhere. I felt some rocks go from under my weight a couple of times and I thought, 'Wouldn't it be so typical to reach the European Cup Final and get injured walking down a bloody hill!' Honestly, someone could have picked up any sort of injury, turning an ankle or worse. Thankfully, we made it safely to our sanctuary. So, instead of being out on the batter with Wispy and Bertie, I was bumbling around in the pitch black of Estoril. Now that's the truth.

I wonder what height Bobby Lennox would have been if someone had straightened his legs. Probably about 6ft 10in! My wee pal had slightly bandy legs, of course, and was never too pleased when you made the observation that a Jumbo Jet could fly through them without the wings touching his knees. 'Where's your horse, cowboy?' he was asked on countless occasions. Actually, Bobby - Lemon to everyone at Celtic - was never one to take offence. He must have been born with a smile on his face and it remained that way ever since. He's a lovely, bubbly character. He scored 273 goals in 571 appearances for the club and that's simply phenomenal shooting. However, Lemon was so fast I'll bet there were scores of perfectly legitimate goals ruled out because he looked miles offside. His pace was frightening and he must have been an absolute nightmare for any defender facing him. In his heyday I would have taken him to beat any player in the world over a short distance.

Big Jock used to tell us to knock the ball inside the full-backs and, inevitably, Bobby had timed his run to perfection to swoop onto the pass and leave defenders in his wake. He was told to play on the shoulder of the last opponent to keep himself onside and I'm sure he would have followed that instruction. Let's face it, Bobby hardly needed a head start on anyone. To emphasis how fast he was, he scored a goal against Feyenoord in the 1970 European Cup Final that experienced Italian referee Concetto Lo Bello ruled out. No-one complained at the time. We watched the replay later on and, astonishingly, Bobby was played onside by no fewer than THREE Dutch defenders. It's there on film for all to see. That would have given us the lead and, of course, I might have netted another shortly afterwards. I realise the entire pattern of the game would have been altered had Bobby's goal stood and there was every likelihood I might not have got the opportunity to score when I did. But you can't help wondering. A two-goal advantage might have seen Feyenoord fold. It just wasn't our night in the San Siro in Milan.

I'll tell you another thing about Bobby Lennox that you cannot say about too many players who make their money hammering the ball into the net. He was totally unselfish. If he was in the penalty box and in a reasonable position and he saw a team-mate better placed he would pass the ball to his colleague ten times out of ten. That's unusual for a goalscorer. Normally, they are greedy buggers who see nothing else when they are put through. How often have you seen a player attempt to score from awkward angles when an unattended team-mate is screaming for a pass? It happens all the time. Not with Bobby Lennox, though. Goodness knows how many goals he set up for Willie Wallace,

Stevie Chalmers, Joe McBride, John Hughes and the others. Hundreds, probably, and I don't think that is being too far-fetched.

So, here's the team that will live forever in Celtic's heritage: Ronnie Simpson; Jim Craig, Billy McNeill, John Clark and Tommy Gemmell; Bobby Murdoch and Bertie Auld; Jimmy Johnstone, Willie Wallace, Stevie Chalmers and Bobby Lennox.

Not too shabby, is it?

CHAPTER FOUR
SCOT (TAX) FREE

Jock Stein never said it to my face, but I had been informed by some of his closest associates that he regarded me to be the best left-back in the world. But it was the same Jock Stein who restricted my international appearances for Scotland to a mere eighteen. No doubt a lot of people will find difficult to comprehend or even believe that statement. Take it from me, it's the truth.

After my debut in 1966, if anyone had told me I would represent my country only another seventeen times in a playing career that stretched a further nine years, I would have guessed I was the victim of a wind-up. Unfortunately, the history books show that to be an absolute fact. And that was down to one individual - Jock Stein. Big Jock was always a difficult man to argue with. At Celtic, his word was law. When an international game was on the horizon and I was a cert to get a call-up, Jock would sidle up to me and I had a fair idea of what was coming next. 'You don't want to be bothered playing against that lot, do you?' he would ask. It was, of course, a rhetorical question. If Scotland were preparing for a match against one of the smaller nations, Jock would have much preferred his players resting before an important club game the following Saturday. He didn't like his players risking injury in friendlies against the minnows of the football world.

However, if we were due a crucial qualifying encounter in the World Cup or the European Championship, that was a different story. He wouldn't even attempt to pull any of his players out of those squads. But if he thought it was an international against countries of lesser stature, then there was always the chance of Big Jock getting a hold of you and letting you know it might be a good idea to withdraw. 'Say you've got a hamstring or something,' he would 'advise' you. 'I'll get someone from the club to put in a call for you.'

In those unenlightened times, the SFA would take an individual at his word and clubs weren't expected to provide a medical certificate to prove you were, in fact, injured. Back in the late sixties and early seventies, the standard international fee was £50 and, once tax and other deductions were made, you were left with around £36. The SFA knew they didn't have to throw money at the players because most, if not all, of us would happily have given our services for free. Personally speaking, I know how much it meant to for me to don the dark blue of my nation and how proud it made my entire family. But that would have meant little to the Celtic manager whose concentration would be completely focused on what was happening at a club in the east end of Glasgow.

Jock would add a sweetener - a £50 tax free payment for not representing Scotland. Imagine that, you got more by not playing for your country than you could for playing! Money, of course, had nothing to do with it. You can't buy those sort of memories, pride doesn't have a price. But Jock could be very, very persuasive and he was always quick to tell anyone, 'There are other players out there who are just as good as you and who could do your job for Celtic.' It was a thinly-veiled threat, of course. He couldn't actually force you to pull out, but you wouldn't have to be Einstein to work out you might be putting your first team place in jeopardy if you went against his wishes.

But, please believe me, playing for my country meant the world to me. One of my most magical moments - right up there with Lisbon - was making my Scotland debut against England in Glasgow on the Saturday afternoon of 2 April, 1966. We lost 4-3 to the Auld Enemy, but it couldn't take away the overwhelming feeling of honour I had when I stepped onto the pitch that day. Of course, I had been in the Hampden stand to witness Scotland games, but to actually go out there and participate and to be taken aback by the sheer volume of noise and all those waving Lion Rampant flags was just something else altogether. Hampden was just awash with tartan and that was something I had never experienced before as a player.

Naturally, I was used to big and vociferous crowds at Celtic Park, but this was something different. I don't know about Braveheart, but it made Tommy Gemmell's heart beat a little faster, I can tell you. I loved it and I revelled in it. That particular memory has a special place in my heart. Jimmy Johnstone netted twice and Denis Law beat the great Gordon Banks with a jack-in-the-box leap to fire a header high into the net. And I remember, too, that we might have got a draw in the last minute when Willie Wallace, later to become a superb Celtic team-mate and loyal friend, had an effort cleared off the line by Nobby Stiles. Now, if that had gone in...

Being asked to withdraw from an international squad wasn't unique to me, of course. Jimmy Johnstone was easily the best outside-right in the world in his heyday. He could have walked - or waltzed - into any of the great Brazil teams. No argument. How many caps did Jinky pick up? Twenty-three. Bobby Murdoch was one of the best midfielders on the planet. How many caps? Twelve.

The situation involving Bertie Auld was simply downright bizarre. He was one of the most magnificent passers of the ball I have ever seen. He was a crucial cog in the engine room of the Celtic team that conquered Europe and dominated the home and foreign fronts for so long. How many caps? Three. And they were all won back in 1959 and 1960, long before he switched from an orthodox outside-left to a midfield berth where he excelled with his range of passing, incredible vision and quick thinking. If you ever want to see two guys at the top of their game and taking over the middle of the park to dictate the entire ninety minutes of a football match, just watch a rerun of Bobby and Bertie against Inter Milan in the Portuguese capital in 1967. They were unbelievable. Unstoppable. Unmatchable.

81

But Big Jock never had to offer Bertie a £50 tax free 'inducement' not to play for Scotland. Curiously, Bertie, one of the most wonderful exponents of the measured through ball in football, was never selected for any Scottish squad. To be honest - and I'm not saying it because he is still a very good friend of mine - I find that unfathomable, simply beyond comprehension. Did Scotland have so many excellent left-sided midfield players back then that they could continually overlook Bertie? It would appear the selectors thought so. I know it didn't bother my wee mate one jot. He would look at a pool of players for an upcoming international and say, 'I must be doing something right - Big Jock keeps picking me for Celtic every week.'

Oddly, every other player who won a European Cup medal would get a call-up at some point afterwards for Scotland. Ronnie Simpson, Jim Craig, Bobby Murdoch, Billy McNeill, John Clark, Jimmy Johnstone, Willie Wallace, Stevie Chalmers, Bobby Lennox and yours truly. However, there was never any sign of the name Bertie Auld. As my pal might have said, 'Ach, there's no accounting for taste.'

Mind you, Bertie might not have done too much to push his claims by being sent off on his international debut while playing against Holland in Amsterdam back in 1959. I suppose Bertie was determined to mark the occasion. He has always protested his innocence when fists and boots were flying around in a melee between both sets of players near the end of what had been a fairly explosive encounter which the Scots, incidentally, won 2-1. However, a Dutch player took a dull one and collapsed as though he had just been struck by a freight train. The referee picked out Bertie as the culprit and he was immediately dismissed. Two games later and that was his international career consigned to the dustbin. Strange things happen in the beautiful game.

Something else Big Jock was fond of informing you was the fact that you were on the payroll at Celtic and Scotland would only pick up the tab whenever they chose to give you a call. 'Remember who pays your wages every week,' he would growl. 'You'll not be able to pay your mortgage with three or four fifty quids a year.' He had a point, of course. I've no idea if there were any compensation claims back then if a player missed a chunk of games for his club after being injured on international duty. I suppose there was that risk factor to consider, too. Look at Rangers left-back Eric Caldow, for instance. He suffered a broken leg after an accidental collision with England's big, burly frontman Bobby Smith at Wembley in 1963. I'm reliably informed that Caldow, so steady and consistent for an Ibrox side that virtually dominated in Scotland in the early sixties, was never quite the same again when he returned. As a matter of fact, rather sadly, Caldow never played for his country again. Did Rangers get a penny? Honestly, I don't know, but it would have been most unusual in those days for a club to sue the SFA.

By the way, it wasn't only Big Jock who wasn't slow to attempt to persuade his players it might be better for them to put their feet up on a Wednesday evening rather than be pitched into an international confrontation. Bill Shankly, at Liverpool, and Matt Busby, at Manchester United, did exactly the same. Stein, Shankly and Busby, three great Scots. But three great Scots who wouldn't think twice about asking - or demanding? - their star men to have a night off instead of turning out for Scotland. And those managers weren't alone, either, but they were the most high profile.

Busby, though, was always wasting his time if he tried to get Denis Law to pull out of a Scotland squad. Denis would have none of it and, at the peak of his powers, his would surely have been among the first names on Busby's team sheet alongside Bobby Charlton and George Best. Not even Busby could have afforded to leave out a fully-fit Lawman. Denis was fanatical about playing for his country. He was an outstanding patriot and God help the guy who stood between him and a place in the Scotland team. Busby would have had to put him under house arrest to prevent him getting to Scotland to play for his country. If Scotland had arranged a fixture on the moon, you could be sure Denis would have got there somehow, some way. Okay, a slight exaggeration there, but you get the drift.

Denis would often tell me, 'I loved it when we won and I could go back to Old Trafford and let my English mates Bobby Charlton and Nobby Stiles know how well we had played. The other English guys in the dressing room had to tolerate me going on all week about how wonderful Scotland were. If we lost, though, it was a vastly different story. Then I was apprehensive about what was awaiting me when I returned from a trip to face a dressing room grilling. I was helped by the fact I had Paddy Crerand alongside me and he would always lend his support. But, boy, did they know it when Scotland achieved a good victory. I suppose I must have been difficult to live with in 1967 after we had beaten them on their own midden at Wembley. World champions? We proved who were the best that afternoon. It was 3-2 going on a massacre.'

Sometimes, of course, there were other reasons for Jock not wanting players to turn out for Scotland. Wee Jinky was the direct rival of Rangers' Willie Henderson for the outside-right position in the international line-up. And, sadly, the Ibrox fans used to give Jinky dog's abuse when he was chosen ahead of their player, who, by the way, was an outstanding performer in his own right. Jinky was as courageous a character as I have ever encountered, but being continually booed and jeered while playing for his country did get through to him. You would have required the skin of a rhino for it not to. Jock would see that could affect his performance a few days later for Celtic with the player's confidence completely sucked out of him. There were several occasions when Jinky would get the same treatment as myself. 'I'll get someone to phone in and say you're injured or ill, Wee Man,' Jock would say and a lot of the time Jinky chose to take that line instead of putting himself up for the boo brigade to have a field day at his expense. Honestly, it was pathetic. Scottish fans jeering their own player? You couldn't make it up.

I know Davie Hay had a similar situation when he was settling into the international team. At that stage, if Davie was selected, it normally meant he was taking the right-back berth associated with Rangers' Sandy Jardine. That would make my mate Davie a target for what was always termed 'a small minority'. Small or not, they could kick up some bloody racket. I can tell you that Davie actually got out of his sickbed once to play for Scotland in a game at Hampden. He had been struggling with a touch of flu and had just made it to play for Celtic on the Saturday. He was given some time off at the start of the week to try to recuperate by the-then international team manager Bobby Brown before being picked to play in a European Championship qualifier against Denmark in a midweek tie in November 1970. As you might expect, he struggled before being replaced to huge cheers from a section only too happy to see Sandy Jardine come on in his place thirteen minutes from the end. If only those so-called supporters had known. At least Davie, as ever, had put in a fabulous shift to help Scotland to a 1-0 win with John O'Hare scoring in the fourteenth minute. Frankly, the opposition during those dark days, must have been completely bewildered at the antics of the home fans.

I recall Kenny Dalglish getting much of the same. He was achieving great things at Celtic as he emerged as a potentially genuine world class player and we all knew he was destined for football's pinnacle. Yet he still got it in the neck from some halfwits on the terracing when he performed at Hampden. That all changed, however, when he moved to Liverpool. Soon afterwards, the mob who used to bay for him 'tae get aff' were proclaiming him as King Kenny. Did he suddenly become a better international player when he moved to Anfield? Coincidence? Don't think so.

I must also say there were times when you were omitted from an international squad and that left you more than a little puzzled. Every player knows when he is going through a good spell. They don't need anyone to tell them. They don't need big headlines in the national Press. So, there were occasions when you could see an international looming and, without being big-headed or complacent, you believed you would be involved. Then the pool of players would be announced and the name Tommy Gemmell was missing. You would reread the list of players just to make sure your eye hadn't skipped over your name. Nope, it wasn't there. You were surplus to requirements on this occasion.

Rather amazingly, Bobby Brown, who made his debut in the 3-2 Wembley win over England in 1967, was the first full-time Scotland international manager. It took the SFA an awful long time to catch up with the Twentieth Century. Before Bobby, the team bosses were given a list of players whose names had been put in front of them by the SFA selectors. How antiquated was that? I'm sure there must have been individuals on the selection committee who took their business very seriously, but it must have been seen as a wee jolly for some others. An all-expenses trip to London or Manchester, take in a game and chuck in a player's name for consideration.

Here's another story you'll find hard to swallow. One of these old duffers went to Highbury to watch Arsenal. This guy's knowledge of football must have been next to zilch. He duly returned to Glasgow with a name for the perusal of the international manager. He had taken quite a shine to the Arsenal left-back he was convinced could do a great job for Scotland. At one of their many meetings, this guy pushed the merits of the Gunners defender. He had a good Scottish name, but Bob McNab was already the ENGLAND left-back at the time. So, there was a bloke with his finger on the pulse. Tells you all you need to know about the set-up back then.

Years after I had quit playing, I was having lunch with a Stirling Albion director by the name of Archie Gourlay. He, too, had been on the SFA selection committee and he was quite candid about his role back then. He told me, 'If a club wanted one of their players to get international recognition they really looked after you. They would go over the top in their hospitality. I would go down to the big clubs at the time, Manchester United, Liverpool, Spurs, Arsenal, Newcastle and the like. They would really take care of you. They would lay out these impressive spreads and would make sure you were comfortable before, during and after the game. That would absolutely guarantee one of their players being recommended. If they didn't take care of you, then that was bad luck for one of their players. That was the system in those days.'

I also had to laugh when I heard the story of one player having a word with Big Jock when he started his second stint as Scotland manager - remember, he had been caretaker in 1965 - after taking over from Ally MacLeod following the shambles of the 1978 World Cup Finals in Argentina. I'll do the player a favour and not reveal his identity, but, trust me, this is a true tale. Back then, the British Home International Championship used to be played over the period of eight days at the end of the season. Scotland, say, could start with a game against Northern Ireland in Belfast on Saturday, play Wales in Glasgow in midweek and then there was the Big One, the encounter with our old foes England at either Hampden or Wembley on the following Saturday. Obviously, that was the match every Scot wanted to get involved in; there were no sicknotes flying around before this confrontation.

Anyway, this player, who was a defender with one of the top English sides, went to Jock to inform him he wasn't interested in playing against the Welsh or the Irish, but he would be perfectly willing to turn out against England. Obviously, this guy did not know Jock Stein. My old gaffer didn't swear a lot, but I could imagine this bloke copping an earful. Needless to say, his name was absent whenever Scotland played England and Big Jock was in charge. The guy never got a sniff.

Obviously, I made a lot of good friends on my international sorties. Denis Law, for a start. Then there was Alan Gilzean, as fine an attack-leader as I have ever seen, Jim Baxter, the great Ranger, wee Billy Bremner, a bundle of energy, and Willie Henderson, second only to Jinky as a right-winger in my opinion. This may surprise you, but England's Alan Ball became a big mate, too. Well, wee mate, I suppose. There were so many fabulous pals, so, if there are any of my old colleagues reading this and I have overlooked you, then please accept my apologies. You're in my memory banks somewhere, be sure of that. Okay, it's time to get the party started and put together my all-time Scotland line-up of legends. Easier said than done. Here we go...

I scored over sixty goals for Celtic - not all of them penalty-kicks, I hasten to add - and that's not bad going for a left-back. However, while I was playing for Scotland, I only netted two. Embarrassingly, one of them was in my own net! And, even worse, it was against my old mate Ronnie Simpson. Honestly, you don't need comedy scriptwriters in football. We're all masters of improvisation. So, how did it come about? Sadly, I can't even blame the conditions at Hampden on that sunny Wednesday evening of 10 May 1967 when we faced the USSR.

Our opponents didn't need a helping hand with players such as Albert Shesternev - known as 'Big Al' during the World Cup Finals in England the previous year - Josif Sabo, Valerij Veronin, Igor Chislenko and Eduard Malofeyev in the team. They also had one of the greatest goalkeepers of all time gracing Glasgow that night, the legendary Lev Yashin, known as the Black Octopus. He was the first goalie to wear an all-black kit that so many others copied in the sixties. Octopus? Well, he seemed to have more arms than was considered the norm. Yashin was at the veteran stage at that time and it must have been a rare occasion when my old mate Ronnie wasn't the oldest man on the pitch. Ronnie was thirty-six years old and his Soviet counterpart was a year his senior.

Well, how did my mishap occur? Good question. I blame Ronnie! There were only sixteen minutes gone when I was tidying things up at the back. The game had started off at a genteel pace and maybe I was a bit slow to get into the flow. Anyway, without even looking over my shoulder, I turned to flick a high pass back to our keeper. Imagine my horror, then, when I heard a howl from the Hampden terracings and I swiftly looked round. Ronnie, for whatever reason, had wandered onto his eighteen-yard line. I turned to see our keeper scampering back trying to catch the ball as it sailed serenely into our net.

I looked at Ronnie and said, 'For fuck's sake, why didn't you give me a shout? Why weren't you on your line, you old bastard?' That, you should know, was a term of endearment. Ronnie was always good at returning fire. 'Why the hell didn't you look where you were putting the ball?' Thankfully, the man known as Faither was never a big curser. Mind you, he might not have been too delighted when I said, 'Faither? You should be known as GRANDfaither after that goal!'

It didn't get any better when Fedor Medved netted another just before the interval and that's the way the scoreline finished. We had beaten England 3-2 at Wembley the previous month and, quite possibly, we had gone well into overtime overindulging that success. I also had to face the wrath, not only of Ronnie, but also another five of my Celtic colleagues who had figured in the game against the USSR - Billy McNeill, John Clark, Jimmy Johnstone, Bobby Lennox and Willie Wallace. We all had better fortune, I seem to remember, in a club game that was played in Portugal fifteen days later.

At the end of the match, there was the usual scrum of newspaper reporters waiting to talk to the players. They selected me for the main question. They chorused, 'What on earth were you thinking about at the own goal?' I had to think fast. I answered, 'I looked up and saw an old guy coming out of goal and I thought it was Lev Yashin, so I decided to lob him.' I don't think anyone bought into that.

My other goal while representing my country was hardly memorable, but, at least, it was for Scotland! There is a good story about it, too. We were strolling to a 7-0 World Cup qualifying rout over Cyprus - a country Big Jock would have undoubtedly termed as small fry - when we were awarded a penalty-kick with only fourteen minutes to go. Colin Stein, the Rangers striker, was on fire at Hampden that May afternoon in 1969. He had rattled in four goals in the space of thirty-nine minutes and was doing his utmost to beat Denis Law's Scottish international record. The Lawman had scored foursomes in games against Northern Ireland in 1962 and Norway a year later. The bold Colin wanted to go one better and grabbed the ball as soon as the referee pointed to the spot. It was natural enough for an in-form hitman to want to take the award. In fact, the penalty was given at what was commonly known as the Rangers End of the national stadium and the fans in there behind that goal were chanting for their Ibrox hero to have a go.

No chance! I was the designated penalty-taker for the team and the onus was on me. Colin could plead all he liked, I was taking that spot-kick. A Celtic player allowing a Rangers player to overtake a legend like The Lawman? Sorry, Colin, it was never going to happen. I put the ball on the spot and I did what I always did. I smashed it as hard as I could in the direction of the goal and hoped for the best. It flew into the net and that completed the scoring. Colin looked a bit miffed at the end. The Cypriot keeper's name was Michalaikis Alkiviadis and someone should tell him he was in legendary company. He became only the second goalkeeper, along with the icon that was Ronnie Simpson, I scored against in an international. That would have been something to tell his grandkids!

I only played alongside Hearts keeper Jim Cruickshank twice on international duty, the first being a goalless British Championship draw against England at Hampden in April, 1970 and a 3-0 hammering against Belgium in Liege a year later. Of course, he defended the Edinburgh side's goal on many occasions when I faced him while playing for Celtic. I thought he was a real Steady Eddie who rarely got involved in the spectacular, much preferring to anticipate where the danger was coming from. Jim, in fact, was linked with Celtic several times over the years, but, obviously, nothing materialised. The word was that he wasn't a huge fan of training and used to do his own thing. That would have had Big Jock climbing the wall. It wouldn't have mattered if Jim had been a combination of Lev Yashin and Gordon Banks, he wouldn't have got anywhere near Parkhead. Actually, I don't see the need for goalkeepers to do cross-country running. What's the point? They aren't likely to go on and run the length of the pitch during a match. They are asked to do quick bursts of about twenty to thirty yards if they are coming out of their area to boot a ball to safety. I would have put them through those sort of routines rather than lung-bursting marathons.

One guy who might have done with a bit more exercise was the Liverpool No.1 Tommy Lawrence. He was in goal twice in international games in which I was involved and I have to say his nickname just about summed him up. He was known as The Flying Pig! Lev Yashin was the Black Octopus and Tommy was the Flying Pig. Wasn't the most complimentary of nicknames, was it? Actually, there are some players who are naturally stocky and are mistaken for being a bit flabby. Tommy, I'm sorry to say, looked as though he was carrying a bit of surplus baggage. Having said that, he was good enough to play for Liverpool for many years under the critical gaze of Bill Shankly before the Anfield manager brought in Ray Clemence.

Bobby Ferguson was the goalkeeper in place when I made my debut against England in 1966. He conceded four that that afternoon and, to be honest, didn't greatly impress me. A year later West Ham shelled out £65,000 to take him from Kilmarnock and that was a British record fee at the time for a keeper. Old Upton Park manager Ron Greenwood must have detected something in his handling that I was unaware of. I played in the same team as Ferguson on three occasions and he never had a shut-out, conceding six goals. My old mate Ronnie Simpson eventually nudged him aside to become his country's No.1.

I thought Jim Herriot was a terrific goalkeeper when he was with Dunfermline in the mid-sixties. It looked as though he had everything. He was agile, possessed a good pair of hands and had sound concentration. He played in eight games when I was at full-back and I have to say I wondered what had happened to him when he returned to Scotland after a period with Birmingham City. For whatever reason, he didn't look the same goalkeeper. I didn't think he was as confident as he had been with the Fifers. He was a character, though. I remember him preparing for an international against England at Wembley in 1969. It was played on a Wednesday night to try to dissuade the Scottish fans from turning up in their thousands after our support thought it was a good idea to transport the Wembley pitch and the goalposts back across the border after our win over the world champions two years earlier. Some hope.

Anyway, Jim was gazing into a mirror in the dressing room and applying some sort of cream. A lot of players get soaked in liniment and all sorts of other lotions, so no-one took a blind bit of notice until Jim turned round to face his team-mates. He had these great big self-administered black blotches under his eyes. It looked as though he had gone ten rounds with Muhammad Ali. And then another ten with Joe Frazier. Maybe one or two with George Foreman. 'What the hell is that for?' I asked, rightly mystified, possibly believing he had some sort of weird superstition about playing in London on a Wednesday evening. He explained he had seen American footballers applying the same stuff when they were playing under floodlights. Apparently, the black under the eyes killed the glare. Most footballers will try anything to enhance their game, I thought. Didn't help our keeper one bit, though. We were gubbed 4-1. We all got a black eye that night. Back to the drawing board, Jim.

Aberdeen's Ernie McGarr was in my company for all of twenty-four minutes as a Scotland international when he made his debut in a friendly against the Republic of Ireland in Dublin in 1969. Unfortunately, he was injured and had to be replaced by Herriot - I wonder if he had time to put on his black eyes? - in what ended in a 1-1 stalemate. McGarr played one more game, a 2-0 win over Austria, later that year before being replaced at club and country level by Bobby Clark. What do I remember about McGarr? He was tall and skinny. That's about it, I'm afraid, so he didn't quite make a lasting impression.

Now it's time to stand up and be counted. Who gets the nod to be the last line of defence for my country? It's got to be Faither, Ronnie Simpson. As I've said earlier, I just can't see past him. Defenders depend on the man behind them being solid and dependable and being able to drag you out of the mire every now and again. Ronnie had that ability. So, Ronnie Simpson is my Numero Uno Number One.

As I am th manager of this team and I have the final say, I am going to choose yours truly for the right-back position. I wouldn't want to miss out on being involved with this line-up, so, sorry, but I am going to be selfish. Most people will remember me as a left-back - and that's where I played the bulk of my football - but I was quite comfortable switching wings. I was two-footed, so that helped. And I don't have to spend too much time dwelling on who should be my full-back partner. It has to be Chelsea's Eddie McCreadie. He might not have scored too many goals in his career, but he must have made hundreds by the way he bombed forward. He was lightning getting down that line and he rarely squandered a cross when he whipped one into the danger area.

He was quite compact and looked to be just about the perfect build for a full-back. Eddie was quick on the turn and any winger who thought they only had to knock the ball past him and run into space with a bit of freedom to spare were, more often than not, caught out by the speed of his recovery. He was crisp and clean in the tackle, too, and it's amazing he started his career at little East Stirling and a quality player like that wasn't picked up by one of the bigger clubs in Scotland. Chelsea didn't hesitate, though, and they got years of sterling service out of an excellent footballer. And a thoroughly nice guy, too.

Central defence is a little more tricky. I played twelve games with Rangers' Ronnie McKinnon as the man in charge of the No.5 shirt. Billy McNeill and I were international team-mates on a mere four occasions. So, I realise I am about to be accused of being biased towards my old Celtic mate, but I have to pencil him in ahead of his Old Firm rival. Billy and Ronnie both had different strengths. The Ibrox man, for a start, was a lot quicker across the ground than Billy. I think Ronnie was helped by the fact that he had started his senior career as an old-fashioned wing-half at Rangers. I believe he also played at centre-forward in the juveniles before stepping up. Undoubtedly, that would have helped him be a lot more mobile on the deck than his Parkhead counterpart. Billy had plenty of pluses, but I have to admit pace was not among them. Being the honest citizen he is, he will probably be among the first to admit to that.

Yet, look at his prowess in the air. He was awesome. Of course, being around the 6ft 2in mark would have helped, but his timing was also immaculate. I've seen wee guys outjumping blokes about six inches taller just because their judgement is faultless. Look at Dixie Deans, at Celtic, for instance. Dixie was no skyscraper - I think he was about 5ft 7in - but he must have put the fear of God into taller opponents simply by his reading of the play and his ability to time things perfectly. Denis Law was no giant, but take a look at the goals he scored with his head. Take a trip back in time and watched footage of the incomparable Pele and the West German Gerd Muller. Neither would get snow in their hair when they took off, but they knew how and when to attack the ball when it was in the air. But I doubt if any of those blokes would have got much change out of Billy in aerial duels. There can be no argument that Billy was more masterful than Ronnie when the high balls were dropping into the penalty box. I like my centre-backs to be commanding in that crucial area. Caesar, look out your boots, you're in.

If you wanted a ball-playing left-half performing alongside Big Billy, you must go for Jim Baxter. The Rangers idol wasn't a great defender, but don't believe all you may have read or heard that he was lazy. That is a myth. He made the forward passes from opponents look predictable such was his anticipation. He was rarely put in a position where he had to fly into tackles. His ability on the ball was breathtaking. He was so nonchalant the way he used to flit across a football pitch. 'Just gie the ba' tae The Glove,' he would shout in that unmistakeable Fife accent. The Glove, by the way, was his name for his left foot. And after the leather sphere did, in fact, drop at that magical set of twinkling toes then you knew in an instant the opposition were in trouble. He could thread that ball through the best organised of defences. I couldn't possibly leave Slim Jim out of this team.

As far as the midfield is concerned, I would expect both wingers to do their bit in the team's cockpit and, of course, Baxter would be having his say in there, too. One guy who puts forward a forceful claim for a place in the side has got to be Billy Bremner, the inspiration of Don Revie's emerging Leeds United team of the mid-sixties and early seventies. He was a feisty, fiery character with the same sort of temperament as another wee flame-haired guy of my acquaintance. We got it every week at Celtic with Jimmy Johnstone and you wondered if, in fact, he was a blood relative of Bremner. They would quite happily fight with their image in a mirror.

The Press often referred to Wee Billy as the Bristling Bantam and he probably took that as a compliment. In fact, he was more like a terrier the way he snapped at rivals' heels. An opponent must have thought he was facing up to a mini-combine harvester when my pal was zipping around. If the ball was there to be won, Billy was convinced it was his property. And what a brave player. He never ducked out of a challenge or shirked a responsibility. Actually, I never thought he received the credit he deserved for his all-round ability. People will talk about his tenacity, but what about his talent? That guy could play, alright. His passing was wonderfully accurate, even in the tightest of situations. And, believe me, Billy could get himself into some tight situations. I know what I'm talking about - I was there on several occasions.

I will never forget the evening of our 3-2 victory over England at Wembley in 1967. By the way, I make absolutely no apology for mentioning this game on more than one occasion. I think true Scots will know why.

Anyway, once the smoke of battle had cleared that particular day, all the players, booted and suited, went out for the aftermatch banquet which was being held at London's plush Cafe Royale. It would be fair to say a few cocktails were partaken by the Scottish entourage that night. The English guys were at the dinner, too, and, once all the formalities had been taken care of, both sets of players repaired to the bar. You could say one set of blokes were just a tad more raucous than the other. Bobby Charlton, Bobby Moore, Nobby Stiles, Alan Ball and the rest of the England mob retreated to a little corner where you could hear a pin drop. Denis Law kept looking over at his Manchester United colleagues, Bobby and Nobby, smiling and waving a drink in the air.

For some obscure reason, the Scotland team was invited to the Shaftesbury Theatre where there was a celebration going on for the 10,000th production of Agatha Christie's world famous whodunnit The Mousetrap. It made its debut in 1952 and was still going strong sixty-two years later when I put this book together. Anyway, it was getting on a bit and it was obvious Billy had thoroughly enjoyed the evening. You could say he was as happy as a newt. The electric soup had been in full flow and who could deny him and the rest of us our day in the sun? We had all had the fact rammed down our throats that England were the world's finest team ever since they had beaten West Germany 4-2 in extra-time the previous summer. It seemed they had been unbeaten since God was a boy until we derailed them, of course, to become the best on the planet. It seemed a logical thought to all of us Scots at the theatre as the booze continued to flow.

Anyway, in the midst of all this frivolity and merriment, two famous faces loomed into view. Cilla Black and Frankie Howerd had decided to join in our celebrations. I think the conversation went along these lines.

Cilla (talking to Billy), 'Well, chuck, you must be really delighted with that win. What a wonderful surprise. I think it was a great result for you and Scotland. I thought you deserved it.'

Billy (gazing at Cilla), 'Eh?'

Frankie (talking to Billy), 'I rated that a masterful performance. Nothing short of excellent. Scotland were superb.'

Billy (to both), 'See you, Cilla, you're one of the worst fuckin' singers I've ever heard in my fuckin' life. Hey, Howerd, you're the biggest fuckin' poof in the fuckin' world.'

In that instant , it seemed evident to me why Eamonn Andrews had never asked Billy to pay any tributes to showbiz personalities on his TV programme This Is Your Life.

Interesting lad, on and off the field, was our Billy. But I'm afraid he will have to take a place on the sidelines in my all-time greats. I'm going to be accused of wearing my green-tinted specs again, but I am going to have to award that place to Bobby Murdoch. I've talked about Bobby elsewhere, so I don't want to go over old ground. But, suffice to say, if Bobby Murdoch can get in to my team in front of Billy Bremner then that tells you all you need to know. I picked up a reputation with my shooting power, but Bobby was devastating, too, when he set his sights. To him, falls the honour of claiming one of the finest goals I have ever witnessed in a football game anywhere.

We were playing West Germany in a World Cup qualifier at Hampden on an April evening in 1969. We were losing 1-0 after a goal from Gerd Muller, who could use his backside better than anyone else in the game when it came to barging into defenders and spinning to have a shot at goal. That's what he did that night when he collected a short free-kick on the edge of the penalty area, bumped Ronnie McKinnon to one side with his Red Rum backside, swivelled and shot low into the net. Tommy Lawrence - the Flying Pig - didn't exactly soar as the ball eluded him. So, there were only two minutes to go when Bobby, chest thrust forward in that proud manner of his, strode upfield. I think it was Charlie Cooke who rolled the ball in front of my team-mate who didn't even break stride before unleashing an unstoppable right-foot drive from about twenty-five yards that almost tore a hole in the net. Sepp Maier did well to get out of its way. What a goal. And what a player. His versatility just shades Billy.

A guy I would definitely have on my bench would be Rangers' John Greig. The Ibrox legend played in a variety of international positions during my time and never let his country down. Greigy played at full-back and midfield and his enthusiasm and dedication were second to none. He didn't have the finesse of Bobby, but he had wonderful leadership qualities. He had a marvellous engine, too. I look back at the team that won at Wembley in 1967 - yes, that game AGAIN! - and he was another that day who never got the applause he deserved. All the talk was of Jim Baxter playing keepy-uppy, Denis Law's overall dynamic display and the performance of the debutants, Ronnie Simpson, at thirty-six, and twenty year old Jim McCalliog. Somewhere in there, though, we should never forget the immense contribution of Greigy.

Now for the wingers. No-one is going to take a step back in surprise when I name the outside-right. Of course, it has to be Jimmy Johnstone. How could I possibly leave out the Wee Man? He and Billy Bremner were great mates on and off the field and barmen in any pub must have known they were in for a hectic evening when these two came through the door. Both liked a swally, as it's known in the west of Scotland, but it must be pointed out they were great trainers. There's no way either could have had the careers they had if they didn't punish themselves on the training ground to compensate for a night on the tiles. Like a lot of footballers, they could let their hair down when they were let off the leash. Okay, as Cilla Black and Frankie Howerd might testify, they could go a bit over the top at times, but I can tell you both made up for it and that undoubtedly helped their fitness levels.

Jinky's nocturnal escapades on a rowing boat at Largs have been well documented. There was another hilarious adventure concerning Jinky and Billy, but, unfortunately, it had dire consequences for the Celtic player. Davie Hay was in the Scotland squad that had gone on a two-game trip to Belgium and Norway to prepare for the 1974 World Cup Finals. He told me the story of the Scottish players on their way to Norway after losing the first game 2-1 in Bruges. There were five days between the matches and the cabin crew had been very generous with the champagne on the flight to Oslo. Apparently, the bubbly was flowing and things can get a bit out of hand in these circumstances. I've been there, seen it and got the T shirt, as they say. It continued into the bar of the team's hotel where Jinky and Billy broke manager Willie Ormond's curfew. According to Davie, the team manager discovered they had gone AWOL and wouldn't have required the aid of a Private Eye to track down the offenders to the bar. Words were exchanged and the Oslo Two appeared to be very unhappy about being reprimanded by their nation's manager, preparing for Scotland's first appearance on the World Cup Finals stage in sixteen years.

They both decided the football extravaganza would go ahead without their input. They were going home. Davie put it this way, 'I got wind of what was going on and I tried to talk some sense into them. They had gone to their rooms, packed their bags and were making their way to the lifts with the full intention of going home. Dishevelled and obviously the worse for wear, they were teetering about with their luggage undone while their clothes, sleeves, trouser legs and ties were hanging out of their bags. Goodness knows how they were going to get back to Scotland. They had no air tickets and there was the little matter of the North Sea separating the two countries. That didn't seem to bother them too much at the time. Jinky, in that condition, might have contemplated hiring a boat! Eventually, they were talked out of going home and returned to their rooms.

'I understood the seriousness of the situation, but it was comical seeing them standing there with their half-packed bags ready to make their escape. Neither Willie Ormond nor the SFA saw the funny side of things as the players surfaced the following morning. It looked as though they might be going home, after all. But this time it wouldn't be their decision. I believe there were some at the SFA who wanted the pair sent packing on the first available flight. The team manager didn't want to take such stringent and drastic action, of course. For a start, Billy was our captain and on-field organiser. He was invaluable as to how the team was set up. Eventually, sanity kicked in and peace broke out. The players weren't being sent home. They both got a stiff reprimand, instead.'

There were repercussions, though, for my wee Celtic pal. He never got to kick a ball in those World Cup Finals while Billy, of course, captained Scotland against Zaire, Brazil and Yugoslavia. Isn't it amazing to discover that players of the quality of Jinky, George Best and Alfredo di Stefano never got the opportunity to display their God-given skills during soccer's showpiece on that glittering platform? Never mind, Jinky, you're in my dream team. If it was fairly predictable to work out who I would nominate for the No.7 berth, I'm willing to bet it wouldn't have been so easy to fathom out who would get the nod for the outside-left place.

Step forward, Willie Henderson! Yes, the same Willie Henderson who used to make my life hell while playing on the right wing for Rangers. But I have seen Willie operating on the opposite wing for Scotland and been very impressed. He might have looked all right foot, but if you have the talent he had at his disposal, I reckon you could play a bloke like that in a variety of attacking positions. Mind you, he might have struggled at centre-forward. The only drawback with Willie was that he was as blind as a bat. I remember going out for a pint with my wee mate while we were still with our respective Old Firm clubs. Willie was talking about an evening game he had played at Ibrox. Straight-faced, he said, 'I'm pretty sure I set up three goals that night, but it was so bloody dark I couldn't be certain.' I wasn't sure if he was joking.

On the field, Willie was a real nuisance who never gave you a moment's peace. He was fast and tricky and, once he was away from you, there was no way back. You knew you were never going to catch him. Off the field, he became a great friend, a special bloke. Jinky was the Wee Man and Willie was the Wee Barra. Both graced the game of football and I would have to put them in my line-up.

That means apologies to my old Celtic colleague John Hughes. On form, Yogi, as he was affectionately known after the TV cartoon bear Yogi Bear, would get into any world eleven. Off form, Yogi would struggle to get into any street team. There was no middle ground with that man. He could be a juggernaut at times, completely unplayable. He was a giant of a man with the deftest of touches. Yogi could play through the middle or on the wing, mainly the left. It was his sheer unpredictability that let him down. I hope he won't mind me making that observation.

Charlie Cooke was another delightful player. He had perfect balance, bewildering poise. Charlie weaved towards players with mesmerising ability. They loved him at Chelsea where they encouraged flamboyance. They had the likes of Eddie McCreadie, Peter Osgood and Alan Hudson and cheeky Charlie fitted right in with a positive attacking attitude. However, like Yogi, he could be a moody player. You could watch him and wait for him to explode into action and go on a mazy run. Ninety minutes later, you could still be waiting. Both these players at their best would have terrorised any defence. Leeds United's Eddie Gray deserves a mention, too. Another exceptional ball-playing wide man with a style all of his own. He liked to take the ball right up to the full-back, wiggle those hips and then take off. Right or left? That was the defender's problem. Eddie could go down the flank or come inside and he always looked comfortable.

No beating about the bush for my main attacking positions - Denis Law is an absolute must. The guy was pure showbiz, a glamorous personality who was as tough as nails. His upbringing in a tenement in a council estate in Aberdeen formed his outlook, not only on football, but life, as well. He shared a bedroom with three brothers, his three sisters commandeered another and his mum and dad had the third bedroom in their small apartment. Denis's dad was a fisherman who could be away for up to a week at a time when the trawler headed for the Faroe Islands and suchlike places. Denis always admitted his family were 'poor, but happy' and that upbringing didn't do him any harm, did it? He had the most electrifying reflexes I have ever seen in any footballer. He summed up situations in an instant. It could be a packed penalty area with bodies and boots flying all the place and Denis would have it under control in an instant. He was lightning swift.

I remember playing against him when I was at Nottingham Forest and we were due to face Manchester United. I was put in at centre-half that day and was right up against Denis. Yes, I admit there was a bit of an edge to both Denis and myself during the game. He was a mucker, but you didn't want him ripping you apart. And I knew he had the ability to do that very thing. I just didn't want to be on the receiving end. I was getting in about him right from the off and the Lawman didn't say a thing. I continued to dive in and never give him a chance to get the ball under control. Throughout the first-half there wasn't a murmur. Same at the start of the second period. And, following another clattering challenge after about an hour, Denis calmly looked round and said, 'Hey, Tam, would you stop fuckin' kicking me!' That was all he said. I believe it ended honours even at time-up and we had a pint or two in the club bar afterwards. The game wasn't mentioned. A wonderful bloke. A real man's man.

Another who didn't quite earn the reputation as a shrinking violet was Alan Gilzean, or Gillie as he was known to everyone. The Spurs man was simply magnificent. He had a sublime touch, was awkward to dispossess, could gallop with the ball at his feet, fabulous at link-up play, was deadly in front of goal and was a terror in the air. What else do you need? The Lawman and Gillie, two formidable forwards who could have played in and graced any footballing era.

I really liked Gillie. I played against him a few times when I was first coming through at Celtic and he was at Dundee before his move to London. I do recall he gave Big Billy a tough time in aerial duels and anyone who can achieve that against Caesar has got to be special. I spent a lot of time in his company when we were at Largs preparing for international games. More often than not, the players would assemble at the North British Hotel in Glasgow on a Sunday before our trip down to the Ayrshire coast. It wouldn't be an understatement to say Gillie could sink a drop or two. Back then, we were pretty much left to our own devices before the serious stuff kicked in and we got prepared for the forthcoming game. Walter McCrae doubled up as trainer with the national side and his club outfit Kilmarnock. Walter was normally left with the thankless task of trying to round up the players and getting them to their bed at a decent time. We used to stay at the Queen's Hotel which was just back from the promenade on the North Ayrshire holiday resort.

Gillie, myself and a couple of the other lads found a wee pub smack in the middle of the Largs front. We were made most welcome and, needless to say, we were never thrown out at closing time. There would always be the luxury of a wee lock-in for the Scotland international players from a very generous mine host. Midnight would come and go and there was never any sign of Gillie being the first out the door. One or two would make their excuses and leave, but the Spurs man remained propped up at the bar as the bevvy kept flowing. It would get to around 1am and I would say, 'Are we ready to go now, Gillie?' He would look at me. 'Are you finished?' I would answer, 'Not quite.' 'Well, shut up and get them in, then,' I would be advised. Hollow legs? He had a hollow body! And, yet for all that boozing, I don't think I ever saw Gillie the worse for wear. Seriously. I had heard the stories about Gillie and his fellow-Scot Dave Mackay frightening the hell out of their English team-mates at White Hart Lane when they suggested going for a drink. I could see why. Eventually and invariably, Gillie and I were the last men standing when we decided to call it a day.

Now we knew Walter McCrae would be situated somewhere near the frontdoor in the hotel's foyer, probably doing a crossword puzzle or something as he whiled away the hours waiting for the rest of the squad to return from their night-out. What Walter didn't know was that Gillie had worked out a way of getting into the Queen's Hotel without going through the front or back door. He always organised one of the squad to leave a window open at the top of one of the landings. Then he would climb up the drainpipe at the side of the building, clamber through the window and make his way to his room. I had to follow suit. Can you imagine the fun today's newspaper photographers would have with those images? Two Scottish international players shinning their way up a drainpipe in the wee sma' hours to get to our rooms?

The following day, McCrae would see me and Gillie at breakfast, getting prepared for a good day's training and he must have wondered how on earth we managed to get home the previous night. Do you know, he never twigged? Mind you, I don't expect anyone would believe two of the country's best-known footballers would take such a curious route to their bedrooms. 'Morning, Walter,' we would say as the trainer took his seat at the table. It must be said we looked in better nick than him. He probably only got about two hours' sleep!

So, that's ten down and one to go. There were plenty of candidates for the third striker's role. I'm talking about the likes of Jim McCalliog, Joe McBride, Colin Stein, Stevie Chalmers, Willie Wallace and John O'Hare, among others. However, I have gone again for a Lisbon Lion and I honestly believe I have chosen a guy who would dovetail magnificently with Denis and Gillie - Bobby Lennox. Bobby Charlton once said Bobby was one of the best frontmen he had ever seen and I'll take his word for it. For a start, he played most matchdays with a certain Denis Law, so he could make worthwhile comparisons.

Bobby was - and still is - one of the most unassuming guys you will ever meet. You could forget he was in the dressing room before a game, but you knew when he was out on the pitch alright. He used to run on the sands at Saltcoats where he was brought up and, in fact, still lives. That must have really strengthened his ankles. It was no wonder he could buzz around with effortless ease when he stepped onto a football pitch. It must have been like coming out of a quagmire and onto a manicured lawn. He must have been an absolute nightmare to play against. I think I might have been tempted to bring along a lasso if I was facing him. That would be the only way I would ever have caught him and I would like to think I was no slouch myself.

So, there you have it - my collection of Scotland greats. Let's run through the line-up again. Ronnie Simpson in goal with yours truly and Eddie McCreadie at full-back. Billy McNeill in the middle of the defence with Jim Baxter not too far away. Bobby Murdoch strutting his stuff in the middle of the park with Jimmy Johnstone on the right and Willie Henderson on the left. Alan Gilzean, Denis Law and Bobby Lennox forming a three-pronged attack. It would be difficult to tie these guys down to a rigid formation. They were all individuals, but were also all excellent team men. It's all fantasy football, of course, but you can't help letting your imagination run riot at the thought of what those guys could have provided if they had all got together.

We'll never know, but it is a nice thought.

CHAPTER FIVE

THE RUDE, THE FAB AND THE BUBBLY

Somehow I got the impression very early on in my Celtic career that John McNamee and I were not destined to become great friends. It's not too easy to warm to some bloke who continually called you 'an Orange bastard'.

Sadly, that was the case with this fairly flawed character who obviously never excelled at the Charm School. Back then, I genuinely didn't know if he was joking or being serious, but I certainly sensed humour and this bloke were not on the same wavelength. Upon reflection, at the tender age of seventy, I am now willing to give McNamee the benefit of the doubt, although I admit that wasn't always my train of thought. However, I did get the impression he might have been the school bully.

I was a Protestant, of course, at a club that was predominantly, but not exclusively, Catholic. Let's get this straight, I had never been in an Orange Lodge in my life. And, despite what you may have heard elsewhere, I am happy to tell you that Alfie and Margaret Gemmell had been wed some considerable time before I made my debut on the planet on 16 October 1943.

Undoubtedly, McNamee could be a pest and an irritant. At times I found the guy obnoxious, even if he was under the impression he was being hilarious. I never bothered too much about religion as I was being brought up in Craigneuk. It was never a big deal to me or my family. Bob Kelly, the Celtic chairman, was a devout Catholic who, I believe, went to mass every morning. He liked me and I liked him and I don't recall either of us having a discussion about religion. I was there as a young player trying to learn my trade and hoping to get into the first team to do a job for Celtic. That's all that mattered to Bob Kelly, who, of course, made all the major decisions at the club. Quite right, too. I was never going to allow an individual, misguided or otherwise, to sidetrack me from my targets, my aims, my ambitions. I used to look McNamee and think, 'I thought you had to be dead before you donated your brain to medical science.' I never said it out loud, but I did think it!

Ian Young, my full-back partner, was also a Protestant and got similar treatment, but he admitted he thought it was all a bit of a joke. Fair enough, maybe my sense of humour didn't match that of McNamee and possibly Ian's did. These things happen at football clubs and people may be surprised, or even shocked, to discover that. It's just like a big school, really. You've got the good guys and the bad guys. You've got the loud and you've got the quiet. You've got the brash and you've got the shy. It's an eclectic mix and it's impossible for anyone to keep a twenty-four hour watch on what is happening within the walls of a big football club. That's where you have to show a character, a strength and a determination to see your way through all sorts of obstacles. So, John McNamee and I were never to become Christmas card buddies, but I will give him some sort of credit - he was a hard bastard.

Vinnie Jones, or any other of football's so-called tough guys, would have thought twice about picking a fight with McNamee. Hell, John Wayne would probably have preferred to square up to Sitting Bull at the Little Big Horn than take on Big Bad John. He was the type of guy who made a post-spinach Popeye look like a pansy. He was not a man to mess around. His sporting prowess owed more to Frank Bruno than Franz Beckenbauer. If he could attempt to intimidate his own team-mates, you had to wonder what he had in store for opponents!

I can say these things now safely in the knowledge he is seventy-two years-old and happily retired in Cumbria. Apparently, he worked as a postman in the Lake District after quitting the game. God help any terrier who thought it might be a good idea to have a bite at his ankles. Silky skills and frills were not for this lad. It didn't seem to matter too much to John if a rival player ended up in Row E along with the ball when he made a clearance. Anyone managing to get past him might discover they had left a part of their anatomy behind them. As we say in football, he was effective. I wouldn't have been surprised to have discovered he shaved with a chisel. Yes, he was THAT hard.

The name John McNamee might not be well-known to a lot of Celtic fans and the reason for that can be summed up quickly - Billy McNeill. It wasn't easy to get a first team place at centre-half when Caesar was around. McNamee, in fact, only made twenty-seven appearances in the top side between 1961 and 1964 before moving to Hibs, bought, incidentally, by a certain Protestant called Jock Stein! He was in the line-up when I made my debut against Aberdeen at Pittodrie in January 1963 and we only played alongside each other on another seven occasions. We won that match against the Dons 5-1, saw off Queen of the South 5-2, Falkirk 2-0, East Stirling 5-2 and Basle 5-1, but suffered defeats against Rangers (0-3), St.Mirren (1-2) and, finally, had a 1-1 draw with Queen of the South during our time as colleagues.

Big Bad John took no prisoners and was afraid of no-one. There was an evening in Glasgow when he was quite happy to antagonise 75,500 Rangers supporters back in 1969. He was part of the Newcastle United team that won the now-defunct Inter-Cities' Fairs Cup and they beat the Ibrox side in the two-legged semi-final on their way to the Final. John thought it would be a jolly wheeze to wear an old Celtic top when he went out for a kickabout before the start of the game at Ibrox. John v. 75,500 Rangers fans? He probably thought it was a fair fight. Mind you, that was presupposing he could actually count.

There was another occasion when he went to his mother-in-law's flat for lunch after training. She stayed just along the road from Parkhead and John often nipped round for a bite to eat at her place. On this day, though, she was out. The solution was simple - John booted in the frontdoor! He came back for an afternoon training session and told us what he had done. It was very matter-of-fact. Goodness knows how his mother-in-law reacted when she got home to find her frontdoor hanging by its hinges. I don't think it could have done much for harmony between the families. But that was John. On other occasions he could be playing cards with the other players whiling away some hours on train journeys to away games. If he was losing he would simply take the cards off the other players, put them back in the pack and throw it out of the window. That was the end of that particular card school. No-one ever argued with John.

I've given him the nod to take care of things in the central defence of Celtic players I have performed alongside outwith the Lisbon Lions. I'm sure John McNamee would make some sort of impact. Probably on the opposing centre-forward.

John Cushley played several times at centre-half, too, and was actually chosen ahead of Caesar on occasion. Bob Kelly picked the team before Big Jock arrived and he believed John was better on the deck than our captain. Billy was never the speediest guy around, that's for sure. Of course, he was unbeatable in the air, but Kelly would often opt for Cushley. To my recollection, he did this at least a couple of times against Rangers. He reckoned Cushley was a better bet against the Ibrox side's prolific striker Jim Forrest who did his best work with the ball at his feet. Forrest was fast over those vital ten yards or so. I recall Cushley coming into the side for an Old Firm game in September 1964 and doing very well against Forrest as Celtic won 3-1. He got the go-ahead to play against the Ibrox men in the League Cup Final a month later. We lost 1-2 and Forrest netted both the Rangers strikes. Back came Caesar!

Right, let's have a look at the candidates for the number one position. One thing any manager would demand from his goalkeeper would be consistency. It's all very well for your last line of defence having a blinder one week and then getting lost in blunderland the next. That has team bosses sucking out their fillings, trust me. It was often levelled at Jock Stein that he could not spot a goalkeeper and there may be an element of truth in that criticism. In his twelve years at Celtic, he certainly brought in plenty. I'm talking about the likes of Gordon Marshall Senior - his boy also performed between the sticks for my old club - Bobby Wraith, Graham Barclay, Bent Martin and Jack Kennedy. I realise that not one of those names will probably be instantly recognisable to most Celtic supporters.

No wonder. Five names, five games. Each of those goalkeepers had only one first team outing before being handed their P45. They were the lucky ones. Geir Karlsson, a giant of a man, arrived from FC Copenhagen and Lief Nielson was signed from Morton. Neither played in the top side. Big Jock could be as subtle as a landslide when he assessed some players' ability. He never held back. It wasn't his style to ponder too long about the merits of individuals. Outfield players could be judged in the blink of an eye, but, I'm afraid, he had a bit of a blind spot with his men at the back. For instance, Bent Martin was signed from Danish side Aarhus after he had two excellent games against us in Europe back in 1965. We beat them 3-0 on aggregate and it was mainly down to Martin that we didn't score more. He was hailed as the bloke who would eventually take over from Ronnie Simpson when Faither decided to spend even more time - if that was possible - on the golf course without being encumbered by interfering things such as football and training.

I've no idea what happened to Martin and why he just didn't produce the goods at Parkhead. He was tall, athletic, well-built and had a good pair of hands. However, I do recall him flapping about all over the place when he performed in his solitary first team game. It was a Glasgow Cup-tie, so there wouldn't have been too much pressure on him, but, as they say in football, it looked as though his backside had fainted. Obviously, Big Jock was neither impressed nor amused and the keeper was on his way shortly afterwards.

To be fair to the likeable Dane, he had a reasonable career with Dunfermline later on and actually won a Scottish Cup medal in 1968, so his move to Scotland wasn't a complete waste of time. By the way, Bent was a very interesting character. He was called up once for the Danish international side for a game against Norway in 1973, but knocked back the opportunity to represent his country because he had a banking exam that same day. Now there's dedication. And, yes, he did later become a bank manager. Hope he was better at handling accounts than he was the ball!

Taking Ronnie Simpson out of the equation, I only really played in front of three other keepers on a consistent basis at Celtic. Frank Haffey was the man in charge when I made my debut against Aberdeen at Pittodrie in 1963. John Fallon was installed about two years later and then along came Ronnie in 1964, sold by Jock Stein to Celtic. And then in came Evan Williams from Wolves. Let's examine the merits - or demerits - of Haffey, Fallon and Williams to see who guards the goal in this particular dream team.

Haffey, I have to admit immediately, gave me palpitations on a regular basis. I was just a young guy trying to settle into the first team and here was a goalkeeper behind me who would swing from the crossbar going through all sorts of gymnastic routines while the other team was attacking us. I'm not too sure how seriously Big Frank took playing football. There's no doubt he was a colourful character and playing for Celtic was never dull with this guy around. Of course, he will be forever remembered as the goalkeeper who conceded nine goals to England when Scotland were thrashed 9-3 at Wembley in 1961. That was his second international appearance for his nation. Hardly surprisingly, that was also his last. A crushing, overwhelming defeat like that might have left some others devastated and completely humiliated. Not our Frank. He was singing in the bath only minutes after the most embarrassing result in Scottish football history. He could hold a note, but he wasn't too hot with a shot.

Actually, it might have taken a blowtorch to give my old mate a red face. There was a league game against St.Johnstone in February 1962 when Frank achieved something that I would have thought was virtually impossible. Somehow, he managed to put the ball in his own net from a goal-kick. The TV cameras couldn't have been at that game because surely that would have featured heavily among compilations of the all-time outrageous sporting bloopers. I wasn't at that game - I was with the reserves - but I'm reliably informed that Frank put the ball down and tried a quick pass to right-back Dunky MacKay. Unfortunately, the goalkeeper was facing the wrong way and sent the ball trundling over his own goalline. Frank's excuse afterwards? He was still dazed following a collision with another player. He must have been dazed every day of his five-year career at Celtic! Of course, it wasn't a goal because the ball hadn't gone out of the eighteen-yard box and the referee ordered a retake. Celtic still won 3-1 at the end of the day, but the main talking point in the pubs after full-time was Haffey's performance. The fans just didn't know what to make of their team's goalkeeper. You can take it from me, neither did his team-mates. Big Frank later emigrated to Australia - after one year at Swindon Town - and went into showbiz. I'm told he was a fair chanter. If you were being cruel, you might say it would have been a good idea for him to have made that career switch a lot earlier.

John Fallon took over from Big Frank and proved to be an excellent shotstopper. Whereas his predecessor loved being in the limelight, Fallon was quite content remaining in the background. He was reasonably consistent, but, to be honest, I would never have rated him international class. He wasn't showy or flashy and just got on with his job. At least, with John behind you, no-one had to worry about looking over their shoulder and wincing as their keeper performed all sorts of acrobatics on the goalline. Unfortunately, all goalkeepers are judged on the ones that got away. The fans rarely recall the days when the goalies have put in a good shift and made some fine saves at crucial times in the game. That comes with the turf when these guys decide to don the No.1 shirt and look out the gloves. They know what they are letting themselves in for.

A game where Fallon hit the headlines for all the wrong reasons was a 2-2 draw against Rangers at Parkhead in January 1968. There's no easy way to put this - our goalkeeper chucked two into the net to cost us a valuable point in the tightest league championship during Celtic's nine-in-a-row sequence. It was a dire display from our keeper and he knew it. Big Jock didn't like goalies at the best of times, but he was fuming after that game. Fallon, by his own admission, was sent to Coventry and didn't play a solitary first team game again that season. Yet this was the same John Fallon who performed so heroically when we played Real Madrid at a sold-out Bernabeu only a week or so after we had won the European Cup in Lisbon in 1967. Over 130,000 spectators were there to say farewell to the legendary Alfredo di Stefano. The Man of the Match was easily Jimmy Johnstone, but Fallon wasn't far behind. I think Big Jock fielded John because he didn't want anyone to beat his Lisbon Lions side. Ronnie was given a rest and John was in. If that was the first time anyone was watching Fallon, they would have undoubtedly rated him world class. However, I don't think he ever replicated that inspired performance as he shut out the Spaniards and Bobby Lennox fired in the only goal of the game.

John, by the way, must be the only player in history to have a European Cup medal in his possession without touching a ball in the tournament. He was on the substitutes' bench for our games against Zurich, Nantes, Vojovidina, Dukla Prague and Inter Milan and wasn't called on once. You could only name a back-up keeper as a substitute in those days and John got the nod from Big Jock to warm the bench on those occasions. Strange game, football.

And what about Evan Williams? He was virtually unknown when Big Jock plucked him from the Wolves reserve team back in October 1969. I knew he had played for Third Lanark for a couple of seasons, but they were a struggling outfit and, of course, went defunct in 1967. My old Celtic mate Mike Jackson was with the Cathkin outfit around the time of their demise and used to tell wonderful stories about the players being paid their wages with pennies from the slot machines in the social club. They took their cash home in holdalls before getting to the bank to convert them into notes.

There was also a Scottish League edict at the time that all clubs had to use brand new footballs for their home games. That was obviously a luxury item around Third Lanark. How did they get round it? Mike told me he and his team-mates were ordered by the directors to fire the ball into the terracing as soon after kick-off as possible. Then the new ball would be retrieved and on would come a tatty and scuffed replacement. To make the object look in reasonable condition, it had been whitewashed! So, it couldn't have been easy for Evan to have embarked upon a career in football in this environment. A lot of others might have chucked it to look for employment in some other more profitable industry. It is to Evan's credit that he toughed it out.

However, not even his wildest dreams, could he have ever believed he would be playing in the European Cup Final only a year after leaving the Molineux second team. The men with the white coats would have been heading in his direction if he had made predictions like that. Of course, though, that is exactly what happened with Evan. I think he proved that night against Feyenoord at the San Siro Stadium in Milan that he was a class act. It was a miserable evening in the history of Celtic Football Club with the Dutch winning 2-1 in extra-time, but no-one could point a finger at our goalkeeper. He was outstanding. I still don't know what happened on that fateful occasion. I got the opening goal, of course, after Bobby Murdoch back-heeled a free-kick in my direction and I let fly from the edge of the box. They got back to level it within three minutes and that didn't do our cause much good.

Maybe we were a bit complacent. Certainly, Big Jock hadn't been quite as thorough in his preparations for this confrontation as he had been three years earlier in Lisbon. However, no-one is blaming our gaffer. We won as a team and we lost as a team. However, Evan's contribution that evening was immense. He was about three minutes away from throwing us a lifeline. That's how long remained on the clock and there would have been a replay with no penalty-kick deciders back then. Sadly, they got their late goal and you have to say the better team won on the night. Take my word for it, though, it would have been a vastly different story in a second game. But football is packed with such stories. I suppose that's the romance of this wonderful game.

Everyone felt sorry for our goalkeeper. He made a collection of breathtaking saves and, ironically, one that sticks in my mind came from an explosive shot from a bloke called Wim Jansen. I wonder what happened to him? He was a busy, bustling little midfielder and he raced through from a deep position to let fly from about thirty yards. I would have been proud to have claimed that pulverising effort as one of my own and I have to admit I thought it was a goal from the moment it left his boot. It was arrowing up towards Evan's top right hand corner, but our keeper took off on a mighty leap and not only stopped the shot, but held onto it. A fabulous save and if anyone in our team deserve a winner's medal that night it was Evan.

To my mind, Evan Williams was a reasonable successor to Ronnie Simpson, but it was never easy to replace a legend and a man who was such a favourite with the fans. Evan did his best and I would say he was the most consistent keeper I played in front of with the exception of Ronnie, of course. If you took the strengths of Frank Haffey and John Fallon and managed to combine them, you would have had one helluva goalkeeper. As there was no sign of a Doctor Frankenstein around Celtic Park in the sixties, this merging of talents never materialised. So, Evan would get the No.1 jersey and John would get a place on the substitutes' bench. Sorry, Frank, I don't think my heart could stand any more of your antics!

Dunky MacKay, in my opinion, was years ahead of his time as an attacking right-back. He wasn't the fastest, but he had the ability to build up play from defence with some slick passing. He would never have been encouraged to cross the halfway line, anyway, back in the early sixties before Big Jock took over in 1965. Sean Fallon used to holler from the dug-out, 'Cross that line and you'll be in the reserves next week!' Honestly, that was the coach's theory of how his full-backs should play. If you could hoof the ball from one end of the pitch to the other then you were in. Believe me, I know what I'm talking about. I used to get it in the ear from Sean on a regular basis. Dunky started his career as a wing-half, so that might explain his desire to push forward into attacking areas. He left Celtic just before the return of Big Jock and he definitely missed out on the presence of a man who actively encouraged his full-backs to get up the park.

Dunky was good enough to win fourteen Scottish international caps and, remember, he was in a Celtic team that was struggling at the time. He really deserved more from his career. He was sold to Third Lanark in 1964 and disappeared off the radar when the club shut up shop three years later. He emigrated to Australia and, alas, a lot of Celtic supporters will never have realised what a fine player he was. Take my word for it, though, he was an exceptional professional and, with the guidance of a bloke like Jock Stein, you would have heard an awful lot more about this player.

Okay, I've already discussed John McNamee's abilities as a rugged central defender, so, to bring a bit of balance to that area in the line-up, I would look for a ball-player. Step forward, George Connelly. Like Dunky MacKay, George's career path was a fairly strange one. Unlike Dunky, though, it was of his own choosing. Of course, he gave up the game three years before his thirtieth birthday and that was a terrible waste of talent. George was a magnificent passer of the ball, long or short, and had a superb touch. He could kill the ball in an instant no matter the circumstances. He could have an opponent breathing down his neck, but that never fazed the elegant Fifer. I never saw him flustered; not once.

He liked to play alongside the centre-half instead of being the main defender. That wasn't his type of game. One illustration is the 1971 League Cup Final against Partick Thistle at Hampden. Who will ever forget that game? Billy McNeill was injured and out of the team and Big Jock went with George as centre-half with Jim Brogan beside him. Didn't work out, did it? We were hammered 4-1 and, to be honest, George didn't look comfortable all afternoon. Mind you, that could have been said about every Celtic player that day. That was as bad as we have ever played in all my time at the club and I don't wish to take anything away from a Thistle team who were right up for it. We were four goals down by the interval and no-one in a green and white jersey could quite fathom what on earth was materialising at the national stadium that day. I doubt if George ever played as the main central defender again.

It would be fair to say George had happier times at Hampden. Just look at his performance against Rangers in the Scottish Cup Final in 1969 in his first full season as a regular in the top side. He was awesome that afternoon as we won 4-0 and he scored one of our goals. My old mate Willie Wallace told me an interesting story about George as we prepared for that Old Firm encounter. Willie recalled, 'I was rooming with Big Geordie for three nights at our hideaway in Seamill. I'll never forget it because I hardly got any sleep the night before the big game.

'Geordie had been told early by Big Jock that he would be playing because we would be without Jimmy Johnstone, who was suspended, and John Hughes, who was injured. Geordie must have been fairly confident as emerging as a winner because he was already trying to figure out how to spend the bonus money. I was trying to get some shut-eye when Geordie stretched across from his bed and nudged me on the shoulder. "Wispy, do you think I should get a new bathroom suite?" I was asked. "Aye, goodnight," I answered.

'A few minutes later there was another nudge. "Wispy, do you think I would be better off with a new kitchen?" I replied again, "Aye, goodnight." Another couple of minutes. "Wispy, how about a conservatory?" "Get some bloody sleep!" "Wispy, how about an extension to our dining room?" It just went on throughout the night. I was knackered by the time we sat down for breakfast the next day. And, no, I haven't a clue what he spent his money on. Probably a car!'

I thought playing off the stopper was George's best position, but, to be honest, with his God-given talent he could have performed in a variety of roles. Just don't ask him to hold the defence together! However, McNamee would have revelled in having a player with such outstanding skills alongside him. Big Bad John could win the ball and knock it a few yards to George to set things in motion. They would have been a very interesting double-act.

To complete my back four I have to go for Danny McGrain, who was, of course, equally at home in both full-backs positions. I don't think Danny had a weakness. Okay, he may not have been brilliant in the air, but he compensated for that with what he achieved on the deck. I can't remember any winger ever giving Danny the run-around. He was quick going forward and coming back. He read play wonderfully, anticipated where the danger was coming from and his tackling was as clean and crisp as anyone I can think of. Danny would probably be the first to admit he would get a nosebleed when he was right in on goal and he will never be famous for the goals he scored. But how many did he set up on a plate for others? Has anyone got a calculator handy?

I liked Danny's style. At one stage in the seventies he was winning every Player of the Year award that was possible. I was at one function when Danny was making a speech. I think he nailed it when he said, 'I've become so popular that I'm thinking about having the number on my shorts changed to ex-directory.' That just about summed up this fabulous player. I was watching a SKY sports programme a few years ago and they were doing a compilation of the world's greatest players. Normally, Scots are overlooked in these sort of shows, so imagine my delight when a panel of judges, mainly English, voted Danny in at right-back. Having said that, they overlooked me for the left-back spot!

Jim Kennedy - known to everyone at the club as Pres - played in the No.3 slot before I came on the scene and he moved into the old left-half role. I think his style of play was more suited to that position. Pres had many attributes, but speed off the mark wasn't one of them. However, as I have already said, he would not have been encouraged to flash up and down the wing, anyway. Like McNamee, he was as hard as nails. He didn't take prisoners, either. I recall an incident where Airdrie's Billy Reid must have taken some brave pills. According to my old mate, Pres said Reid had called him 'a Fenian bastard'. Not the wisest thing the Airdrie guy had ever uttered. There was no hesitation from Pres - he stuck the head on Reid. A good old Glasgow Kiss. His opponent collapsed to the turf with blood spurting from his nose and mouth. That was the end of the matter. The referee and linesmen completely missed the incident and Reid didn't go within twenty yards of Pres for the remainder of the game.

So, that's a back four of Dunky MacKay, John McNamee, George

Connelly and Danny McGrain. There's a real fusion of all sorts of strengths and skills in there and, if I was a manager, I would think anyone attempting to score a goal against this lot would have to work hard for any rewards. A jackhammer might be required to make a dent on that foursome. Now let's have a look at the midfield pairing. Davie Hay is an absolute must in here. This may surprise you, but Davie has told me he believes his best position was at right-back. However, I've got to say I liked him in the middle of the park where he got the opportunity to show the full range of his skills. He was a powerful, strong-running character and a completely dedicated team man. I don't think many realised the pace Davie possessed. If you're still unsure, have a look at his performance against Leeds United in the European Cup semi-final second leg at Hampden in 1970. Davie zipped up and down that right flank all night and I would like to think I was contributing something similar over on the left.

Davie, of course, was a genuine competitor and that's probably why Big Jock moved him into midfield in the first place. Rangers were always strong in this department in the early to mid-sixties. John Greig was a ferocious opponent and he could dominate a game with his awesome will-to-win and leadership qualities. However, Big Jock sought to nullify Greig's strength in there by putting Davie into that area. Greigy soon knew he was in a game when my old mate was around. People talk a lot about the power of the man Tommy Docherty nicknamed 'The Quiet Assassin', but no-one should ever overlook his all-round ability. Davie could win the ball and he could use it, too. That's a rare combination. Priceless in this day and age.

At one point it looked as though Kenny Dalglish might turn out to be the natural successor to Bobby Murdoch on the right-hand side of the Celtic midfield. Early in his career, Kenny came into the team in that position and it was obvious he had an eye for accurate passing. He wasn't the fastest, but, like Bobby, he made the ball do all the work. Then, of course, he discovered the knack of putting the ball in the opposition's net and that was his career as a midfielder over and done with. Kenny became the main striker at Celtic and he backed up Big

Jock's judgement with a barrage of goals. He rattled in 112 in total and then another 118 at Liverpool. Don't forget he also shares the Scottish international goalscoring record alongside the incomparable Denis Law on thirty goals. Impressive stuff. But I would put him into midfield alongside Davie and urge him to get forward at every opportunity to use the full range of his shooting prowess. So, there would be a lot of invention and industry in the middle of the park with Davie and Kenny in the engine room.

Charlie Gallagher and Tommy Callaghan are two other midfielders who deserve a mention. Both were entirely different types of players. Charlie was a beautiful striker of the ball. It was Charlie who took the corner-kick nine minutes from time for Billy McNeill to power in the winner in the 3-2 Scottish Cup Final victory over Dunfermline in 1965. That was Celtic's first trophy success since the 7-1 League Cup Final win over Rangers at the same venue in 1957. It also helped us get the gorilla off our backs. Charlie also launched over a perfect delivery - this time from the right - for Caesar to head in the deciding goal in the fading seconds to give us a win over Vojvodina in the European Cup quarter-final second leg with the aggregate tied at 1-1. Charlie was a cousin of Paddy Crerand and both were brought up in the tough Glasgow district of the Gorbals. If you expected a street-fighting man in Charlie Gallagher, you would have been very disappointed. He was an artist who, I have to say, didn't particularly enjoy it when the opposition put the mix in. That wasn't Charlie's style, at all.

Tommy Callaghan could run all day with the ball at his feet. He just covered the ground at a hectic rate of knots, racing from one penalty box to another. Another plus was the fact that he could throw in the odd spectacular strike or two. And he wasn't bad in the air, either. TC never put in anything other than a full shift. He wasn't a flair player and possibly the fans didn't quite realise what he was giving the team, but I can assure everyone that his colleagues were well aware of his unselfish contribution. He was always in space, looking for a pass and covering your back. Charlie and Tommy would both get places among my stand-by players.

With Jimmy Johnstone around, not too many other players were utilised to play wide right during my time at Celtic. John Hughes could play in that position, but I've named him as my outside-left - where I thought he was more accomplished - and, of course, I can't select Lisbon Lion Stevie Chalmers, who wore the No.7 shorts on more than a few occasions. I've trawled through a pile of names and one I kept coming back to was Harry Hood. He was a versatile player who could perform wide right although he was never an out-and-out winger. Harry was at home in the middle of the park, playing as support to the main striker as he did often enough with Kenny. And, of course, Harry was adept at putting the ball in the net, so could also take on the role as the lone attack leader. I thought Harry oozed class. It's another of the game's little mysteries that he never won a full Scotland cap. Harry's game was based on confidence, like just about every other player, I suppose. When Harry was buzzing he was something else altogether. He was a plus factor in the team with his versatility. He was a smooth operator, alright. And, of course, he could come into midfield to supplement Davie and Kenny to make the formation a fluid 4-3-3 as opposed to 4-2-4. A handy guy to have around in so many ways.

Lou Macari was another of those blokes who lived the dream, playing for the team he had supported all his life. It was a pity that the club did not cough up the cash to keep him at Celtic when his contract expired back in 1973. Manchester United were happy to quadruple his wages and I think my old club wouldn't have been too upset to accept £200,000 for a player who had cost them nothing. Wee Lou was a dynamo and must have been a nightmare to play against. He was in the opposition's faces right from the off. There wasn't much of him, but, my God, was he brave. He put himself about big-style and laughed off the warnings of bigger, stronger defenders who threatened all sorts of retribution if he didn't calm down. That was a waste of their time.

Lou was a bundle of raw energy and you knew you would always get 100 per cent from him. Manchester United's gain was very definitely Celtic's loss. Unfortunately, I didn't get a lot of playing time with Lou on the pitch, but in the couple of years we did have together he certainly made a lasting impression. Another selfless team man who had the remarkable knack of always being in the right place at the right time in front of goal. Lou was my type of player, effervescent and bubbly, and just had to be in my line-up.

Joe McBride's scoring rate at Celtic was simply sensational. He was an absolute phenomenon. Joe came into Parkhead like a whirlwind at the age of twenty-seven and looked as though he was doing his utmost to make up for lost time. Everyone knew of his love for the club, but Celtic missed out a couple of times when they moved for him. Joe had actually played for five senior clubs - Kilmarnock, Wolves, Luton Town, Partick Thistle and Motherwell - before he became Big Jock's first signing in June 1965. Rather remarkably, Joe - known as Jose to all at the club - started at Kilmarnock Amateurs before going Junior with Shettleston Town and then Kirkintilloch Rob Roy.

His goalscoring record with Celtic is nothing short of breathtaking. He collected eighty-nine goals in ninety-two appearances. That meant his goals-per-game record is bettered only by the legendary Jimmy McGrory, who actually hammered in 410 goals in 408 league games. It would have taken something special to beat Jimmy, but Joe gave it his best shot and I think we all agree that he was something special. His tally tells you all you need to know about the amazing penalty box talents of a fearless striker.

Joe had a simple philosophy about scoring goals. He didn't care how that ball got over the line, just so long as it counted. He never held back when the goal was in his sights. He would never take an extra touch, he wouldn't think about playing in a team-mate. He was totally selfish when he came to taking his chances. Don't get the notion he was a glory-seeker, though. He just wanted to rack up goals. Simple as that. He would always work the goalkeeper. Nine times out of ten that finishing effort would hit the target. Sadly, Joe's career was derailed when he sustained a cruciate knee ligament injury in a game against Aberdeen at Pittodrie in December 1966. Joe had struck thirty-five goals by the time he played in that match and was on his way to an unbeatable total

121

for the campaign. Only Stevie Chalmers, with the winner against Inter Milan, achieved more goals - thirty-six and Stevie, of course, had an extra five months to reach that tally.

So, I didn't have to work the grey matter too hard to give Joe McBride a berth in my team. Dixie Deans was very similar in stature and style to Joe. They were both stocky and around the 5ft 7in mark, but both were excellent in the air. Dixie joined Celtic shortly after that League Cup mishap against Partick Thistle. Big Jock knew the team required a penalty box predator and Dixie didn't disappoint. A record 132 goals from 184 outings isn't a bad return for a fee of around the £20,000 mark.

There was a bit of devilment about Dixie. I had played against him several times when he was at Motherwell and he rattled my old bones on several occasions. He could be a bit mouthy, too. And I'm not too sure what the Celtic fans thought they were getting when Big Jock bought him. The only memorable thing Dixie had ever done at Celtic Park was get sent off for jottering Wee Jinky. That didn't go down well with the occupants of The Jungle who witnessed the bout of fisticuffs taking place right in front of them. However, it didn't take Dixie long to win them over. A bundle of goals helped, for a start.

It's a measure of the quality of the Celtic fans that they gave Dixie a rousing reception when he played at Parkhead only three days after missing a crucial penalty-kick against Inter Milan in the second leg of the European Cup semi-final in 1972. Effectively, that miss cost Celtic the opportunity of playing in their third European Cup Final in five years. The Italians got through 5-4 on spot-kicks and the Parkhead support must have been massively disappointed. The club's next outing was a league game against Dixie's former club Motherwell and he has admitted he was nervous before the encounter. Really, he didn't know what to expect. But any fears of a backlash were blown to smithereens at the kick-in before the match when he fans continually chanted his name. And Dixie repaid their support by sticking two in the net in a 5-2 victory. To make things even better, he notched a hat-trick in a 6-1 Scottish Cup Final win over Hibs seventeen days after his spot-kick error. So, Dixie was an exceptional goalscoring talent, but, to be honest,

I don't think he could play in the same team as Joe McBride. They were very similar and would probably been vying for the same ball throughout a game. Dixie wouldn't be a bad guy to have on the substitutes' bench, that's for sure.

Big John Hughes - Yogi to colleagues and fans alike - waltzes into the outside-left position. Yogi was a puzzle. It would be fair to say he was a bit erratic, but I still loved playing behind him on the days he decided he was a world-beater. He was like a tornado going down that left wing. He had the ability to get into his stride very quickly and it was no surprise to learn he had been an athlete during his schooldays. He could take that ball for a run and, in the mood, didn't care how many defenders blocked his route to goal. He would take them all on. As you might have expected, the supporters loved him. Celtic actually spoiled the guys in The Jungle back then. In one half, they would have Wee Jinky and, in the next, they would have Big Yogi. Now that's value for money.

Frank Brogan also had a few games at outside-left as I was breaking through. That guy was as fast as a whippet. Unfortunately, his brain wasn't quite in sync with the speed of his feet. Frank, brother of Jim, would leave defenders stranded in his slip stream as he simply took off down the wing. Anything could happen, though, at his final ball. It could land anywhere from the penalty box to Parkhead Cross. He was bone idle, too. Tracking back was not in his remit. It meant if you were looking for some assistance when a team broke forward and you suddenly found yourself face-to-face with two opponents, the last person you could rely upon to give you a helping hand was Frank. He would be way down the pitch waiting for you to win the ball and present it to his feet. Then he would get on the afterburners and hurtle down the flank with the final destination of the ball a mystery to colleague and rival alike.

So, there you have it, my perfect eleven with five substitutes rarin' to go. Just to repeat, it's Evan Williams getting the vote in goal with a back four of Dunky MacKay, John McNamee, George Connelly and Danny McGrain. I've put Kenny Dalglish and Davie Hay in midfield with Harry Hood, Joe McBride, Lou Macari and John Hughes sharing the attacking load up front. On the substitutes' bench we've got John Fallon, John

Cushley, Charlie Gallagher, Tommy Callaghan and Dixie Deans. Now that's sixteen players I wouldn't mind managing.

In fact, I would even pay in to see that lot.

CHAPTER SIX
BEST BAR NONE

Johan Cruyff was more than just a little perplexed as the minutes ticked down to the kick-off. He grabbed me by the arm and, with a bewildered expression, asked, 'Is he always like that? Is he okay?' The subject of his quizzical attention was none other than George Best.

We were in the dressing room preparing for a Rest of Europe exhibition game against Benfica in Lisbon in honour of their legendary captain Mario Coluna. Unfortunately, my old mate Bestie had over-indulged in the pre-match hospitality. He wasn't quite legless, but he certainly wouldn't have passed any breathalyser test. The Dutch legend might have thought he had seen everything in his glorious career, but he had never shared a dressing room with the Irish superstar. Let's be kind and say Bestie was a bit merry; tipsy, even.

I have to admit, though, I had seen George in that condition before and it didn't prevent him from running amok and giving yours truly a torrid time in another friendly confrontation when Celtic were facing Manchester United in Toronto. Both clubs were staying in the same hotel, the Royal York, and, on the afternoon of the game, Billy McNeill, Bertie Auld, Willie Wallace and myself arranged to have a snifter with our old Celtic team-mate Paddy Crerand at a wee Irish pub, O'Malley's, just round the corner from the hotel. Paddy turned up with Bestie in tow and all our good intentions of just having a quick half-pint went hurtling right out of the window.

We knocked back our half-pint and then someone ordered another. Bestie, of course, was known to down a beer or several, but, on this occasion, he preferred the grape to the grain. And he so capably proved that particular afternoon he was also fairly adept at downing copious amounts of wine. 'Forget the lager,' he said, 'let's get a few bottles of Mateus Rose.' The wine disappeared in the blink of an eye and the chink of a glass. Several other bottles were placed on the table. It didn't take long for them to be demolished, either. Please don't get the impression that this was normal practice for Celtic players - or those of Manchester United, for that matter - before a game, but this was a glorified kickabout with nothing at stake. I think it was due to commence at eight o'clock and, four hours before the match, we were still hammering the vino in O'Malley's. Now, if this had been an important European tie we would all have been in bed at four o'clock. This was different. We were having a bit of harmless fun and we knew we could still entertain the 35,000 fans on the night.

Bestie, though, really should have carried a Government Health Warning. He was dangerous to be around. Good fun, but lethal. Anyway, someone must have had an attack of brains because we decided to get back to the hotel and have a wee rest before going to the ground. I said to Bestie, 'Remember, George, take it easy. I don't want to be chasing you all night. Okay?' He smiled, 'Okay, Tommy, no problem.'

No problem? He was inspired that evening. He was twisting this way and that, racing away from everyone in a green and white shirt right from the off and no-one could get the ball off him. I caught up with him. 'Hey, you wee bastard, I thought you were going to take it easy.' He answered, 'Sorry, Big Man, I just feel so fuckin' good.' Believe me, I was happy and relieved to hear that full-time whistle and get off that pitch. Bestie was unstoppable. After that mauling, I often wondered about the qualities of Mateus Rose. Several glasses certainly didn't do my Irish friend any harm, but if there are any budding footballers out there reading this I must point out that Bestie was a one-off. He could get away with things us mere mortals wouldn't have a chance of achieving.

Of course, stories about Bestie, booze and birds are legendary. There was a movie entitled Yesterday's Hero which came out in 1979 starring Ian McShane, famous for his Lovejoy TV series. Most of the football films are rubbish. This one was no different. McShane, with his long black hair and big sideboards, actually had more than a passing resemblance to Bestie and the movie was based loosely on the life and times of a fictitious character who liked a drink and female companionship. Remind you of anyone? Of course, the film could quite easily have been based on the charismatic Irishman.

There is one scene where McShane, looking uncannily like Bestie, rummages around in his coat in the dressing room at half-time looking for a hidden bottle of whisky. He is caught drinking it by his irate manager. For goodness sake! Does anyone actually believe such a thing could happen? But it all added to the folklore that surrounded George Best. There was also a tale that was doing the rounds back then that Bestie actually had nookie with some obliging blonde during the interval of another game. Good story, but, even by Bestie's admission, was a lot of crap. Sadly, the bevvy did take its toll and the world was a sadder place when he passed away in November 2005 at the far-too-early age of fifty-nine.

He left me with some wonderful memories, though. I first played against this outstanding individual in a pre-season friendly at Celtic Park in August 1966. It was the start of that unique campaign when Celtic won everything in sight, including becoming the first British side to conquer Europe. Manchester United came to Glasgow with their full array of glittering talent. Bobby Charlton and Nobby Stiles had become World Cup winners with England that summer and, of course, two other good friends, Denis Law and Paddy Crerand, were in the team. Bestie lined up at outside-left that afternoon and I was at right-back with Willie O'Neill over on the left.

Of course, I knew all about Bestie's reputation. The first time I had seen photographs of him in the press I didn't think he looked old enough to cross the road on his own. Now, though, I was in direct line of fire. In normal circumstances, it's good to give your opponent a wake-up call early in the game. Just a wee dunt to see if he's got the heart the size of an Aspirin. I duly challenged Bestie and realised immediately he had the heart the size of a building. Other players could quickly fade out of the picture if they thought they were in for a hard time of it. I'm not talking about breaking a leg or anything quite as severe. No, I'm talking about a good, solid tackle that would get your opponent's bones jarring. There wasn't much of Bestie, but he was afraid of nothing. He just kept coming back for more.

At one stage, Jock Stein leapt out of the dug-out and yelled at me, 'For God's sake, Tommy, it's only a friendly. Don't kick him.' I shouted back, 'If I don't kick him he will fuckin' destroy me.' Jock, of course, was a big friend of United gaffer Matt Busby and, clearly, didn't want to upset his good mate by seeing one of his most important players being booted all over the park. I have to say Bestie gave as good as he got. It was the same when I played against Willie Henderson in Old Firm encounters. Wee Willie, like Jimmy Johnstone, was made of stern stuff. He never found a convenient air pocket to disappear into, either. We ended up beating United 4-1 that day and the Old Trafford side, with Bestie in brilliant form, went on to win the English First Division at the end of that season. Possibly, Bestie remembered that afternoon in Glasgow when he decided to turn it on in Toronto a few years later against an unsuspecting Tommy Gemmell.

There was another occasion when he tore Scotland apart during a Home International match at Windsor Park in Belfast in October 1967. It was a crisp afternoon, but that particular pitch was known to cut up quite badly as a game wore on. You could take one look at Bestie's slight frame and wonder if he could wade through tricky underfoot conditions. Wade? He danced. Bestie defied the elements in a devastating display that took everyone's breath away. Mine included. He tormented me throughout a one-sided first-half. He was a wiry, little character who could ride challenges better than anyone I had ever faced. Honestly, he was unstoppable that afternoon. At the interval, our manager, Bobby

Brown, was rightly worried about the skills of the Irishman. 'How on earth do we stop this guy, Tommy?' he queried. My first thought was, 'I suppose a rocket launcher is out of the question?' On a more serious note, I ventured,'The first thing we could do would be to try to cut off his supply. If we get tighter in midfield that might stop the flow of passes coming his way. I'll get in quickly any time the ball comes anywhere near him. If he gets past me, we'll need someone to come out and close him down sharpish.' Easier said than done, of course.

Actually, I wondered if left-back Eddie McCreadie would consider swapping places with me. Of course, I was comfortable at No.3 and Eddie was quite at home on the opposite wing. I practically begged him, 'I'm having trouble with Bestie, Eddie, do you fancy a stint on the right?' 'Go fuck yourself,' was the curt reply. But I was smiling at the start of the second-half. After the brusque refusal of a change in positions from my so-called friend and ally, I had braced myself for some of the same until I noticed Bestie had switched wings and was lining up at outside-right. He must have got fed up torturing me and was now about to do the same to my full-back partner McCreadie. I looked across at Eddie. 'Good luck,' I shouted. 'Bet you wished you had swapped!' Funnily enough, he answered with the same three words as he had at half-time.

I thought Eddie was a first-rate defender and was one of the quickest on the turn. Unfortunately, Bestie was simply awesome on a pitch that deteriorated with every passing minute. Northern Ireland won 1-0 with a second-half goal from Dave Clements after he was set up by You Know Who after a darting run down the right and a low cross into the box. It could have been about five or six if it hadn't been for a superb goalkeeping display from Ronnie Simpson, who made three top-class saves from Bestie. 'At one stage it was me v. Ronnie Simpson,' said Bestie later. No-one could argue. My old Celtic pal also held a penalty-kick from Johnny Crossan low down to his left and if it hadn't been for an inspired performance from him we would have been totally humiliated in Belfast. He was denied the banner headlines. And it was all down to that man Best.

We met up with each other a few times during our careers. I remember one occasion when I was manager of Dundee and Bestie was with Hibs back in 1979. Absolutely no disrespect to the Edinburgh side, but you would have thought anyone was bonkers who had predicted that the Irishman, even in his early thirties, would one day be a Hibs player. A suitable case for treatment, indeed. However, that's the way his career panned out and I don't suppose Bestie was grumbling when he picked up his £5,000-per-week cheque from chairman Tom Hart. That would have made him one of the highest-paid players in Scotland back then.

After the game at Dens Park, I invited Bestie into the manager's room where we had a snifter or two. Or it could have been three. Or four. Actually, I could have bitten my tongue when I asked him, 'What's your tipple these days, Bestie?' I had completely forgotten he had anti-alcohol implants in his stomach to help him curb his drinking urges. These tablets, known as Antabuse, are supposed to make an individual violently sick if they come in contact with alcohol. Bestie didn't hesitate, though, 'A vodka and tonic, please, Tommy.' Maybe Bestie had found a way round combating these pills because he was perfectly okay and we didn't say another word about it. Anyway, I then introduced him to the Dundee board and they were all like wee boys in a sweetie shop. They were excited at meeting Bestie and that's the sort of celebrity appeal he had to everyone. He never changed. There was no big-time stuff from one of the most gifted players the world has ever seen.

He used to tell this story against himself. 'When I was first travelling to North America to sign for Los Angeles Aztecs, I saw a big sign which proclaimed "DRINK CANADA DRY". Well, I gave it my best shot!' Bestie told me a tale that Jim Baxter had passed onto him. The great Ranger was fond of a drop or two, as the world knew, and he said to the Irishman, 'I wakened up one Monday morning with terrible pains in my spine and all down my back. I had been out all weekend on the lash. I decided it would be a better idea to go to my own GP rather than the Rangers club doctor. Now I had been drinking about seven or eight pints of lager every day after training. Then I would go on the Bacardi at the weekend. My GP asked me what was my daily average intake. I lied and told him about two or three pints. The doc gasped, "If you carry on like that, Jim, you'll be an alcoholic!'"

Remember that time Bestie appeared on the Terry Wogan TV show back in 1990? If you saw it, you're never likely to forget it. Bestie was told to appear at the BBC three hours before shooting was due to begin. Someone at the programme was determined to prevent my wee buddy from performing a disappearing act. They stuck him in what is known in the TV studios as the Green Room, a place where the celebrities can prepare before going out to appear on a live show. They might as well have put Bestie in an empty well-stocked bar and told him to help himself. There is always booze around these hospitality rooms and, with three full hours to spare, Bestie poured himself a drink. Then another. And another. He was drinking with Hollywood actor Omar Sharif, but as the bevvy disappeared at an alarming rate, he began calling him Sacha as he was convinced he was now talking to French singer Sacha Distel! By the time he was due to go on as Wogan's guest he was virtually comatose. He was asked what was he doing with his spare time. 'Screwing,' was the reply. What did he like to do away from football? 'Screw,' was the response. A clearly agitated Wogan, grinning inanely into the cameras, managed to fast forward through the interview, cut it short and Bestie, thankfully, was removed from our screens.

I was down in London on business and met up with Bestie shortly afterwards. He told me he remembered little of the interview and was mortified when someone showed him the tape. He also informed me he received a message a few days after the show that said, 'George, dear boy, I didn't think you were too bad at all. You looked perfectly normal to me.' It was from Oliver Reed!

There was another occasion when we arranged to meet at his favourite pub, the Phene Arms, in Chelsea. Once more, I was down at a finance conference in London and, to be honest, it was fairly boring. Then I met up with Bestie and he was sitting at the bar on his own. He was obviously a regular and no-one was bothering him. He was smiling as he went through the racing pages and was about to put on a couple of bets. 'By the looks of your grin, you've just had a couple of winners, 'I said. 'No, no it's got nothing to do with the horses,' replied Bestie. 'The landlord has just passed me the phone and I've had a conversation with a bloke called Patrick Doyle, who owns a firm called Classic Cars in Limerick. He said he has been trying to track me down for ages and has just asked me what do I want him to do with the Mercedes. I said, "What Mercedes are we talking about, Pat?" He answered, "The one you brought in for repairs two years ago!"' I wasn't sure if he was pulling my leg. With Bestie you never knew.

Bestie's professional life must have been in turmoil back on 27 January 1971, but he still made the effort to travel north to play and score for a Rangers/Celtic Select against Scotland in a Benefit Game for the sixty-six victims of the Ibrox Disaster. As we were all aware, he had a dreadful habit of going AWOL, but he made sure he was in Glasgow that evening. Just nineteen days beforehand he had gone on a bender and missed the train taking Manchester United through to London for an important game against Chelsea. He actually caught a later train, but, instead of meeting up with his team, he decided to miss the match and spend the entire weekend at the London apartment of attractive Irish actress Sinead Cusack. Three days later he was suspended for two weeks by the Old Trafford outfit yet still fulfilled his obligation to turn out for that Old Firm X1.

He was around, too, when the Lisbon Lions toured Ireland as part of our twenty-fifth anniversary celebrations. Bestie and Co emulated our feat of becoming the best in Europe when they defeated Benfica 4-1 after extra-time at Wembley in 1968. Bestie, though, was always full of praise for Celtic's victory in the Portuguese capital. 'Celtic showed us that it could be done,' he said on numerous occasions. 'Before them, it was thought only clubs like Real Madrid, Benfica or Inter and AC Milan could be European masters. Celtic broke down the barriers and let the others in. The importance of their win in Lisbon should never be overlooked.' Thanks, Bestie. I couldn't have put it better myself.

I've often been asked who was the better player between Bestie and Jinky. I would say Bestie was a better all-round player, but Jinky was more skilful. They were both incredibly brave, as I have already said, and could make and take goals. Bestie was good in the air, but, so, too, was Jinky, despite his lack of inches. I recall him scoring with a header against Hearts in a game at Tynecastle in the sixties. Big John Hughes set it up after galloping down the left wing. He fired over a blistering cross that was missed by everyone. Jinky, though, was coming in at pace about ten yards out at the back post and his timing was impeccable as he bulleted the ball beyond Jim Cruickshank. If that goal had been scored in a World Cup Final we would still be watching replays of it to this day.

Bestie was the most dangerous opponent I ever directly faced in a competitive match. When you consider some of the opponents I have come up against in games throughout Europe that is saying something. Jinky, though, was a menace when we faced each other in training. He had fabulous balance and liked to poke the ball through your legs just for fun. I could just about stand it two or three times, but when he went looking for a fourth I had to have a word in the Wee Man's ear. It normally went along the lines of, 'Try that again, you wee pest, and I'll boot you up the arse!' I don't think he ever took a blind bit of notice of my warnings.

Bestie obviously brought forward his Christmas celebrations that memorable night at the Stadium of Light in Lisbon when he turned out for the Rest of Europe against Benfica on 8 December 1970. Johan Cruyff may have been baffled at the antics of his team-mate, but I recall it being a very enjoyable occasion. The scoreline didn't really matter, but, if anyone is taking notes, we lost 3-2, despite goals from West Germany's Uwe Seeler and Spain's Jose Garate. It was just an evening of joyous football for Mario Coluna. The West Ham World-Cup winning trio of Bobby Moore, Martin Peters and Geoff Hurst also took part.

I have to say Moore was a magnificent defender. Critics would point out he had no pace. Others said he was useless in the air. People insisted he couldn't pass the ball. Hard to believe he skippered England to the finest result in their history when they beat West Germany in 1966, isn't it? Bobby's strengths were in clever anticipation and crisp, clean tackling. He never tried anything fancy when he was on the ball. He didn't look to ping fifty-yard passes all over the place. And he never dived into a tackle. How many times do you see a defender sell himself by lunging at an opponent and being left on his backside? I was very wary of that, too. I reckoned if I was sitting it out on the ground I would be momentarily leaving the team a man short. My philosophy was to cajole the winger and try to keep turning him onto his weaker foot. Timing in a tackle is a bit of an art form. Bobby Moore had it down to perfection.

Critics may also say he didn't score too many goals. Neither did John Clark. So what? Moore was there to do a job, protect his goal, break up play and set things in motion. And he did that very, very well. I remember seeing him scoring a rare goal for West Ham. I think it was against Derby County when he picked up the ball and came forward looking for one of his quick trademark passes. No-one seemed to be offering themselves for a pass and the defenders were backing off. Obviously, they believed he wouldn't even attempt a shot at goal. But Bobby just kept coming forward until he was about twenty-five yards out and, without too many alternatives, just gave the ball a mighty whack and it flew high into the corner of the net. He actually looked embarrassed. Certainly, he didn't know how to celebrate this rarest of occasions. Bobby simply put his hand in the air and then jogged back to his position in defence.

Bobby got a taste of Argentinian hostility a year before Celtic encountered Racing Club of Buenos Aries in the World Club Championship in 1967. England manager Alf Ramsey will never be forgotten for his rant at Argentina's players after his nation's 1-0 win over them in the quarter-final. He labelled them 'animals' and, being a dog lover, I thought he was being a bit harsh on the canine fraternity. However, I certainly agreed that these blokes were a disgrace after our three games against them. Bobby was always immaculate. I never saw him with his jersey flapping outside his shorts even once, his socks were inevitably right up to his knees and I don't think I ever saw one of his blond hairs out of place, either.

We were comparing notes on the Argentines shortly after Celtic's encounters with them. 'Did they spit in your face, tug your hair, poke you in the eyes and kick you when the ball was nowhere near you,

Tommy?' he asked. 'All of that and more, Bobby,' I answered. 'They are not nice people, are they?' said Moore. I could have put it another way. I have to say I loved Nobby Stiles' take on the match against Argentina. The jolly little Manchester United man, a ferocious opponent on the park but good company off it, said, 'Apart from the violence, it was okay.' The English like their understatements, don't they?

Bestie tells a great story about how ordinary and down to earth Bobby Moore, a true England legend, really was. The Irishman was working for a London radio station as a match commentator and was asked to cover Sunderland's game against West Ham at their old home at Roker Park. Bestie found himself sitting beside his pal and former Fulham team-mate who was also at the game for another radio company. At half-time, according to Bestie, Bobby asked if he fancied a cup of tea. 'It was a bitterly cold afternoon and a cup of tea was more than welcome,' said a frozen Bestie. 'I said yes straight away. Bobby duly went to the stall down the stairs and returned with a cup of tea and a couple of meat pies and chips, too. Keep all your fancy restaurants - that was a veritable feast to two cold guys on an exposed radio gantry. Imagine that, though. The England World Cup-winning captain fetching me a cup of tea, a couple of meat pies and chips. Typical of Bobby. He was always so generous.'

Martin Peters was another player who rarely got the praise he deserved. Ron Greenwood was the attack-minded manager who installed the Academy of Football at Upton Park and so many good players came through that system. They really worked at the finer things of the game at that club. Peters fitted in to the set-up wonderfully well. Geoff Hurst was a big, robust frontman who could put himself about, but Peters preferred to ghost around and suddenly appear out of the shadows at a front or back post with rival defenders constantly taken by surprise. Hurst, of course, became the only man to hit a hat-trick in the World Cup Final - was his second effort over the line? - and that feat once again underlined how fickle football can be. He wasn't even in Alf Ramsey's original forward line when the tournament kicked off and was nowhere to be seen during the opening section games against Uruguay, Mexico and France. Jimmy Greaves received a nasty gash during the game against the French and had to pull out of the quarter-final clash against Argentina. Geoff Hurst took his place, scored the only goal in the 1-0 win and the rest, as they say, is history.

Malcom Allison, surely one of the most colourful football managers the world has ever seen, also came through the Greenwood Academy until ill health cut short his playing career. However, he took his enterprising ideals into management when he teamed up with Joe Mercer and guided Manchester City to the English league championship in 1968. That Maine Road outfit abounded with flamboyance and flair. City looked like Celtic in light blue jerseys! They had Colin Bell, Frannie Lee and Mike Summerbee among other richly talented individuals. Talking about Allison reminds me of another Bestie story. At one stage my wee mate was figuring more on the front pages than the back pages of the national newspapers. He seemed to crash a car every week and, of course, he did a two-month stint at Her Majesty's Pleasure following an early-morning altercation with his vehicle and a lamppost outside Harrods in December 1984. Later on, Bestie admitted he was completely taken in by Allison telling him he had written a book entitled 'How To Beat The Breathalyser'. It wasn't easy to wind up Bestie, but Big Mal managed it with that one. Maybe he should have told him about the planned sequel, 'How To Enjoy Life Behind Bars'!

And what can I say about the truly stupendous Johan Cruyff? If that guy had a weakness I certainly couldn't detect it. He could dribble, he was strong, good in the air, could shoot, had an eye for a pass, was pacy, was fearless. Did I miss anything out? I played with and against him and I thought he was incomparable. If Bestie enjoyed a snifter, that guy certainly embraced a cigarette. I was amazed to discover he could get through eighty to one hundred fags a day. And yet look at how fit he was. He must have been a phenomenon. Having said that, wee Billy Bremner enjoyed a smoke, too, and he was Mr.Perpetual Motion on the park. Maybe I should have taken it up! To be honest, I never thought about smoking as I was growing up. As a confirmed non-smoker, I could never see the allure of shoving a weed between my lips and setting it alight. However, it didn't do Johan much harm as a player, that's for sure. Mind you, he did have a triple heart-bypass later on in life!

Choosing a goalkeeper for my All-Time Favourite Team isn't quite as simple as nominating Bestie, Moore and Cruyff. Three top contenders who immediately spring to mind are Gordon Banks, Lev Yashin and Guiliano Sarti. Let's start with the Italian who, of course, came so close to breaking Celtic hearts in the European Cup Final in Lisbon in 1967. It's hard to believe, but he was actually thought of as being a bit of a weak link in the Inter Milan team that day. Remember, that was the era when you had to rely on information filtering through from the media and little clips of film. There was nothing like the blanket coverage of foreign football we can all get now at the switch of a button on a remote. So, we really didn't know an awful lot about the shotstopper. One thing we should have worked out was the fact he was the last line of a defence so favoured by Inter manager Helenio Herrera. He built his reputation on the dreaded catenaccio, the system that stifled attacking football. Would Herrera have selected a dodgy keeper to play behind his rearguard? Of course not.

Another thing that escaped our attention was the fact that Sarti was actually making his fourth appearance in a European Final. He had already played when Inter had beaten Benfica 1-0 two years previously and had also performed twice in European Cup-Winners' Cup Finals for his former club Fiorentina. As far as experience at that level was concerned, he completely eclipsed the entire Celtic team. Maybe it was all a bit of gamesmanship from Inter before the game to lull us into thinking he was there for the taking. Italian teams, of course, were well versed in all sorts of shenanigans before big games. They would attempt anything to give them the upper hand.

I recall a story when Bill Shankly, Liverpool's legendary manager, caught a representative of an Italian team just before kick-off trying to persuade the referee to change the pressure of the ball. Apparently, he wanted it to be just a shade lighter and softer as he thought that would favour the Italian side. Bill went ballistic. He guarded that ball with his life until it was eventually released for the match official to take onto the pitch.

A little point, possibly, but it might have meant an awful lot at the end of the day.

And a certain Brian Clough, then the Derby County manager, once completely lost the plot after his team had gone down 3-1 in a European Cup-tie against Juventus in Turin in 1972. Cloughie stormed off the pitch straight into a televised press conference and proclaimed, 'All Italians are cheating bastards!' Then he refused to attend the aftermatch press conference to face the newspapers. 'Tell them I won't talk to any cheating Italian bastards!' A bit extreme, Brian. And he was normally such a quiet, reserved bloke...

In Lisbon, Sarti, as we soon found to our horror, was no Aunt Sally. In fact, he looked unbeatable. I can watch that game being rerun to this very day and I still can't fathom how he made some of those saves. I was hitting that ball as well as I have ever struck anything, but it appeared there was no way past Inter's Man In Black. We knew it would take something special to beat him and, thank God, we managed that just after the hour mark. I connected sweetly with Jim Craig's pass from the right and the ball just took off into the top corner. Gallantly, Sarti threw a right hand at it, but, even if I do say so myself, there was so stopping that shot. Of course, Stevie Chalmers then got the winner and the final scoreline was 2-1.

Years later, I was at a football awards' ceremony and the Inter man was there, too. He spoke very little English. Instead, he held up his right hand with his fingers outstretched and smiled. 'It could have been five,' he said in halting English. I put up both my hands. 'It could have been ten,' I said. He laughed and nodded. 'Si,' was all he said. I didn't need an interpreter.

Now, if that performance was indicative of how Sarti played every week in Italy, then there would have been absolutely no debate about who would be in goal for my team. I just don't know, though, if that was ever the case. The Italian international team had Dino Zoff and Enrico Albertosi around at the time and Sarti didn't seem to get much of a look-in at that level. One keeper who did play over one hundred games for his country was the great Russian Lev Yashin. The first time I got a proper chance to see him in action was in the World Cup Finals in England in 1966. He was classed in the veteran category at that stage and was coming to the end of a fabulous career. Again, I wouldn't have seen him play for his club side Moscow Dynamo. It would have been difficult enough trying to get telephone calls out of Russia in the fifties and early sixties never mind film of a football game. Yashin, though, had to be considered, if only on reputation alone.

The nod, though, goes to Gordon Banks, the England World Cup winner. Banksie was amazing. I played against him five times for Scotland and I always thought he was excellent. I had one success against him - the unforgettable 3-2 win at Wembley in 1967. Two others ended even with England victorious in the other two. It's always a plus for any defender if the bloke performing behind him looks poised and confident. That was Banksie. His team could have been under pressure when a high ball dropped into the penalty box and there would be Banksie clearing everything in front of him to either catch or fist the ball to safety. Believe me, defenders loved their goalkeepers taking responsibility at times like that. His distribution was brilliant, too, either by hand or by foot. He looked the complete No.1 to me.

Denis Law used to try to wind him up during international encounters. 'You dirty English bastard,' Denis would say, combining menace with a smile. It didn't seem to faze the Englishman one little bit. He was concentrating completely on the developing ninety minutes and could have his say with Denis later. Mind you, he would have been either brave or crazy if he ever wanted to seek out Denis after a game Scotland had lost. Then he would have really felt the sharp edge of my mate's tongue!

It's a wee bit strange to note that such an accomplished goalkeeper never played for one of the giants in football and I mean no disrespect to Chesterfield, Leicester City and Stoke City in saying that. He won only two club honours in seventeen years - League Cup victories with Leicester in 1964 and Stoke in 1972. Odd, that. You would have thought a Manchester United or a Spurs or a Liverpool might have come in for him at some stage when he was at the height of his powers.

I reckon Banksie pulled off one of the greatest saves I have ever witnessed. It came in that marvellous 3-2 victory in 1967 and Denis Law must have thought he had scored his second goal of the afternoon. He spotted the keeper off his line and deftly flicked the ball up and over Banksie's head. Denis thought it was a goal. I thought it was a goal. Everyone who saw it thought it was a goal. Banksie didn't. Somehow he catapulted backwards, got his right hand to the soaring ball and pawed it round the post. I've watched it since on TV and I'm still spellbound. People often talk about miraculous saves. Let me tell you, this was one of them.

I realise a lot of observers go on about Banksie's save from Pele during those memorable 1970 World Cup Finals in Mexico. It certainly looked spectacular as he raced from his near post to the back after Jairzinho had crossed for the unmarked Pele. The wonderful Brazilian got up to head the ball down and the keeper got back just in the nick of time to push the ball for a corner. I believe if Pele had glanced the ball towards the same spot he would have scored. However, he got up and headed it downwards and it was actually bouncing up behind Banksie when he got his hand to it. Still a magnificent save, though, but I think the one from Denis at Wembley was even better.

Sadly, Banksie's career came to an end at the age of thirty-four when he lost the sight of his right eye in a car crash in 1972. With one eye, he would still have been a helluva lot better than some goalkeepers I played in front of!

Berti Vogts is a name that may bring an involuntary shudder to the Tartan Army after his less than successful stint as manager of the Scotland international side. He got off to a dreadful start on 27 March 2002 when he saw his new charges obliterated 5-0 by France in Paris. The Scots were four goals adrift at the interval and the French, with Zinidine Zidane and Thierry Henry in awesome form, were toying with us. In truth, it was the debut from hell. And it all went downhill after that. To be fair, France were the reigning world and European champions at the time and I'm sure Berti might have chosen any other country to make his baptism against rather than this outstanding French outfit.

There was also talk of a blazing stand-up row with Celtic goalkeeper Rab Douglas at Charles de Gaulle Airport as the team prepared to fly home. Douglas claimed he had been promised a chance at some stage during the game with Spurs' Neil Sullivan in the starting line-up. I can only presume Douglas is a masochist. Did he really want to face a French team firing on all cylinders? Who said all goalkeepers are crazy?

Berti Vogts might have been a loser on that occasion, but I still rated him a first-class right-back. He reminded me a little of Danny McGrain. Both were quite stocky, but had good pace and were excellent tacklers. Neither was a goalscorer - I think you would struggle to get a total of twenty between them - but they knew what they had to do as far as their defensive duties were concerned. I would have Berti in my team in the No.2 shirt.

Over on the left, I would select Inter Milan's Giacinto Facchetti, who, like myself, was a great believer in combining the offensive with the defensive. We knew a lot about the 6ft 2in Italian's reputation long before we encountered him and his team-mates in Lisbon, of course. He was said to be the first of the attacking full-backs and that must have been highly unusual when you consider his country's reputation as being ultra defensive. I got a close-up view of Facchetti when he played against Scotland in the qualifiers for the 1966 World Cup Finals. Jock Stein was caretaker manager of the international side at the time, taking over from the sacked Ian McColl, and I thought I might be in with a chance of getting a game, either at home or away.

Jock pulled me aside before the first game at Hampden and informed me, 'I'm not taking a chance in playing you in this one, Tommy. They've got a wee outside-right called Giovanni Lodetti and I think he would skin you alive!' Thanks for the boost in confidence, boss. He played Rangers' Davie Provan, instead, and if Lodetti was on that pitch I missed him. Facchetti impressed me, though, with his instant control and intelligence. He rarely gave the ball away. Scotland won 1-0 with a last-minute goal from John Greig and it was all eyes on the game in Naples a month later.

I was in the travelling squad, but I realise now it was merely for experience. I had no chance of getting the nod for that one. Eddie McCreadie came in at left-back and a guy called Bruno Mora replaced Lodetti in the wide right role. The encounter turned out to be a stroll in the park for the Italians. Poor Jock. He was hit by a spate of withdrawals with Denis Law, Jim Baxter, Willie Henderson, Alan Gilzean and Bill Brown all pulling out. It was the ideal setting for Facchetti and Co to show what they could do as an attacking force and they didn't pass up the opportunity. They were already a goal ahead by the time Facchetti showed his finishing touch. I have to admit I was well impressed with his precision and coolness.

Adam Blacklaw had replaced the injured Brown in goal and, truth be told, the burly Burnley shotstopper wasn't international material. He was in because there was no-one else available. He flapped at a cross and merely pushed the ball to the Italian defender about thirty yards out. Facchetti could have done a number of things. For a start, he could have smashed the ball goalwards and there was every chance of it hammering against someone in the packed penalty box and being diverted to safety.

However, he summed up everything in an instant and gently flighted the ball high towards goal. Blacklaw was never blessed with the agility of a gymnast and there was no way he was going to do a 'Banksie' and get back in time to push it away. The ball sailed into the net and the Italians won 3-0. The one consolation for Scotland was the fact Italy made such a mess of playing in the World Cup Finals when they lost 1-0 to North Korea and faced a barrage of rotten fruit and vegetables from their infuriated fans when they returned to Rome Airport. Facchetti certainly deserved better because I really rated him an accomplished player.

I was talking to him at a sporting event years later and I was surprised when he asked, 'How is Jimmy Johnstone?' We weren't to know it at the time, but Jinky was winding down his career at Celtic. I answered, 'Oh, he's fine.' Facchetti smiled and said, 'My manager at Internazionale, Helenio Herrera, did me a big favour in that European Cup Final in Lisbon. He asked Tarcisio Burgnich to mark your player. I was very grateful for that because I did not want to face him on his own. Please tell him that.' I doubt if the Italian crossed the halfway line that day such was the attacking domination of Celtic, but I thought that was very honest of him. We swapped a couple of football stories and exchanged telephone numbers and promised to keep in touch. Sadly, this great sportsman passed away a few years ago and I didn't get the opportunity to say farewell.

By the way, I did not copy Facchetti's style in any way. Until the 1965 game at Hampden I had never even seen him play. I had read about him, but I had little or no knowledge of how he performed in my position. So, please don't call me the second Giacinto Facchetti. I was the first Tommy Gemmell! The Italian was certainly good enough to get a place at left-back in my line-up.

As I've already stated, Bobby Moore is a must for a role in central defence. I have to admit it wasn't so easy to pick a partner for the stylish Englishman. He played alongside Jack Charlton for England and they were a good enough double-act, but I wouldn't place the Leeds United man in the world-class variety. I saw plenty of Mike England in Scotland v. Wales clashes and I rated him highly. The word back then was that he was signed by Spurs after they failed to land Billy McNeill and I think there is a lot of truth in that. He dominated in the air, but was fairly limited on the deck. Northern Ireland had Terry Neill, but he pretty much fell into the same category as his Welsh counterpart.

One name, painful though it was, kept coming into focus; that of Feyenoord skipper Rinus Israel. His performance against us in the 1970 European Cup Final defeat in Milan was fairly faultless. The Dutch were well drilled that night in the San Siro and Israel stood out among eleven heroes who, I will admit, deserved their success.

I'm told he scored around twenty in his eight-year career with the Rotterdam outfit and that makes it even more agonising that he headed in Feyenoord's equaliser only three minutes after I had given us the lead with a drive from the edge of the penalty area. He played a captain's part that night. Unfortunately. Well after the game, both sets of players were leaving the San Siro Stadium, heading for our respective coaches, and, of course, all the kudos were going to our rivals. Wim van Hanagem, with a left foot Jim Baxter would have been happy to possess, was getting photographs taken wearing a Celtic tammy and smoking a huge cigar. Israel saw me looking at his club's playmaker and said, 'He has always been a fan of Celtic.' He destroyed us that night with his range of passing. Some way to show his appreciation of a team whose style he appreciated. Alas, he only saw a shadow Celtic side in Milan.

If I struggled to find a worthy partner for Bobby Moore it was quite the opposite with the midfield. Here are just a few of the top quality candidates: Gianni Rivera (Italy), Johan Neeskens (Holland), Josef Masopust (Czechoslovakia), Amancio (Spain), Wolfgang Overath (West Germany) and Alan Ball and Bobby Charlton (both England). And that's just some of the guys who didn't get into the side!

Without a doubt Franz Beckenbauer would get a place, but you would need someone in there to complement his strolling style of play. He was probably a harder grafter than a lot of onlookers appreciated and will be forever remembered for stroking the ball around in that elegant way of his. But he could get in there, too, with a tackle when it was needed. My choice to play alongside him might surprise a few, but I would plump for my Portuguese mate Mario Coluna. He was a well-built specimen, but he wasn't one of those muscle-bound, leaden-footed defensive midfielders who could turn as quickly as the Queen Mary. He was surprisingly sprightly on his toes for such a big man. In fact, he was a natural athlete. He had a wonderful lazy-looking gait, but he got around that pitch.

He always looked as though he had time on the ball and, as I've said a few times, that's the sign of a good player. He could pick up opponents, but, inevitably, was also in the right place at the right time to accept passes and keep the flow of the team going forward. Of course, the style of Benfica and Portugal was just about identical which came as no surprise when you considered there were so many Benfica players in the national line-up. They could have renamed the international side as Benfica plus a couple of guests.

I was thrilled when Coluna phoned me personally to ask me to play in his Testimonial Match in 1970. He said, 'You must play, Tommy, I already have a watch with your name engraved on it!' I didn't need any extra inducements to play in that fabulous player's big night. By the way, I've still got that watch to this day, a treasured memento of another unforgettable night in football. Well, it was unforgettable for me, but maybe not for George Best! That guy could sleep walk his way into my dream team. I will always be a fan of that gifted Irishman. Okay, let's look for some guys who could score a goal or two for this team.

Eusebio became known as Europe's answer to Pele when he exploded onto the scene during the World Cup Finals in England in 1966. His shooting power was terrifying. He scored two goals as Portugal beat Brazil, then the holders, 3-1 at Everton's ground at Goodison Park in one of the section games. I can still recall one of his efforts that evening so vividly that he could have scored it yesterday. The Brazilians failed to clear a corner-kick and it dropped right at the feet of the man from Mozambique about ten yards out at a slight angle. The next thing we knew the ball was bulging the net with goalkeeper Manga still waiting for Eusebio to shoot! I have still to see that effort crossing the line in normal time. Slow motion shows you the perfect technique of Eusebio as he got his head over the ball to strike it first time. I have to say I felt sorry for Eusebio and his international team-mates that they didn't win the trophy that year. And, before you say it, I am not being anti-English.

However, would anyone argue that there was a more attractive team than the Portuguese in those finals? With Pele carrying an injury and Brazil relying on players such as Djalma Santos and Garrincha, who were probably past their best, it was left to Portugal to add a splash of colour to proceedings. I thought they looked good enough to take Brazil's prime position in the global game. I was as bemused as anyone when news was filtering through that North Korea had taken an early lead against their celebrated rivals in the quarter-final clash, again at Goodison. I didn't take too much notice because I thought Eusebio and Co would come back and pulverize them. Then the Koreans netted a second. 'This is getting interesting,' I thought. Then we were told it was

3-0. Was there a massive shock on the cards? Remember, this was the North Korean side who had knocked out Italy, the nation who had beaten Scotland in the qualifiers. It was obvious they were no mugs, but a 3-0 lead against the Portuguese was just outrageous.

Eusebio then came to life. Final score? North Korea 3, Portugal 5. And Eusebio netted four of them, two, admittedly, from penalty-kicks. Jose Augusto got the other, but by then it was already 4-3 and Eusebio had done the damage. So, with so much going for them, why didn't Portugal go on and win the trophy? They had the likes of Eusebio, Torres, Augusto, Simoes and my old friend Coluna among their ranks and they were managed by the celebrated Otto Gloria. Unfortunately, they couldn't find a goalkeeper of equal stature to match the outfield players. They had to rely on Jose Perreria and he was undoubtedly their Achilles' Heel. Eusebio was the tournament's top scorer with eight goals, but the Portuguese defence conceded seven - two in the semi-final defeat against England - and that's the difference between success and defeat in this game.

I think the only team I've ever seen get away with having a dodgy keeper was that magnificent Brazil team in 1970 who had Felix in goal. He certainly wasn't Felix The Cat. However, with players such as Pele, Alberto, Jairzinho, Rivelino, Gerson, Tostao and Clodoaldo around they could probably have played Ronnie Corbett in goal and still won that World Cup in Mexico.

Eusebio was a sporting megastar by the time Benfica visited Parkhead to take on Celtic in the European Cup second round in 1970. Those were two of the most dramatic ties I have ever played in with the most sensational of climaxes. I scored the opening goal in the first leg at Parkhead in the second minute when Bertie Auld tapped a free-kick into my path and I just let loose first time with my right peg from about twenty-five yards. The keeper didn't even move as the ball zoomed straight and true into the top corner of the net. I enjoyed that strike and I was smiling, too, when Willie Wallace and Harry Hood added to it to give us a three-goal cushion going into the second game.

The encounter in Lisbon was nothing short of torrid. Eusebio scored their second goal and we were hanging on deep into injury time when they got the equaliser through a wily wee winger called Diamatino. That took the game to extra-time and, if I'm being honest, the men from Lisbon fully deserved it. Eusebio was leading by example that evening and we had to take care of him. The guy, like Coluna, was a natural athlete and an extra thirty minutes didn't seem to daunt him one little bit. Somehow we managed to hold on. The tie would then be settled on the toss of a coin as there were no penalty-kick deciders back then. In these circumstances, tensions were running high as you might expect. There had been several personal feuds in extra-time with tempers becoming frayed and players on a knife edge. There was a fracas in the tunnel as the stress and pressure of the evening took over. A lot of scores can get settled in that cramped little area.

Bodies were flying about all over the place and punches were being thrown wildly and blindly. Suddenly, out of the corner of my eye, I could see the great Eusebio pinned to the wall and, naturally enough, he looked more than a little alarmed. I could see the sleeve of the guy who wanted to punch out Eusebio's lights and, I have to admit, it had green and white hoops on it. In all the melee, I couldn't quite make out the identity of the assailant, but I had my suspicions later on although no-one admitted to it. Remember, this was the same Eusebio who actually championed Celtic before our European Cup Final against Inter Milan in Lisbon only three years earlier. The same Eusebio who acclaimed Jimmy Johnstone as one of his favourite players. And, there he was with his back against the tunnel wall, with a genuine look of fear in his face and with a fist round his throat. It didn't get any better for him - Celtic won the toss and got through to the quarter-final.

That night in the Portuguese capital was a strange one altogether. The dressing rooms in the Stadium of Light are not too far away from the referee's office. Billy McNeill went in with Benfica captain and my old mate Coluna for the toss of the coin. There was absolute silence coming from both sets of players as we waited expectantly to discover our fate. There was a loud yell at one point. From whom? Was it Billy? Or was it Mario? We didn't realise it at the time, but there was a first flip of the coin to see who would get the opportunity to toss the coin for the right to get the first call. You got that? There was a toss of the coin to see who got the toss of the coin! Then there was another loud outburst. Again, was it Billy? Or was it Mario? All was revealed when we heard those wonderful words, 'Ya fuckin' beauty!' We were through and Benfica and Eusebio were out. Later on, I hoped he forgave the over-exuberance of my team-mate.

So, we've got Best, Cruyff and Eusebio in attack, but who else could possibly grace this sparkling front line? Come in the White Arrow, Alfredo di Stefano. He was so good he played for THREE international teams, Colombia, Argentina and Spain! That has got to make this exceptional player even more unique. Underling how odd football can be, he never performed in the World Cup Finals, despite having three times the opportunity than most other players.

Alfredo came into focus as part of that magnificent Real Madrid team that ruled Europe from 1956 to 1960. They won the inaugural European Cup by beating France's Rheims 4-3, followed that up with a 2-0 success over Fiorentina, then overcame AC Milan 3-2, and Rheims again were the 2-0 losers in the 1959 final. They looked unstoppable by the time they reached Hampden in 1960 and a crowd of 127,261 packed into Scotland's national stadium to see what Di Stefano, Puskas and Gento could do against the redoubtable West Germans of Eintracht Frankfurt, who had taken twelve goals off Scottish champions Rangers while dismissing them over two legs in the semi-final.

I was sixteen years old when I watched that game on television with my dad at home in Craigneuk. I had never witnessed such perfection on a football field. The Spaniards actually gave Eintracht a goal of a start that evening in Glasgow. Then they ran amok. Alfredo thumped a hat-trick beyond the West German keeper Heinz Loy and the man known as the Galloping Major, Ferenc Puskas, fired in four in a fabulous 7-3 triumph. It was all breathtaking stuff. Gento, on the left wing, was a flying machine. I'm sure he could have won a gold medal at the Olympics in the 100-yard sprint. I would have put my wages on it.

I was enthralled by the spectacle and there's one moment I will never forget in the game. Eintracht had just scored another goal and the ball was re-centred. Puskas shoved it in front of Di Stefano and he took off like a hare, skipping past about three challenges before unleashing a low shot from about twenty-five yards low into the bottom corner. The perfect response, I think. That was only one of 526 club goals the player scored in a career that spanned from 1945 to 1966.

Never in my wildest dreams could I ever have thought I would meet up with this icon. Of course, that's what happened seven years later when he asked Celtic to provide the opposition in his Testimonial Match at a sold-out Bernabeu Stadium. He met us at the airport and had his photograph taken with us. His English wasn't very good, but he got the message across that he was happy Celtic had won the European Cup. 'Very good,' he said. 'Yes, very good for football.' He was forty years old at the time, but insisted in kicking off on his big night. He was on the park for about fifteen minutes before going off to a deserved standing ovation. I joined in and then Jimmy Johnstone took centre stage. The Wee Man put on the performance of a lifetime and I can assure you this was no friendly after Alfredo bade his farewell.

Real Madrid wanted to show the Scottish upstarts who were the genuine European champions and they came at us with a verve and gusto. My mate Bertie Auld and his opposite number Amancio emphasised the combative nature of the game by doing their best to knock each other out and being sent off in the process! I wondered what the great Alfredo, who was by then sitting in the presidential area of the directors' box, made of that.

There was hardly a sound in the ground, not that easy when there's 135,000 in attendance, when Bobby Lennox scored the game's only goal after some marvellous leading-up play by Jinky. The game had been put together in a bit of a rush after our European Cup success. I think Real were waiting to see who won in Lisbon before putting out their invitation. So, our fans wouldn't have had the time to get the money together or make travel arrangements to get to Madrid for the match. There was hardly a Scot in the stadium. However, when Bobby's shot struck the net to be greeted with stupor from the home fans, suddenly there was a solitary shout of 'G-O-A-L!' It was unmistakeably Glaswegian.

I would loved to have included Pele, the best player I have ever seen. Unfortunately, our paths never crossed. As I have stated elsewhere, I passed up the opportunity of playing against him and his Brazil mates at Hampden in the summer of 1966 to go on holiday with about sixteen other footballers to Lloret de Mar. I can only look back now and kick myself. In my defence, I couldn't have been thinking straight. Who would knock back the chance to grace the same field as Edson Arantes de Nascimento, otherwise known as Pele? I might just be in an exclusive band of one.

Anyway, here is a full run-through of my All-Time World Football line-up in a 4-2-4 formation: Gordon Banks; Berti Vogts, Rinus Israel, Bobby Moore and Giacinto Facchetti; Franz Beckenbauer and Mario Coluna; George Best, Eusebio, Alfredo di Stefano and Johan Cruyff.

Manager? It has got to be Jock Stein. He would have loved to have been in charge of such a collection of excellence and quality. Although how he would have got on with Bestie is anyone's guess!

CHAPTER SEVEN

HOORAY HENRIK!
LAUDABLE LUBO!

Henrik Larsson was so exceptional I wouldn't hesitate even for a nano-second in giving him a place in the legendary Lisbon Lions line-up. If we could have fielded twelve men!

The Swede was everything I love in football. When I gave up playing and managing I would, more often than not, be found at a Celtic game watching my old team and lending my support. I have witnessed so many excellent players over the years in those famous green and white hoops and I would rate Henrik Larsson the best of the lot. I can't pay him a higher compliment.

The parade of talent I have watched has been beguiling and fascinating. When I sat down to compile the best eleven I have seen as a fan watching from the stand, I just didn't realise how daunting the task would be in attempting to narrow it down to one team. So, I've put together a Team A and a Team B, but, in all honesty, I could have gone all the way to Team Z such was the conveyor belt of skilful operators from whom I had to choose. Who would be a manager?

When the idea was first mooted by my co-author Alex Gordon, two names immediately sprung to mind for my best-ever line-up - Henrik Larsson and Lubomir Moravcik. I could turn up on matchday on a freezing cold February afternoon safe in the knowledge I would be entertained by these two guys. They would warm the cockles of the coldest heart. These blokes were born to play for Celtic. They embodied everything the club stood for; flair, flamboyance, attacking instincts and sheer class.

Henrik was a quiet sort of guy. On the evening he was voted into the Greatest-Ever Celtic team by the supporters in the millennium poll, he mixed with the rest of us, but never sought out the limelight. He thought it was our night and seemed quite content to take a back seat. However, he certainly deserved to be among the elite. I told him I thoroughly enjoyed watching him play. All he said was, 'Thank you, Tommy. I have watched videos of you and your friends. I enjoyed the way you played, too.' A mutual admiration society was born in that moment.

Silent off the park, but what a startling transformation out on the pitch, though. You couldn't keep your eyes off him. His movement, pace, anticipation and touch were quite mesmerising. Wim Jansen bought him from Feyenoord for £650,000 in the summer of 1997 and, at that price he has got to be the best bit of transfer business in Celtic's history. Around about the same time, Alex McLeish, then the Hibs manager, paid £750,000 for Ulises de la Cruz. Who do you think got the better deal?

Mind you, the Swede hardly got off to the best of starts in his Celtic career. You only get one chance to make a first impression, but, thankfully, Henrik's debut against Hibs at Easter Road on the opening day of the 1997/98 league season turned out to be a false start. Wim put him on as a substitute in the second-half with the game tied at 1-1. Henrik set up the winner. Unfortunately, though, it was for the Edinburgh outfit. He mishit a pass out of defence that swept straight into the tracks of that well-known Celtic fanatic Chic Charnley and he did his favourite team no favours whatsoever by striking an unstoppable twenty-yard drive low past Gordon Marshall. Henrik showed great character to quickly overcome that early setback.

In fact, I thought Larsson was sublime. I would have loved to have played alongside that guy. His consistency was unbelievable. I'm not just talking about his phenomenal goalscoring rate although that is fairly breathtaking, too. In seven years at Celtic, he rattled in 242 goals. Breathtaking! However, I'm talking about his overall play and his work-rate. He wasn't just an out-and-out striker although his fantastic goal tally may suggest that. Look back to that awful evening in France when he broke a leg in the European tie against Lyon. Henrik was actually in the right-back position when he was chasing deep into his own half to put in a tackle on an opponent. I played with and managed a lot of lazy buggers who would never have been in that position in the first place.

Henrik was a very private person, but my old Lisbon Lion mate John Clark, is his capacity as a backroom man at Celtic, tells me he was a bit different in the dressing room before a game. Then Henrik was as noisy as the next man. I have to say I liked his style. I was at a Player of the Year awards night in Glasgow back in 2002, the evening after Rangers had beaten Celtic 3-2 with a last-minute goal from Peter Loovenkrands to win the Scottish Cup. The Ibrox side also won the championship that year. Anyway, Henrik had been voted Best Player and, as a man of few words, he accepted the award and thanked everyone who had voted for him. Then I was amazed by what he did next. He fixed Dick Advocaat, then the Rangers manager, in his gaze and said, 'Enjoy your moment. We will be coming after you next season.' He didn't say a lot, but when he did open up he didn't miss his target.

I was intrigued, too, when a friend of mine, who was a neighbour of Larsson in Thorntonhall on the south side of Glasgow, told me a story about the player. Celtic and Rangers were neck-and-neck in the title race in 2003 and the Ibrox side were due to play a game on the Sunday which was being televised live. My pal said there was about half-an-hour played in a dramatic encounter when he happened to gaze out of his frontroom window. 'I could hardly believe my eyes,' he told me. 'There was Henrik taking his dog for a walk! Every Celtic fan in the world must have been tuned into that match because it was so important for us, but Henrik, instead, decided to take his pooch for a stroll.' Now that's what I call laidback.

Lubomir Moravcik was a bit of an unknown when Dr.Josef Venglos bought him for Celtic from German team MSV Duisburg. I think he cost something like £300,000 and that was just loose change to most clubs back in 1998. To be honest, the transfer hardly caused a ripple of interest among most of the support when you consider that even mediocre players were moving for £1million fees at the time. Dr. Jo knew him, of course, from his days as manager of the Czechoslovakian international side. Possibly a lot of fans thought he was coming to the club to top up his pension at the age of thirty. I'll admit I didn't know too much about the player, either, but I realised he must have been of a reasonable pedigree to have played seventy-odd games for the Czechs who were a good team at the time.

'This guy's no mug,' I told everyone. 'We might be onto a winner.' My God, was that an understatement. When Lubo knocked in two goals against Rangers in a 5-1 triumph at Parkhead on 21 November only a couple of weeks after his transfer to the club we all knew we were in the presence of something special. He arrived as an unknown and left as a legend.

It was a shame that he did not come to Celtic at his peak. We only saw two or three years of an individual who was one of the best, if not THE best, two-footed players I have ever seen. It was impossible to work out which was the stronger of his feet. He was more than capable with both. He was the type of player it would be difficult to pin down. I think both Dr. Jo and then Martin O'Neill basically gave him a free reign in the team. He would move around the pitch, get the ball and build and destroy. He took a wicked free-kick, too. I thought Lubo brought a new dimension to the team, he added that something extra. If Henrik Larsson was Celtic's best-ever buy at £650,000 then Lubo wouldn't have been far off at £300,000.

So, that's two players in place from the many who have graced Celtic during my days as a fan. Selecting a goalkeeper wasn't too difficult, either. I've gone for Pat Bonner, the Republic of Ireland legend. You look for consistency in your last line of defence and I think Pat gave Celtic that valuable commodity and his managers some peace of mind over his years as the club's guardian. He was reliable and didn't always get the headlines, but any team boss will tell you they know when a goalkeeper is producing. I remember Davie Hay telling me about a European tie against Sporting Lisbon at Parkhead in 1984. Celtic, two down from the first leg, were winning 3-0 at the interval and had changed things around completely. Davie recalled, 'It was looking good and then the Portuguese were awarded a direct free-kick about twenty yards out. Sporting seemed to have a team packed with deadball experts. My heart was in my mouth because a goal at that time would have turned the game on its head. Their player whipped his effort up and over our defensive wall and I feared the worst until Packie got across his line to pluck the ball out of the air. We scored two more to win 5-0 and I read the reports in the newspapers the following day. Big Packie's save didn't merit a mention anywhere. I appreciated it, though. If that had gone it would have been a different game altogether and, possibly, a very different outcome.'

Tommy Boyd was never a guy to hit the back page splashes, either, but, in my opinion, he was the best right-back at Celtic since the days of Danny McGrain. He was a workmanlike defender with a great engine as he got up and down that flank. Tommy was a good user of the ball, too, and rarely mistimed a tackle. Celtic got him a straight swap from Chelsea in a deal that took Tony Cascarino to London. Laim Brady paid £1.1million to sign his former Republic of Ireland striker from Aston Villa and he turned out to be a colossal waste of cash. Celtic definitely got the better of that bit of transfer business.

My choice at left-back may surprise many. There are guys such as Andy Lynch, who was my assistant manager during my second stint at Albion Rovers, Tosh McKinlay and Stephane Mahe who were good enough to stake a claim. But I'm going for Derek Whyte, who could also play at centre-half. I preferred him on the left flank, though. I thought he was an elegant player who, like Boyd, rarely gifted possession to the opposition. He was as honest as the day was long and was a thorough professional. I believe Celtic should have done more to hold on to him after wage negotiations broke down and he moved to Middlesbrough. Obviously, I wasn't party to the pay talks, but I do know Derek was upset at what was on offer at the time. Pity, that, because I think he could have been a quality Celtic left-back for years.

In central defence, I would pick two players I believe would have been an awesome partnership - Roy Aitken and Paul Elliot. I would make Aitken the anchorman in the back four, but, with his energy, it would be difficult to curtail his enthusiasm for going forward. I can hardly remember him having a bad game. Honestly, I can't recall too many occasions when I have come away from Parkhead thinking he could have done so much better. And he always gave 100 per cent to the team. He was a born leader and a perfect captain. Again, I was talking to Davie Hay over a snifter or two in a wee southside establishment one day and Roy's name cropped up in the conversation. He was Davie's skipper, of course, during his years as manager between 1983 and 1987. Davie couldn't speak more highly of the player.

'He never gave me a single problem,' said my mate. 'If you asked him to do something, you knew it would be done. Look back at the Scottish Cup Final against Dundee United in 1985. We were struggling and were a goal down with time running out. A manager earns his money in moments like that. I took off Paul McStay and Tommy Burns and put on Pierce O'Leary and Brian McClair. I'm sure most of the fans must have thought I had taken leave of my senses with my double substitution. I put McClair into a forward position because I knew he was always liable to nick a goal and I pushed O'Leary into central defence alongside Tom McAdam. I asked Roy to play on the right flank because I thought United could be vulnerable in that area with someone running at them. Davie Provan equalised with an excellent free-kick and then Frank McGarvey netted the winner with a header from a cross provided by Roy from the right wing. It was a different role for Roy, but he didn't even question my judgement. When I told him what I wanted him to do, he simply said, "Right, gaffer," and carried out my instructions to perfection.'

NINETY MINUTES FROM GLORY... the Lisbon Lions are rarin' to go. Back row (left to right): Bobby Murdoch, Jim Craig, Ronnie Simpson, Yours Truly and Bobby Lennox. Front row: Willie Wallace, Stevie Chalmers, Billy McNeill, John Clark, Bertie Auld and Jimmy Johnstone. Thankfully, we didn't line up in this formation!

THE GODFATHER... Jock Stein with some of the former Celtic players who became managers. They are (clockwise from the top): Willie Wallace, me, Willie Fernie, Benny Rooney, Billy McNeill, Mike Jackson and Bertie Auld.

WELL, AT LEAST, JIMMY JOHNSTONE IS PREPARED FOR THE TEAM SNAP BEFORE KICK-OFF IN LISBON!... Willie Wallace is about to join him as Bertie Auld and Bobby Lennox get prepared. Jim Craig, myself, Ronnie Simpson, Billy McNeill and John Clark get set to take our positions. Bobby Murdoch and Stevie Chalmers are awol.

HIGHLAND FLING AT HAMPDEN... I talk to Spurs midfielder Alan Mullery as we take to the pitch for a pre-season friendly to kick-start the 1967/68 season. Willie Wallace follows on. We drew 3-3 with the London outfit in a rousing encounter.

BALL BHOYS... Willie Wallace and I show why we never made it as jugglers before the same game. Ronnie Simpson, Bobby Lennox, Stevie Chalmers and Jim Craig follow our lead.

ME, BERTIE AND WISPY ARE FLYING HIGH AS EVERYONE KNOWS WE ARE THE
BEST IN EUROPE.

WHO'S THAT WITH TOMMY GEMMELL?... Real Madrid legend Alfredo di Stefano (second from the right) mixes in good company. That's me and Billy McNeill at the front with Willie O'Neill, Bobby Lennox and Davie Cattenach at the back. We played in Di Stefano's Testimonial Match only a few days after Lisbon and won 1-0. Wee Bobby scored the only goal.

WORLD-BEATER... I blast the penalty-kick past Racing Club goalkeeper Augustin Cejas to put us 1-0 up in the second leg of our World Club Championship in Buenos Aires. The rest is history!

RUSSIA COMES TO ROTHESAY... I'm carrying this bottle of vodka for a friend. Honest! My pals and I used to enjoy wee breaks on the Isle of Bute.

HAIR-RAISING... That's me making my Scotland international debut against England in 1966. I wasn't smiling afterwards - we lost 4-3.

PEEK-A-BOO!.. That's me almost out of the frame third from the left in the back row. It's the Old Bhoys' network again! The others are (back row left to right): Sean Fallon, Stevie Chalmers, Charlie Gallagher, Jim Craig, Billy McNeill, John Hughes, Bobby Murdoch, Bertie Auld and Willie O'Neill. Front tow: John Fallon, Jimmy Johnstone, John Clark, Bobby Lennox and Joe McBride. And, of course, the Big Cup!

SILVERWARE SMILES... John Clark, me, Billy McNeill and John Hughes celebrate yet another Hampden victory. Happy daze!

THE GREATEST... what an honour to be chosen by the Celtic fans in their best-ever side. They hardly need an introduction, but here goes, anyway: Bobby Lennox, Henrik Larsson, Kenny Dalglish, Paul McStay, Jimmy Johnstone, Bertie Auld, Billy McNeill, me, Danny McGrain and Ronnie Simpson. Unfortunately, Bobby Murdoch had passed on by this time. What would that little lot cost today?

HAPPINESS IS... me and my wife Mary enjoy a relaxing moment.

STREETWISE... Bertie and I return to Celtic Park after a training stint at Barrowfield.

THE LIONS ROAR... Stevie and I sign copies of the video that showed our run all the way to Lisbon.

MOVE OVER, JOCK... here I am with Bannockburn Amateurs, a great bunch of youngsters I coached for a spell.

DUG-OUT DELIGHT IN DUNDEE... here I am celebrating a win during my managerial spell at Dens Park.

LOVELY BUBBLY... the air hostess helps us celebrate a victory on our flight home. The usual suspects are (left to right): Bertie Auld, Bobby Lennox, me, John Clark, Billy McNeill, Willie Wallace and Jimmy Johnstone.

THE MAGNIFICENT SEVEN... here I am (extreme right) lining up with my Scotland team-mates Billy McNeill, Alan Gilzean, Colin Stein, Peter Cormack, Eddie Gray and Jimmy Johnstone. We lost 3-2 to West Germany in a World Cup qualifier in Hamburg in 1969. Worse still - I was sent off!

BHOYS TO MEN... we line up again at the start of 25th anniversary celebrations. Back row (left to right): Jim Craig, Yours Truly, Billy McNeill, Ronnie Simpson, Bobby Murdoch and John Clark. Front row: Jimmy Johnstone, Willie Wallace, Stevie Chalmers, Bertie Auld and Bobby Lennox.

BHOYS ON SONG... Jinky and Bertie are the Elderly Brothers as they lead the hit parade (left to right): Jim Craig, Me, Charlie Gallagher, John Clark, John Hughes and Billy McNeill.

Paul Elliot arrived in an £850,000 deal from Italian side Bari in 1989 and was only at the club for two years before shifting onto Chelsea. I liked the big Englishman and I just wished he had hung around a wee bit longer. He played with a lot of poise and was just about unbeatable in the air. I remember a League Cup Final against Rangers in 1990 where Celtic should have been awarded a penalty-kick every time he went forward for a set-piece. The Ibrox side had ordered their defender John Brown to pick up Elliot at deadball efforts and I think he took his manager quite literally. I could hardly believe what I was witnessing as Brown didn't even look at the player taking the corner-kicks or free-kicks. He was facing Elliot all the time and, fairly obviously, wasn't even attempting to get to the ball. His role was to prevent his Celtic opponent at all costs. To me, that's obstruction, at the very least. And if it is preventing the other team from a goalscoring opportunity then it is a penalty-kick. Rangers won 2-1 in extra-time, but they knew they got away with murder that afternoon.

I would play four in midfield with Moravcik taking one of the central berths. Paul Lambert was the sort of player I would have liked to operate in front of me. He was that unusual combination of industry and ingenuity. He worked hard and also possessed a wide range of skills. He supported the players around about him and was always thinking that one move ahead of the opposition. He could strike a good ball, too. As a player, he gave me the impression he was an excellent student of the game and I am not surprised he went into management.

Paul McStay was similar to Lambert in many ways although he wasn't as crisp when it came to tackling. However, his vision was magnificent and his passing ability matched it. He was a quiet lad off the field, but he certainly did all his talking on matchday. He read the game well, kept the play flowing and, like Lambert, was a willing worker who supported the front players. He had a fair dig in him, too. I can still see his goal against Rangers at Ibrox in a crucial league game in March 1988 as Celtic enjoyed a title triumph under Billy McNeill in their centenary year. It was a must-win encounter for my old team and it was goalless before McStay launched a rocket from about twenty-five yards beyond Chris

Woods. Celtic triumphed 2-1 on their way to their historic championship triumph.

No Celtic dream team would be complete without Tommy Burns. He just happened to be a Celtic supporter who played for the club. I liked his idea of how football should be played. As a performer, he was graceful on the ball and gifted with an outstanding left foot. He could ping passes all over the place with breathtaking accuracy. He was always elegant and, like every good player, always seemed to have time and space in which to work. As a manager, you could see what he was trying to achieve at Celtic. He brought in the likes of Paolo di Canio, Jorge Cadete, Pierre van Hooijdonk - the Three Amigos, according to former owner Fergus McCann - Andreas Thom and Phil O'Donnell. The first thought from all of them with the ball at their feet would be to go forward. These were Tommy Burns' type of players. I thought he was desperately unlucky as manager of Celtic. He came up against Rangers who were powering their way to nine successive titles and had players such as Paul Gascgoine, Brian Laudrup, Richard Gough and Ally McCoist in their ranks.

You only have to look at Tommy's time in charge during the 1995/96 season to see how unfortunate he was as a gaffer. Remarkably, Celtic only lost three domestic games throughout that campaign, all to Rangers, and those losses knocked them out of three competitions. I was at Parkhead for the opening Old Firm encounter of that season and I thought Celtic were doing reasonably well right up to the stroke of half-time. Rangers broke away and Alec Clelland, who scored a goal every time we witnessed Hally's Comet, netted with a header that Gordon Marshall should have saved. Peter Grant hit the bar in the second-half and Rangers raced up the park to hit a second through Gazza. At the end of that match I had to be reminded that Celtic had actually lost. A goal from Ally McCoist gave the Ibrox side a 1-0 win in the quarter-final of the League Cup with Andy Goram defying Celtic all night. And it was 2-1 for Rangers in the Scottish Cup semi-final with Marshall practically presenting the opening goal to McCoist.

Walter Smith, quite rightly, won the Manager of the Year award that season and was very magnanimous when he was presented with his trophy. He said, 'I am honoured to be chosen, but I have to say there is another man who should be in this place tonight. And that man is Tommy Burns for the way he has had Celtic playing this season. He deserves massive credit.' Now that's what I call style. Walter Smith had class. So, too, did Tommy Burns. On and off the football field.

Okay, who is going to play up front alongside Henrik Larsson? I looked at the list of striking options and realised I would have to put in a bit of overtime in selecting just one player. Names such as Mo Johnston, Brian McClair, Frank McGarvey, Charlie Nicholas, Chris Sutton, John Hartson, Frank McAvennie, Andy Walker, Gerry Creaney, George McCluskey, Alan McInally, Tommy Coyne, Joe Miller, Jacki Dziekanowski, Mark McGhee, Jorge Cadete, Mark Viduka, Joe Craig, Harald Brattbakk and Pierre van Hooijdonk, among a cast of what appeared to be thousands, all had to be looked at and their merits analysed thoroughly. This was a tough one. I could see the Ovaltine coming into play!

At the end of an exhaustive search through the claims of each player I decided on Charlie Nicholas. Alongside Henrik, I think cheeky Charlie would have excelled. He was a superb ball-player and was never afraid to take on defenders. Okay, he was not the most industrious of players, but he more than made up for that lack of graft by sprinkling star dust at the other end. I always enjoyed watching Charlie in action. He had wonderful control and it was a joy to behold when he ran at an opponent and left him for dead by dropping his shoulder and sidestepping him all in one movement. Then there would be the inevitable shot at the end of it and, my goodness, that lad knew how to work a goalkeeper.

We should have known Charlie was quick thinking even before his Celtic career took off. He used to tell the story about standing in a long line of hopefuls waiting for trials at the Boys' Club. Someone was going along the line asking the youngsters what was their favourite position. Charlie twigged that everyone was saying right-sided places in the team. When he was asked his position he unhesitatingly answered, 'Inside-left.' He was given a game immediately! He was no inside-left, of course, but he must have done enough during that trial to be offered a place at Celtic. Initiative like that deserves to be rewarded.

So, there you have it, the best line-up of Celtic players I have seen over the years of supporting the club from the stands. I'll go through it one more time. Pat Bonner in goal, a back four of Tommy Boyd, Roy Aitken, Paul Elliot and Derek Whyte. A midfield four of Paul Lambert, Paul McStay, Lubomir Moravcik and Tommy Burns and a front two of Henrik Larsson and Charlie Nicholas. Pardon me while I drool!

Okay, who's good enough to get into the shadow team, the guys who came so close to gaining a place in the elite eleven? Who would get the goalkeeper's jersey? It came down to a straight choice between Artur Boruc and Fraser Forster. The Pole reminded me a little bit of my unpredictable old team-mate Frank Haffey. You never knew what you were going to get from him. I've seen him make world-beating saves, but he conceded a few howlers, too, in his time. If he could have allied concentration to his undoubted ability he would have been rated one of the best in the world. I think Celtic struggled to replace him when he left for Fiorentina in 2010. Personally, I would have fought tooth and nail to keep him. Remember his penalty save from Manchester United's Luis Saha in the Champions League game at Parkhead in 2007?

Quite rightly, a lot of people still rave about Shunsuke Nakamura's fabulous long-range free-kick winner that night, but we should never overlook Boruc's plunging save to his right to thwart Saha late in the game. That moment of magic meant sure Celtic had qualified for the last sixteen of the tournament and that brought millions of pounds into the club's coffers. I would have quite happily have delved into that cash pile to get some extra dosh to persuade the Pole to remain in Glasgow.

But, despite having huge admiration for Boruc, I'm going to give the nod to Forster. Who could overlook what he achieved in setting a new Scottish record of thirteen successive league clean sheets in season 2013/14? That topped the best by Aberdeen's Bobby Clark set forty-three years ago. I wasn't too sure about the keeper when he first arrived on loan from Newcastle in 2010. However, his improvement over four years has been fairly dramatic. He looks a very accomplished last line of defence these days and just edges past Boric.

Chris Morris was virtually unknown when Billy McNeill brought him to the club from Sheffield Wednesday in 1987, but I really took a shine to him. He worked his socks off getting up and down that right flank. Certainly, he wasn't a typical full-back. I think he struggled a bit in his tackling and he wasn't particularly strong in the air, but he made up for these deficiencies in so many other ways. His use of the ball was first-rate and I was at Parkhead on 2 January 1988 when he displayed his polished crossing from the wing in a 2-0 win over Rangers. Paul McStay engineered the move with a searing thirty-yard pass out to the right. It was a magnificent ball, but Morris deserved an awful lot of credit in seeing the space behind the Rangers defence and exploiting it to the full. He took McStay's pass in his stride before delivering a perfect pass into that vulnerable area between the goalkeeper and his defenders. Frank McAvennie, arriving at full pelt, tucked the ball beyond Chris Woods. That's as neat a goal as you'll ever see.

On the left, I would go for Boruc's fellow-Pole Dariusz Wdowcyzk. Like myself, he liked to go forward and was a man after my own heart. However, I think he should have made more of his pulverising left foot shot. He possessed frightening power, but rarely used it to its best effect. I thought he was slightly under-rated, but I think he gave a lot to the team. He must have been fairly confident of his striking ability because he elected to go first when Celtic and Aberdeen tied 0-0 after extra-time in the 1990 Scottish Cup Final. I would have put my house on him sticking it behind Theo Snelders. Possibly his confidence was misplaced because he swept his effort just wide of the upright. He did everything right except hit the target! Anton Rogan missed another and Celtic eventually lost 9-8 on spot-kicks. But, despite that error, I thought Wdowcyzk was a top defender who was solid and reliable. Well, most of the time!

I'm afraid I couldn't find a place for Rafael Scheidt in my central defence. Well, I would like to send out a team that's got a chance of actually winning! Scheidt will remain one of the great mysteries of our time. Why did Celtic sign him? Who told him he could play football? Was he the only Brazilian on the planet who couldn't pass the ball six yards? I'm told it took Martin O'Neill about five minutes to realise the lad had no future at Parkhead. Or probably in the game altogether. Scheidt, bought the previous year for a ridiculous £5.5million during the Kenny Dalglish-John Barnes regime, went with Celtic on their pre-season tour of Ireland in O'Neill's first summer in charge.

A friend of mine was at the first game and he told me Scheidt, with no-one in the vicinity, looked up and then launched a screaming pass out of play that almost beheaded the new Celtic manager. He had to duck for cover in the dug-out as the ball zoomed overhead and far too close for comfort. Goodbye Scheidt. At least, he did live up to his surname. Another who didn't quite make it was Olivier Tebily who was nicknamed 'Bomb Scare' by anyone who saw him in a rare first team appearance after signing from Sheffield United in 1999. Scheidt and Bomb Scare would have been the defensive double-act from hell.

Actually, there were a few contenders for a place in this department. There were guys such as Mick McCarthy, Johan Mjallby, Marc Rieper, Alan Stubbs, Brian O'Neill, Bobo Balde and Tom McAdam to ponder over. However, after much deliberating, I would pair Tony Mowbray with Pat Stanton in the heart of my rearguard. Mowbray was a good, old-fashioned centre-half who stood no nonsense. He was a big, strapping lad and there was nothing fancy about his game. He saw his role in the team as clearing his lines and he did that to great effect. Mowbray was first-class in the air and was fearless in going for the ball. He would put his head where other players might think twice about putting their feet. Well, with his looks he had nothing to lose! Only joking, Tony. He made a pig's ear of the job during his disastrous few months as Celtic manager, but I thought he was a top-notch defender.

Pat Stanton may have only played forty-four games for Celtic in his years between 1976 and 1978 and is better known for his years as a Hibs stalwart, but I thought, even in the twilight of his career, he was superb at Parkhead. He was great at organising things at the back. His anticipation was unbeatable and you could see he had spent a lot of his career in midfield with his intelligent use of the ball. In his first season, after his swop deal with Jackie McNamara Snr, he had a profound influence on central defensive partner Roddie MacDonald. He actually made the youngster a more commanding presence and a better all-round player. It was a great pity that he couldn't have had a longer career at Celtic, but injury put paid to that. In his relatively short stay in Glasgow, he picked up league and Scottish Cup medals. Contrast that with his 680 games with Hibs where he only won a League Cup medal, ironically against Celtic in 1972. There were two successes in the Drybrough Cup, but that was a largely meaningless trophy that was used at the start of the season to get the summer rust out of your system. Stanton, though, did enough in his forty-four games in the hoops to show me he was special.

As with Team A, I'll go for consistency and nominate four across the midfield. Once more, I'm spoilt for choice. I looked at players such as Neil Lennon, Peter Grant, Billy Stark, Alan Thompson, Ronnie Glavin, Dom Sullivan, Morten Wieghorst, Eyal Berkovic and Shunsuke Nakamura. However, I'm confident I have come up with the right mix. First to get the nod would be Stilian Petrov, the hard-working Bulgarian with an eye for goal. To be fair to Kenny Dalglish and John Barnes, he was signed by them - a real bargain at £1.2million from CSKA Sofia. He was a great distributor of the ball, possessed a superb engine and had good positional sense. He was excellent in timing his forward runs. It says a lot for him that he was Martin O'Neill's first signing when he took over as boss of Aston Villa. Celtic got six years' good service out of the player plus a £6million cheque when he moved on. That's sound business.

Craig Burley would be a more than suitable companion for Petrov. Craig was another who wasn't afraid of hard work and really put himself about. He could pinch a vital goal or two and that's always a plus from your midfield men. He and Paul Lambert, along with a certain Henrik Larsson, of course, were crucial in Celtic halting Rangers' march towards ten titles in a row. We would never have heard the end of that! Wim Jansen sorted things out very quickly and one of the most important wins in the 1997/98 season was Celtic's 2-0 victory over Walter Smith's team in the New Year game. Burley scored the first and Lambert lashed in the second and Celtic didn't look back afterwards.

Murdo MacLeod was known as 'Rhino' to his team-mates and you didn't require Sherlock Holmes-like detective qualities to work out how he came about his moniker. He charged around that pitch from start to finish and was a real ninety-minute man. He was a powerhouse with a left-foot shot like a sledgehammer. He would win the ball and get forward to support the front players. Murdo was definitely my sort of player. A great man to have by your side.

John Collins would come in here, too. He was a creative player and very easy on the eye. I believe he liked to be the main man in the middle of the park, but he was sacrificed sometimes to play in a right-sided berth with Paul McStay taking the main role. I saw him have some cracking games for Celtic and he took a mean free-kick, as well. One goal I will always remember that he scored from open play came in a European tie against Cologne at Parkhead in 1992. Celtic had lost the first leg 2-0 and were two up and drawing on aggregate near the end of the game. Collins then spirited up a devastating finish from the edge of the box, sizzling an unstoppable drive high into the net. He must have been watching videos of yours truly!

Now we come down to the front two. I've gone for two blokes with similar qualities and who certainly knew the route to goal. I haven't picked a winger for either of my teams and that is no slight on the likes of Davie Provan, Johnny Doyle, Didier Agathe and others. The way I have structured my line-ups, I would like to think my full-backs could get forward and also the midfield men would look to break on the flanks, too. Two guys who would thrive on such a service would be Chris Sutton and Pierre van Hooijdonk. Both were 6ft-plus and, naturally, were powerful in the air. However, they were very adept with the ball on the deck, as well. Big Pierre took a ferocious free-kick and Davie Hay said that was one of the things that swayed his decision when he put his name forward to Tommy Burns. Davie was chief scout at the time and had to choose between Pierre and Michael Mols. Celtic couldn't afford both at the time and Davie could hardly separate the players. But he went for Pierre when he noticed that he rarely wasted a free-kick. Mols? As we all know he ended up at Rangers, but he could have been a Celt if Pierre hadn't been a deadball expert.

And Chris Sutton was as rugged as anyone I have ever seen play in the old centre-forward role. He was Martin O'Neill's first signing for the club and you could say he cost Celtic nothing. Martin didn't have to dip into the coffers - which must have been a relief to the board - because he sold Mark Viduka to Leeds United for £6million and paid the exact same fee to Chelsea for Sutton. I think Celtic got a great deal. It must have been hellish being a defender facing Celtic back then. O'Neill could pair Sutton with Larsson and have John Hartson waiting in reserve. I thought long and hard about the big Welshman, but in the end Sutton just shaded it.

Here's Team B again. Fraser Forster in goal with a back four of Chris Morris, Tony Mowbray, Pat Stanton and Dariusz Wdowcyzk. A midline of Stilian Petrov, Paul Lambert, John Collins and Murdo MacLeod with a front pairing of Chris Sutton and Pierre van Hooijdonk. I've got to say a game between Team A and Team B would be a certain sell-out. They would probably have to build an extension onto Celtic Park for that one.

I deliberately didn't consider any of the present-day outfield players because some of them haven't been around long enough. I have to say I like the look of Emilio Izaguirre in my old position at left-back. Victor Wanyama looked a genuine prospect in the middle of the park and persuaded Southampton to write a £12million cheque for him in the summer of 2013. He reminded me so much of Chelsea's Michael Essien. Scott Brown is growing into the responsibility that comes with being captain while the versatile Charlie Mulgrew has proved himself to be lethal at set-pieces. I've seen James Forrest being mentioned in the same breath as Jimmy Johnstone, but he's got a long way to go before he gets anywhere near Jinky's mantle. A fully-fit Beram Kayal is a more than useful asset in the middle of the park.

However, there are absolutely no doubts about the qualities of my twenty-two players in my A and B teams. They are all there in merit, no argument.

CHAPTER EIGHT
NOTTINGHAM FOREST B.C.
(Before Clough)

'You dirty big Scotch bastard.'

Alan Ball's 'Welcome to England' greeting wasn't quite the one I had anticipated.

Celtic had just sold me to Nottingham Forest for £40,000 and I made my debut against Arsenal - and Wee Bally - at the City Ground forty-eight hours after Christmas Day 1971. Of course, I had faced the England World Cup winner on international duty, but this was the first time we would get up close and personal in a club game. As ever, I wanted to let my opponent realise he would be getting no favours. There was a clattering challenge early on and that brought out the first, 'You dirty big Scotch bastard' of the day. 'You dirty wee English bastard,' was my witty riposte. He kicked me. I kicked him. He nudged me. I nudged him. He tugged my jersey. I tugged his jersey. I think you get the picture.

This went on for the full ninety minutes and it will come as no surprise to anyone to learn I was booked for a foul on him. And he was booked for a foul on me. It was all blood-and-thunder stuff and I was determined

I would not mark my first-ever encounter in English club football with a defeat. It was obvious, too, that Bally wanted to make a good first impression because he had just joined Arsenal from Everton for £220,000 earlier that week, a British record transfer fee at the time. The final whistle of a gruelling and entertaining contest brought down the curtain on a 1-1 draw. Honours even between the sides and honours even between myself and Bally. This little terrier of a player had a squeaky, almost falsetto, voice, which could actually be quite comical when he strained his larynx to attempt to sound menacing. At the end of the confrontation, he came over, hand outstretched and said, 'See you in the bar later? First drink's on me, you dirty big Scotch bastard.'

Anyone entering the Players' Lounge at Forest's ground afterwards would never have guessed that the two guys at the bar exchanging old international stories had been kicking the shit out of each for an hour-and-a-half earlier that day. I liked Wee Bally. I always appreciated an opponent who could stand up for himself and the Arsenal man was certainly one who did that. What is it with wee blokes with red hair? Jimmy Johnstone, Billy Bremner, Alan Ball and all the others. They just refused to be intimidated by 6ft-plus guys like myself and just snapped at you all day long. They made you work for your money, these sort of characters.

Of course, I didn't want to leave Celtic. That's been well documented down through the years. I was only twenty-eight years old when Big Jock let me know it was time for me to go and, as far as I was concerned, I still had an awful lot to prove, if not to anyone else but to myself. It was obvious I no longer had a part to play in Jock's future plans for the club. He had selected me for only three league games since the start of the season and we had won the lot against Clyde (9-1), Hibs (1-0) and Dundee (3-1). Thirteen goals scored, only two conceded and maximum points. However, it still wasn't enough to persuade the manager that I still had a role to play for Celtic. I was perfectly fit and, when I wasn't in the first team, I would get the odd supporter enquiring if I was injured. 'Nope, I'm rarin' to go,' I would tell them and they would look a little mystified. I am not being big-headed here, but Jock was replacing me with the players who were, in my opinion, less than ordinary. They weren't fit to lace my boots. There's no point in naming names at this late stage, but I knew these individuals were not offering the team what I could. Presumably, the man on the terracing noted that, too. But Big Jock rarely, if ever, backed down once he had made up his mind. My tea was well and truly oot.

I realised there was no way back when I received a telephone call from Jock on a Wednesday afternoon after returning home from a morning training session. 'We've received an offer from Nottingham Forest for you,' he said matter-of-factly. I took a few seconds to digest this news. 'Okay,' I said, 'are you going to accept it?' Jock replied, 'They've bid £40,000 and I think that's a good fee. Yes, I've told them it's acceptable.' Naturally, all this was new to me. Despite asking for a transfer when I was dropped from the League Cup Final team in 1969, I never thought I would actually leave. 'What happens next?' I asked. 'Get yourself down to Nottingham as quickly as possible and have a word with them.'

I had already made arrangements that evening to go to a show bar in Chapelhall to judge a talent contest. The bar was jointly owned by my wee ex-Rangers pal Willie Henderson and former Ibrox manager Davie White, who would later become my boss at Dundee. I decided I would keep my word to Willie and Davie and go along as their guest. I arranged a flight to the Midlands for the following morning. I was leaving the show bar at around eleven o'clock and waiting at the frontdoor was a veteran sports journalist called Jim Rodger, who worked for the Daily Express. Jim was known as 'Scoop' to most players and he had contacts everywhere. I knew he had been involved in transfer deals such as Denis Law going to Manchester United from Torino, Alan Gilzean to Spurs and Ian Ure to Arsenal, both from Dundee. He was well in with the people who mattered. He spoke in the sort of high-pitched tone that made Alan Ball sound like Charles Bronson.

He called everyone 'son'. He was a portly little guy who always wore a huge coat, no matter the weather. You could imagine this bloke on the beach in Millport during the Glasgow Fair fortnight, sitting on a deckchair, wrapped up in that overcoat with his trilby hat perched on his head. Scoop was a character. He asked, 'Ah, son, how are you? Have a good night, son?' I was a bit baffled. Scoop was a rarity among sports journalists because he never touched a drop of alcohol and was rarely seen anywhere near a drinking establishment. After all my years in and out of football, I can tell you he is the only reporter I have ever met who didn't knock back the bevvy. 'I'm fine,' I answered, still wondering what on earth had brought Scoop over to Chapelhall at that time of night. I knew he stayed in Shotts and didn't drive a car. He used public transport quite a lot when his newspaper would have quite happily picked up the tab for taxis. But, in his eccentric fashion, he rarely treated himself to a black hack.

'Son, are you going to a club in England?' he asked. He had a twinkle in his eye behind his dark-rimmed spectacles. 'Who told you?' Back came, 'Ah, son, I know people who know things.' You got the impression that Scoop loved these moments. I was told by other journalists that Jim could barely write his name, but his contact list was extraordinary. He would get the story, provide the facts and it was up to someone else to put it into a readable form for his newspaper.

I didn't really have time to play games with Scoop. I told him, 'I'm having talks with a club tomorrow. We'll see what happens after that.' He looked up, 'Ah, son, would that be a club in the Midlands by any chance?' He had a notebook out, but I noticed he wasn't writing anything down. It was only too obvious he knew the whole story. Who had told him? An educated guess would be Big Jock. And uneducated guess would be Big Jock. 'I'm going down to see what Nottingham Forest have got to offer, Jim.' He nodded. 'Right, son, good luck, son.' And with that he shuffled off into the night. I walked towards my parked car and there was a guy selling the first editions of the Daily Express and the Daily Record at the corner. I bought both. Imagine my surprise when I looked at the Express and their back page splash was an exclusive story by Jim Rodger. The headline read: 'CELTIC SHOCK! GEMMELL IN TALKS WITH FOREST'. Aye, Scoop liked his little games.

Anyway, I duly travelled down to meet the Forest contingent at the City Ground about six o'clock the following evening. Matt Gillies, a fellow-

Scot, was manager of the club and it was quite obvious he was eager to sign me. It was nice to feel wanted again. Armed with that knowledge, I was determined to get the best deal possible. I wasn't going to sell myself short. After all, if the move had fallen through because of personal terms it wouldn't have broken my heart to go straight back to Celtic. There was a bit of haggling, as there always is, and eventually we agreed a three-year deal. I had trebled my basic wage, going from £60-per-week to £180. I was leaving the top club in Scotland, one of the biggest in Europe with a massive worldwide fan base, to join an English outfit who were struggling in the old First Division with a fraction of the support Celtic enjoyed. And I was getting three times my money. As they say in America, go figure.

I admit it was all a bit strange and it had all been done at breakneck speed. I left the City Ground just before midnight and the club booked me into the Trent Bridge Hotel. I did some light training with my new team-mates the following Friday morning and accompanied them on the coach to Bramall Lane on the Saturday for the match against Sheffield United. I was going along as a spectator to gauge the strengths of my new colleagues. I looked around me on the team bus and realised I hardly knew anyone. There was no Bertie Auld. No Jimmy Johnstone. No Billy McNeill. No Bobby Murdoch. There were two young lads at the back of the coach, though, I didn't recognise at all. But I would get to know them better much later in life. Two ambitious kids called Martin O'Neill and John Robertson.

I had been registered as a player the previous morning and I was now Tommy Gemmell of Nottingham Forest and not Tommy Gemmell of Celtic. It had a slightly weird ring to it. I returned to Celtic one last time to tidy up a few things. Big Jock wanted to see me. I went to his office and he gave me the impression something was upsetting him. He never displayed personal emotions in front of players, but I detected there was a change in his demeanour. He said, 'Good luck with Nottingham Forest, Tommy, I hope you do well. I'm sure you will.' Then, rather oddly I thought, he added, 'You know, it didn't need to come to this.' Before I could say anything, he waved his big left paw at me, as he had done on so many occasions during my time at the club, and said, 'Ach, on you go. Good luck.' It was clear he didn't want to continue the discussion. I shook his hand and left his office. I never returned.

I have to say Forest was a Holiday Camp compared to Celtic in so many ways. It felt as though I had gone from Barrowfield to Butlin's! It was a bit of a culture shock. For a start, the expectation levels were hardly on a par with those at Celtic where it was anticipated you would win everything every season. The supporters treated defeats - especially to Rangers - like a death in the family. Heaven forbid you lose an Old Firm Cup Final. Then there is no hiding place in Glasgow for a couple of weeks, at least. At Forest, there was a more genteel feel to everything. It was just so much more relaxed. I hadn't gone down to England for a vacation, of course, but not having pressure piled on you almost on a daily basis was a welcome interlude after being constantly in at the deep end following my Celtic debut against Aberdeen in January 1963.

There was a lot about Nottingham that I liked. For the first three months or so I stayed in hotels. Then I bought a lovely house in a wee village called Burton Joyce, with the River Trent flowing through it, which was about five miles east of Nottingham. It was a beautiful spot and my son David was born there. I loved the rural setting and I had plenty of company. Fellow-Scots Neil Martin and Peter Cormack, two former Hibs players, lived in the village, too, and were both about 100 yards from my front door. Next to Neil lived former Celtic player Jimmy Sirrel, who was manager of our rivals Notts County. It really was a very pleasant setting. Neil, Peter and I could go down to the little local pub, all rustic charm and oak beams, and have a couple of beers without any hassle. I didn't have to look over my shoulder and wonder if someone was phoning Big Jock to inform him one of his players had popped in for a drink.

A Monday evening normally saw a few of the players, the usual suspects including me, Neil and Peter, having a beer or two at the Nottingham Knight pub where a young John Robertson would join us. He was always keen to be part of our group, but Martin O'Neill was a bit more withdrawn and seemed happy enough in his own company. There was a relaxed air about the entire environment and I must admit I was surprised, maybe even shocked, at the lack of discipline about the place.

Training was supposed to start at ten in the morning, but some guys wandered in late every day and weren't even fined. They would get a slap on the wrist and a 'please try to be more punctual in the future' speech. And then they would do the exact same thing the following morning. Big Jock would have demanded the return of capital punishment for the serial offenders. I quickly realised we had good players, but I could also see why the team was toiling at the wrong end of the table. At Celtic, we had to be sharp in training. You were performing under the watchful gaze of Big Jock and he missed nothing, absolutely nothing. At Forest, a lot of the guys simply went through the motions and hardly broke sweat. A lot of them mucked about and couldn't possibly have been properly match fit.

I had a few run-ins with Matt Gillies' right-hand man Bob McKinlay, a big Scot who adopted the sergeant-major outlook. He had been a fans' favourite during his playing days as a robust centre-half. But I could hardly have been less impressed by his training routines. He would gather the players around him on a Thursday morning and put us through hell. Even the slackers couldn't hide. We never saw a ball for two-and-a-half hours of sheer torture and tedium. A lethal mix. He would have us going on long runs, then sprints and then jogging. Then it would start all over again. It was excruciatingly monotonous and it did the players absolutely no favours on matchday. Going into the last half-an-hour of a game our tongues were hanging down around our knees and our legs, the muscles drained, were just about gone. We were knackered and it showed in the results by the amount of late goals we conceded.

I had a word with the barrel-chested McKinlay. Reasonably, I asked, 'Why don't we move this training session to a Wednesday and that will give our legs an extra twenty-four hours' rest and we'll be in better shape come Saturday?' McKinlay looked incredulous. You would have thought I had just asked him to recite the Magna Carta backwards. In his best Brian Blessed impersonation, he bellowed, 'Move it to a Wednesday? No chance. The manager plays golf on a Wednesday.' Oh, well, that explained everything.

Big Jock was always going to be a hard act to follow as far as tactics and game plans were concerned. I was amazed to learn that McKinlay had played 614 league games for Forest in a career that spanned 1950 to 1971. In fact, I played for Celtic in his Testimonial Game on the Monday following Scotland's 3-1 defeat from England at Wembley in 1971. I hadn't an inkling I would be meeting up with him again as a Nottingham Forest player before that year was out. What astonished me, though, was the fact that McKinlay had been involved in football for so long and seemed to know damn all about the sport. Tactics? What tactics? He was a big lad, but he didn't like it if someone answered back. He wasn't confrontational, despite his size. He would back down very quickly. I may have been surprised at that, but I wasn't surprised to later discover what new profession he had taken up after leaving Forest. He became a prison warder at Nottingham Prison where, ironically, one of his work mates would be a former Forest player, Dougie Fraser. Both may have been Scots, but you got the impression they hated the sight of each other. That must have been an interesting sideshow for the inmates. Who needed television when these two were around?

When I joined the club in December I looked at the league table. Forest weren't in the happiest place, but I could see that the drop was avoidable. It was hardly inevitable. There would be no need to press any panic buttons. However, after the turn of the year, we suffered a sequence of defeats that saw us hurtling towards the trapdoor. We had three consecutive losses and I detected a few heads going down. We had to get the players out of that frame of mind. It's all too easy to wave the white flag of surrender in these circumstances. Then it was four defeats on the bounce. That all too quickly stretched to eight and alarm bells were ringing all over the place. In truth, we were in freefall.

I recall a game against Leeds United, Billy Bremner, Peter Lorimer, Eddie Gray et al, at Elland Road and I thought we were doing reasonably well. I was getting the opportunity to bomb forward and had a couple of long-range shots that had their keeper David Harvey, who would guard Scotland's goal in the World Cup Finals later that year in West Germany, scrambling around. It was 1-1 at the interval and I went for my half-time cuppa quite pleased with the way things were going. Matt Gillies and Bob McKinlay were sitting in a corner of the dressing room discussing the first forty-five minutes. I wondered what masterplan they were going to come up with. 'Tommy, you'll need to stay back and defend, 'I was told. 'We'll hold onto what we have. A draw here is a good result.' I argued, 'For fuck's sake, we've still got another forty-five minutes to go. Are we going to invite them down on top of us? I'm tying them up on their right and giving them a problem when I go forward.' Neither Gillies nor McKinlay listened. 'Stay back. Do as you're told.' It was like the bad old days at Celtic before Jock Stein when Sean Fallon used to threaten defenders if they crossed the halfway line. I had stepped into a time warp. So we let Leeds United come at us after the turnaround. Final score: Leeds 6, Nottingham Forest 1.

My mood wasn't helped, either, when I had a post-match drink with my wee mate Bremner. He asked, 'What happened there, Big Man? You were doing well in the first-half. You made it easy for us in the second.' I couldn't be bothered explaining what Gillies and McKinlay had cooked up during the interval.

It wasn't all doom and gloom, though. There was a notable victory over a strong Chelsea side at the City Ground in March. We triumphed 2-1 and I'm delighted to report I scored both our goals. The Stamford Bridge outfit were favourites to win that night and rolled into town with players such as Peter Bonetti, Ron Harris, John Hollins, David Webb, Charlie Cooke and Chris Garland in their line-up. We hadn't exactly been performing, so once you looked at that calibre of opposition, it wasn't difficult to reason why they probably thought the points were already in the bag. I don't know who threw the switch, but Forest were a different team during that ninety minutes. Neil Martin, Peter Cormack, Dougie Fraser and myself, all Scots, and a young Irishman called Martin O'Neill all answered the rallying call on that occasion. We won 2-1 in one of our best performances of the campaign.

I scored with a penalty, as John Hollins did for the Londoners, but I really rolled back time with my other effort. It was a real belter. I let go with a left foot drive from about twenty-five yards and the ball screamed

179

past Bonetti into the net. I was chuffed because, after I had hammered in my first goal for the club in an earlier game, Matt Gillies took me aside and said, 'You took your time scoring, didn't you?' I got the impression my new manager believed I would knock in a goal every week. Nice thought. Unlikely, though.

I got particular pleasure from my howitzer-like effort when I bumped into Chelsea player Peter Houseman as I accompanied team-mates Peter Cormack, Ian Storey-Moore and Peter Hindley to the Cheltenham Festival a week later. The Chelsea lad came over and we were having a wee natter about the game at the City Ground. He told me, 'You really made our manager Dave Sexton angry with your goal, Tommy. You weren't supposed to do that.' I looked at him, 'Pardon?' 'Well, he told us not to bother closing you down when you came into our half. He wanted us to operate in behind you because he thought you were wasting your time. He didn't think for a split-second you would be able to beat Peter Bonetti from long range. Hardly anyone managed that feat.' 'Sorry to hear that,' I laughed.

Ian Storey-Moore was an outside-left who appeared to be going nowhere until I arrived at Forest. I know that may sound conceited, but I really mean it. I helped him out by giving him so many tips I had picked up at Celtic. I don't think anyone had really taken the time to properly coach him at Forest. He was twenty-eight years old before he eventually moved in a controversial deal to Manchester United. Ian was known as 'Mugsy' to everyone because he liked a little punt every now and again. There are about five racecourses dotted around the vicinity of Nottingham and our player used to turn up at most of them on a regular basis. He would take the mug's bet hence the unfortunate nickname. However, my mate Mugsy would never have put a penny on himself having a bizarre hand in Nottingham Forest winning back-to-back European Cups in 1979 and 1980 - years after he had left for Old Trafford in 1972. Yet there is every chance the club might not have scaled those dazzling heights if Mugsy hadn't played his unwitting part.

Let me explain. Brian Clough was making a name for himself at Derby County at the time. He appeared to be abrasive and beguiling in equal measures. He was a colourful character and humility didn't seem to have any place in his DNA. Lots of critics wrote him off as merely being a loudmouth, but, as his record would prove, he had a lot more to offer than just bluster and bile. There is little doubt, though, that he was a law unto himself and I believe an incident with Mugsy tipped his Derby chairman Sam Longson over the edge. There had been friction between the two almost from day one and wasn't helped when Cloughie was once quoted as saying, 'I've got the team ticking over so well now that even our chairman could take over and not make a mess of things.' Oops. You just know that saying things like that will come back and bite you in a painful place at some stage down the line. But that was Cloughie. TV and newspapers couldn't get enough of this character. However, he was beginning to believe in his own publicity. He must have thought no-one could touch him. He had an ego the size of Brazil. Unfortunately, so, too, did his chairman.

He let it be known he wanted to sign Storey-Moore and that set in motion a series of events that descended into farce. Two years after he had won his solitary England cap, Manchester United bid £200,000 for my team-mate. Matt Gillies accepted the offer and he, Mugsy, Forest secretary Ken Smales and United manager Frank O'Farrell met in the Edwalton Hotel in Nottingham to finalise the deal. Naturally enough, I was interested in keeping tabs on what was going on because Storey-Moore was one of our best players and Peter Cormack had told me Liverpool were also sniffing around him. I could see nothing but trouble ahead if we lost both of them.

The deal looked to be heading for the rocks when Mugsy, for whatever reason, refused personal terms with United. Someone tipped off Cloughie, who had more spies than MI5, and he immediately rang the hotel. He told Storey-Moore to remain there until he arrived and he spoke to Gillies and Smales who gave him permission to talk to their player. The Forest pair then drove off. Cloughie arrived and, with that silver tongue that got him into so much trouble, persuaded Mugsy that his future lay at the nearby Baseball Ground. The player duly signed the transfer papers and so, too, did Derby secretary Stuart Webb. Big problem, though. The absent Smales, when he was contacted later, refused, so, technically, Storey-Moore was still a Nottingham Forest player. A mere trifle to Cloughie. I was told Smales actually phoned Derby chairman Longson and warned him there would be trouble ahead if Cloughie insisted the player was his. Red tape never strangled Cloughie, though. All the time I was being kept up to date with what was happening. It was like a good thriller. What would happen next?

On the Friday morning, Cloughie took Storey-Moore to meet the Derby players and put him up in the Midland Hotel overnight. While all this was going on, there was something to always remember - Mugsy was still a Nottingham Forest player. On the Saturday when he should have been playing for us, Cloughie took him out to the centre circle at the Baseball Ground before a game against Wolves and paraded him in front of the fans. The Sunday newspapers had the usual snaps of Storey-Moore holding aloft a Derby County scarf and waving enthusiastically to his new supporters. He then watched the game from the directors' box. I read the local paper and Cloughie was quoted as saying, 'As far as we are concerned, we have signed Moore and I am not really concerned what any other party may feel.' You can almost hear him say those words.

The problem didn't go away, though. A bewildered Mugsy - and I had seen him in that state more than a few times after a favourite at the races had flopped - went home to his house in Bingham, just outside Nottingham. Forest secretary Smales point blank refused to sign the legal documents. On the quiet, Manchester United were invited to come back into talks with the player. Frank O'Farrell and Sir Matt Busby, who had by this time become a director at United, turned up at Storey-Moore's front door. Busby, the old fox, had a gift of a beautiful bouquet of flowers for the player's wife. Who could say no? Eventually, Mugsy agreed terms, signed a new set of transfer papers, endorsed by Smales and Busby, and he became a Manchester United player. On Thursday he was a Nottingham Forest player. On Friday he was a Derby County player. And on Monday he was a Manchester United player. That's what I call a whirlwind of transfer activity. And, yes, Peter Cormack did join

Liverpool in a £100,000 deal later on and that did the club no favours, either.

Cloughie, as you could have anticipated, blew his top. The media couldn't get enough of this saga. The Derby manager fired off a four-page telegram to English League secretary Alan Hardaker. I've no idea what was in that particular message, but, suffice to say, it was enough to get Derby fined £5,000. A furious Longson was forced to send an apology to Hardaker afterwards. The relationship between manager and chairman, which was never rock solid at the best of times, was deteriorating beyond repair. I agree with the many others who believe this situation was to have massive significance in Cloughie's eventual resignation from the club in 1973. Many years later, he told me, 'That was the most pisspoor decision I ever made.'

He spent about five minutes at Brighton before his brief and explosive forty-four day stay at Leeds United. Then, of course, he became manager of Nottingham Forest in 1975 - two years after I had left. Could it have been possible that he may have remained at Derby County if it hadn't been for the Ian Storey-Moore fiasco? It's one of those great imponderables. And, if he had remained at Derby, what would the odds have been on Forest ever winning the European Cup? Even Mugsy might not have been tempted to put a fiver on that. One thing is certain, that deal-or-no-deal nonsense helped propel Cloughie and his loyal sidekick Peter Taylor towards the Baseball Ground exit.

I'm often asked if I could have worked with Brian Clough. Why not? I don't think he took himself too seriously all of the time. I heard him say some outrageous things that must surely have been tongue-in-cheek. I recall him admitting, 'I'm not that sure I know too much about this game of football. I'm the manager who paid £1million for Justin Fashanu, after all!' When he won his first European Cup, his left-back was a veteran called Frank Clark. I was thirty-five years old at the time, the same age as Frank. So, the manager wasn't one of those who believed a player should be carted off to the knacker's yard as soon as he passed the thirty-year mark. You never know what might have happened if I had stuck around. I might have had three European Cup winners' medals today!

I remember getting a telephone call one evening early in August 1974. It was Billy Bremner on the line. 'Christ, Tommy, do you know who Leeds have just appointed as manager? Brian fuckin' Clough. Would you believe it? BRIAN FUCKIN' CLOUGH!' My wee pal was somewhat distraught. It was a shocker of an appointment. Cloughie would regularly appear on TV and slate Leeds United. And I realised Billy must have been more than just a little disappointed because he had told me there was a possibility of both him and Johnny Giles getting a joint manager's role at Elland Road after Don Revie, heading for the England international post, had departed. I knew for a fact Revie had recommended both as his successors with Giles as boss and Billy as his assistant. My mate clearly wasn't happy. 'He's just had a meeting with the players and you wouldn't believe what he said. Christ, I couldn't take it in.'

Years later I went to see the movie 'The Damned United' which was based on Cloughie's short reign at the Yorkshire club. There is a memorable line delivered by actor Michael Sheen who was playing the part of Cloughie. Addressing his newly-acquired players at training, he tells them, 'Gentlemen, I might as well tell you now, you lot have won all the domestic honours there are and some of the European ones, but, as far as I am concerned, the first thing you can do is to chuck all your medals and all your caps and all your pots and pans into the biggest fuckin' dustbin you can find because you've never won any of them fairly. You've done it all by bloody cheating.' Now I don't know if those were Cloughie's exact words that day, but I can tell you Billy was bristling when he spoke to me later on. Hardly the opening speech the Leeds United players would have expected.

I was talking to Leeds and Scotland outside-left Eddie Gray around that time and it appeared he was as traumatised as Billy. Eddie, who, like his Leeds skipper, was Celtic mad, was one of the nicest blokes you could ever meet. It couldn't have been easy to upset this chap. Cloughie managed it. Eddie told me, 'On the very first day he took me aside. "I want a word with you, young man." I wondered what was coming next. "If you were a racehorse, you would have been shot." Charming. Obviously, he was referring to the injuries that I had picked up and I had missed a few games, but I didn't see that one coming.'

I met Cloughie several times during our travels and I have to say I quite liked him. Let's just say he was a brusque individual. On one occasion we bumped into each other at a sporting function. He came over to me, extended his hand and said, 'Tommy Gemmell.' Before I could reply, he added, 'You've got one European Cup medal and I've got two.' And then he walked away.

Another time I was chatting to him about Leeds United. I knew he had picked up a lump sum of £25,000, a lot of cash at the time, for leaving the club and he told me it was his FO money. I asked him, 'FO money? What's that?' He answered, 'Young man' - actually there were only eight years between us - 'that stands for Fuck Off. I don't have to put up with any more idiots. If someone wants me to do something and I don't fancy it, I tell them to fuck off, I don't need their money.'

I also quizzed him on another story that had been doing the rounds. 'I'm told you fined your players for playing passes across the pitch,' I said. 'Is that true?' Even by Cloughie's standards it seemed an extreme punishment. He didn't hesitate, 'Aye, a fiver a time. Nobody ever scored a goal going across the pitch. The goal's at the other bloody end. Some of my lot need bloody shooting. They don't listen, but they do when they get their pay packet and it's a bit light. Then they get the bloody message.' I shudder to think what would have happened to the players if they were ever daft enough to pass the ball backwards. That would probably have merited a public flogging in Nottingham Town Square.

There was another fabulous story flying around the Midlands after Cloughie had returned from a training session with the Derby County apprentices. He fancied a pot of tea. He made a call to the dressing room and a youngster picked up the wall phone.

YOUNGSTER, 'Hello!'

CLOUGHIE, 'Young man, I would like a nice cup of tea bringing up to my office straight away, please.'

YOUNGSTER, 'You what?'

CLOUGHIE, 'A cup of tea. To me. Right now. Please.'

YOUNGSTER, 'Fuck off!' And the phone was slammed down. A fuming Cloughie phoned back immediately.

CLOUGHIE, 'Do you know who are you talking to?'

YOUNGSTER, 'Yeah, Brian Clough. Do you know who you are talking to?'

CLOUGHIE, 'No.'

YOUNGSTER, 'Well, fuck off again, then!'

Davie Hay rates the man a genius. He was the Celtic manager when they took on Forest in the UEFA Cup in December 1983 and he never tires of telling this story. 'We were due to play the first leg at their place. It was very frosty and he invited me over to have a look at the pitch and have a chat. He was very pleasant, indeed, and when someone came in to say my wife Catherine and my mother-in-law Margaret were outside, he insisted they came into see him. He made such a fuss of the pair that my missus was charmed off her feet. I had my pub in Paisley at the time, just five minutes from Glasgow Airport, and I told him to pop in any time and we would repay his hospitality. I didn't think any more of it, but he clearly clocked it. Honestly, I didn't give the matter another thought. Then I got a call from my brother-in-law Gerry the night before the second leg.

'He was running the pub for me and he said, "Davie, you'll never believe who's just come in the bar. Only Brian Clough, Peter Taylor and his entire bloody squad! There's a coachload of them. What do you want me to do?" I told him to serve them and pass on my regards, but I have to admit I was staggered by the news. Twenty-four hours before a European tie, after they had drawn 0-0 in the first leg, and he was out boozing with his players! It was like he was saying there was nothing for him or his players to worry about. The more I thought about it, the more I realised he was a real canny bugger. A night in the pub completely deflected the pressure off his team. My wife and mother-in-law were completely won over by him. So, in one fell swoop, my missus thought he was one of the most charming men on the planet, he's had a drink with all my regulars and then he's gone out in front of 66,000 fans at Parkhead and knocked my team out of Europe. We were favourites, but we lost 2-1. I still think it was an astonishing thing for him to do and, for me, underlined what a genius the man was.

'I was working on tactics with my players at Seamill and he was swanning around my pub in Paisley. He did once say that it was players who lost a manager games and not tactics. He put it this way, though, "There's so much crap talked about tactics by people who couldn't win a game of dominoes." The man was class.'

Former England international Peter Withe once asked for the matchball after scoring four goals for Forest against Wolves. Cloughie's reply was priceless. 'You'll get the ball, young man, when you know how to play with it properly.' And former Hibs and Falkirk player Brian Rice was on the receiving end of some barbed wit when Cloughie said, 'I'm not saying he's thin and pale, but the maid in our hotel made his bed the other day and didn't realise he was still in it.'

Goalkeeping legend Peter Shilton, who eventually signed for Cloughie from Stoke City for £250,000 in 1977, turned up at the City Ground for the initial talks. He had two agents with him. Big problem. Cloughie didn't want to know about the financial advisors. It looked as though the move was off when Shilton and his money men left after about an hour without any paperwork being completed. Later that week the deal was done without any outside interference from the financial people. Cloughie said, 'The only agent I ever knew was James Bond and he only shafted women and not entire bloody football clubs.' The Forest manager also warned the keeper that he was the only one around the club who was allowed to have an ego. 'Just call me Old Big 'Ead, young man, and everything will be hunky dory.'

Aye, it would have been mighty interesting to have served under that guy as a player. Sadly, I missed out by two years. I was at Nottingham

Forest BC (Before Clough). Actually, I never had a lot of say in leaving the club, anyway, in January 1973. In total, I played thirty-nine league games and two Cup-ties while scoring six goals. We were relegated in my first season when we could not arrest our slide out of the top division. A good result here and there, like the one against Chelsea, was never allied to consistency. Our fate was sealed when we played Crystal Palace who were also fighting the dreaded drop. Willie Wallace and John Hughes had both been sold to the London club two months before I left for Forest. Willie Wallace - known as 'Wispy' - was one of my best mates at Parkhead during the good old days. Who scored the goal that relegated us? Wispy! Isn't football just wonderful for throwing these unexpected curve balls at you? 'Sorry, TG,' said Wispy. 'I had to do it. It was you or us.' He didn't need to apologise because I knew he was the consummate professional and he was scoring a crucial goal for the club that paid his wages. He knew I would have done exactly the same at the other end.

So, at the age of twenty-nine, I tasted football outside the top flight for the first time in my career. In a bizarre twist, I was actually better off financially. There was nothing in my three-year deal that stated I would be forced to take a drop in my basic wage if we were relegated and, although the win bonuses weren't quite as high as they were in the First Division, I was guaranteed a few more in the second-tier. There wasn't a lot of skill in the Second Division. That much was obvious right from the first day. There was a lot of effort, though. Mediocre players made up for their lack of talent with an abundance of endeavour, application and industry. It wasn't pretty. As expected, Matt Gillies was shown the door and Dave Mackay, the former Scotland international, was given the manager's job. He brought in Des Anderson, who had been his assistant at their previous club, Swindon Town. I had played against Mackay a few times in friendlies when I was at Celtic and he was at Spurs. He was known as a hard man. At Forest, I thought he was more like the Invisible Man.

He would come down to training and play a bit of keepy-uppy on his own. Des Anderson was the man who effectively took charge of the training and so on. Mackay would look up every now and again. Then he would go back to practising his ball skills on his own. Maybe he was thinking of making a comeback as a player. It didn't bode well. I guessed that Forest and I would be parting company some time in the near future. I suspected Mackay might believe an attacking full-back was a bit of a luxury in this division. And, while I didn't necessarily agree with him, I could read the signs. I played my last game for Forest against Carlisle on 20 January and I returned to Scotland just over a year after leaving Celtic.

Mind you, my career at the City Ground could have ended a little earlier. Nearing the completion of the 1972/73 season I was injured and, as I had some time on my hands, I decided to do a little bit of gardening. I got out the Flymo and about an hour later I was in the Accident and Emergency at Nottingham General Hospital. I hit a stone with the lawnmower and it took a jump sideways. I couldn't get my right foot out of the way in time and the whirring blade cut through the top of my big toe. I didn't immediately feel any pain, but then I saw the blood seeping through. I had a squint at the damage. It didn't look too clever.

My missus phoned Neil Martin and he came over immediately to drive me to hospital. The surgeon performed a minor miracle in putting me together so quickly. You could say he quite literally got me back on my feet. He gave me a local anaesthetic and I watched as he sliced a bit off my toe, removed the toenail, took a skin-graft off an arm, folded it neatly over the toe and then stitched it on. He did a marvellous job. I wasn't in shock or anything like that, but I persuaded Neil that we should stop off at the pub on the way home for a quick snifter. He was playing the next day and didn't seem too keen, but I gave it the Dying Swan act and he relented. I had a couple of beers while he had orange juice. I do like a happy ending.

Big Neil would be a shoo-in to my favourite Forest line-up. So, too, am I, but don't accuse me of going on an ego trip. I was just about an ever-present in the team in my spell there, so I don't have too many alternatives. The same goes for the goalkeeper, Jim Barron. I watched him some days and wondered if he was in some way related to a whole host of custodians I had played in front of. So many of them had the same strengths and, unfortunately, the same weaknesses. Not bad at shotstopping, but woeful on crosses. When I was manager at Dundee I used to scout around and look at different training techniques.

Naturally, I picked up a lot from Big Jock at Celtic, but I was always inquisitive about other methods. I discovered a top continental club used to place about four or five life-sized cardboard figures in the goalmouth and then players would fire over a barrage of crosses from the right and left for their keeper to attempt to come and take. He had to manoeuvre through the motionless traffic in front of him before trying to get to the ball. Brilliant! All you needed, then, were opponents who didn't move around the penalty area. There was no-one to jostle your keeper or barge into him. Waste of time.

At right-back, I would go for a Northern Ireland international by the name of Liam O'Kane. I thought he was under-rated although he did win twenty full caps in the seventies. Stuffy, quick and a solid tackler, everything, in fact, you would look for in a defender. Peter Hindley would be the ideal man to have in central defence. Back in the early sixties Celtic had a centre-half named John Kurila, who was imaginatively nicknamed 'Gorilla'. Actually, even if his name had been Smith they would still have given him the same nickname! The Celt was a beast of a player; totally uncompromising on the ground and reasonably competent in the air. Just like Hindley. Sammy Chapman would be the ideal fit. Again, he wasn't the most spectacular, but could always be guaranteed to give you his best. A real 100 per cent performer with virtually the same ability as his back-four team-mate.

I would settle for two in midfield in my selection and the onus to do a lot of hard work in there would fall on Dougie Fraser, a former Aberdeen player, and Northern Ireland's Tommy Jackson. Dougie joined Forest from West Brom after making two international appearances in 1968 and Jackson actually played thirty-five times for his nation. Dougie played his two Scotland games at right-back, but could fit in well to the midfield. We just missed playing alongside each other three years earlier than we did. Jackson was a workaholic. He started off at Everton, moved to Forest and then onto Manchester United. He was a dynamo from start to finish.

Martin O'Neill would get a place wide right on the attack. I didn't see an awful lot of him, to be honest, but I don't want him on the blower giving me pelters for leaving him out! Actually, I liked his enthusiasm and industry. He was a confident chappie and constantly demanded other players to give him the ball. When he got it he invariably did something useful with it. Neil Martin was a brilliant attack leader and was completely fearless. His prowess in the air was breathtaking. He started at Queen of the South before Big Jock bought him for Hibs. He paid something like £7,000 for him. That is tantamount to theft. He then transferred to Sunderland before landing at Forest. Big Jock had him for a year at Easter Road and it is somewhat surprising that the Celtic manager was never tempted to take him to Parkhead. I heard something about a 'gentleman's agreement' between the clubs and that might have had something to do with it. But, at his peak, he was a magnificent striker.

Before John Robertson settled on a left-wing spot, he used to play in midfield. Okay, he was never the most industrious and players operating in the middle of the park alongside him realised they were in for a full shift. I know he used to drive Cloughie crazy when they were at Forest together. The manager would call him a tramp, but, apparently, Robbo took that as a compliment! Cloughie once said, 'When I am feeling a little off-colour, I go and sit beside John Robertson and then I feel like Errol Flynn.' Another went along these lines. 'When I first saw John Robertson he didn't look anything like a professional sportsman. In fact, there were times when he didn't resemble a member of the human race.' Robbo told me, 'He would often use me as the brunt of his jokes or smart arse remarks. Whether he was making fun of me being a scruff, or my smoking, or my weight, but, looking back I probably quite liked the attention. I really admired him. I think he quite liked me.'

Robbo, of course, became world class when he moved to the wing where his stop-start style drove a lot of right-backs to the brink of a nervous breakdown. Deserved every bit of success that came his way. Smashing bloke all round. On the left it has to be Mugsy himself, Ian

Storey-Moore. It took him a long time to realise his potential and, like many wingers at Manchester United, was burdened with the tag of being the new George Best. That was an unfair comparison. Mugsy was pacy, but he never possessed anything like the range of quality of Bestie. I always thought it odd that Storey-Moore didn't add to his solitary cap he won while at Forest in 1970. The weight of expectation may have got to him at Old Trafford, but, unfortunately, he didn't do himself justice. I don't think injuries helped, either, but one thing is certain - he was a good servant to Forest. And you could bet on that.

A quick rundown of the team in a 4-2-4 formation is: Jim Barron; Liam O'Kane, Peter Hindley, Sammy Chapman and Yours Truly; Dougie Fraser and Tommy Jackson; Martin O'Neill, Neil Martin, John Robertson and Ian Storey-Moore. I would have been quite happy to have spent more time in their company, but, as I found at Celtic, there is no point in arguing when your face doesn't fit and you are no longer wanted.

The short-lived Forest stay was just a step towards a move that would change my professional life forever.

CHAPTER NINE
DARK BLUES' BOOZE BROTHERS

Jinky and Gordy may sound like a comedy double-act. But when those two got together it was no laughing matter. Certainly, I didn't see the funny side. Morecambe and Wise they weren't. Okay, maybe I can afford to smile now, but that wasn't the case back in 1977.

I thought I had pulled off the signing coup of the century when I tempted my old Lisbon Lion team-mate Jimmy Johnstone to Dundee during my first few weeks as boss of the Dens Park club. He had left Celtic two years earlier in 1975 on a free transfer, first to San Jose Earthquakes and then onto Sheffield United. After his stint in England, Jinky was up for grabs again. He was only thirty-two years old and I had every faith there was still mileage in those little legs of his. I believed he could do a real turn for Dundee and help me settle into management at the same time.

I contacted my wee pal and the whole town was buzzing when the news leaked that there was the possibility of the great Jimmy Johnstone signing for Dundee. Ten years earlier, he had been my Celtic colleague when we beat Inter Milan to win the European Cup on a glorious day in Lisbon. I had brought in Willie Wallace as my assistant and now there was the chance of three of that historic outfit teaming up on Tayside. Could the magic rub off once more? It seemed beyond the most outrageous hopes and dreams of the Dundee support. One telephone call put the wheels in motion.

Jinky agreed to have a chat and I promised him I would put together a contract that would suit him and the club. I can tell you that if Jinky had stuck to the deal and all had gone well, he would have earned more than me at Dundee. I was on £10,000-per-year and, to help with the comparisons of the time, Ally MacLeod was the Scotland manager on £15,000-per-year. If Jinky kept himself fit and played in all our games, he would have walked away with fifty per cent more in his pay poke than yours truly and the same as the country's international team boss. I was perfectly happy with that situation. But, of course, I knew Jinky better than most, possibly better than the Wee Man himself. Basically, he had to be making appearances and performing for the two-year deal to be worth everyone's while.

I had arranged a reasonable basic wage with an excellent signing-on fee spread over the length of the contract. There would be bonuses for points and our position in the league. There were all sorts of other add-ons that would have made Jinky one of the best-paid players in Scotland although we were a First Division side at the time. In all honesty, if I had still been playing, I would have snapped up a deal like that and made sure I spent the next twenty-four months earning every penny. Jinky, though, saw the world from a different angle from most people.

I was delighted when he said he would sign for us. I then laid it on the line that he would have to work hard to get his financial rewards. He assured me he would and I believed him. He may have been a bit wayward, a happy-go-lucky character, if you like, but there was another side to Jinky that a lot of people never saw. He was a very sincere, well-meaning person. The reason he couldn't retire at thirty when he left Celtic was because he hadn't put together a pot of gold. He wasn't financially secure.

Jinky earned good money at the club, but he wasn't the type of individual to save for a rainy day. Believe me, that is the case with most footballers. I realise it is totally illogical, even to the ones who don't have all their brains in their feet, that a day will dawn when the ability you possessed for such an important part of your life has ebbed away. The power in your body has simply dissipated. And one former Scotland international of my acquaintance, who was a genuine tough guy, told me he knew it was time to retire from the playing side when his heart went. He no longer relished thundering tackles and realised he was being bowled over by fitter and younger opponents. It's something you have to accept.

However, I looked at Jinky on his first day of training with us and I was impressed. He had been on a family holiday and looked tanned, fit and ready to go. There was a problem, though, and I hope my wee pal will forgive me for this observation because there normally was with him. He fretted over all the travelling entailed as he wanted to continue living in Uddingston, in Lanarkshire, with his wife Agnes and the family. I had the solution to that particular obstacle. I had bought the Commercial Hotel in Errol for £34,000 as my financial safety net. It was a six-bedroomed nineteenth century building and I knew it was a good-going business concern. I told Jinky he could come and live there free. He could stay during the week and, after the game on Saturday, take off immediately for home to spend the remainder of the weekend. That seemed to do the trick, the final piece in the jigsaw.

The Dundee directors were ecstatic. Jimmy Johnstone joining Dundee was making news on the front and back pages of the press. Our First Division outfit was suddenly vying with Celtic and Rangers for coverage in the national newspapers. The signing caught everyone's imagination. Mine, too. I still had visions of the Wee Man dismantling defences with those mazy runs, cutting a swathe on his way to goal, leaving defenders spinning in his wake. Don't get me wrong, I am not a dreamer. I knew Jinky could never replicate that sort of heyday stuff with Dundee. What I did believe, though, was that he still had the ability with one electric burst every now and again to unlock the back door of our opponents and give the rest of his team-mates the opportunity to capitalise on a moment of sheer brilliance.

One back door he wouldn't be unlocking, though, was the one to the Commercial Hotel in Errol. Or the front door, either. I had deliberately not given him a set of keys to the hotel. I wanted to know what time he was getting home and he would have to knock on the door or ring the bell to get access. If he mingled in the bar with some of the punters he was bright enough not to do anything silly right under the nose of his boss. It was impossible to keep a twenty-four hour watch on the Wee Man and that became a problem.

When he arrived for pre-season training he looked in good shape, as I have said, but his fitness wasn't at a level that satisfied me. The Dundee support, quite rightly, were excited at seeing one of the most exciting footballers ever produced by this country playing for their club. However, there was little point in him going out, showing a sporadic flash of splendour, and then spending the next hour or so absolutely knackered. Being fit and being matchfit are two entirely different things. So, I got Willie Wallace on the case. I told him to work Jinky hard in training. And I also knew the Wee Man would respond. Despite his excesses away from football, Jinky was a great trainer. Jock Stein would never have let him near his first team if he wasn't convinced he could give everything for the entire game. I had the same attitude. Skill is nothing without fitness.

Jinky, I'm glad to say, buckled down. It was great to see he was taking everything so seriously. Listen, we all knew Jinky was devastated when Big Jock told him he had no future at Celtic. Parkhead was his spiritual home, Celtic was his team, the club had become his life. He loved it there. He thrived on those supporters singing 'Jimmy Johnstone on the wing' on matchdays. But, fair play to him, he picked up the pieces when he went to the States and then Sheffield United. To me, that showed a gritty determination to carry on playing. I must say I wasn't surprised.

Apart from the financial situation, I realised only too well there was an inner core of steel within that small and sturdy frame. But, alas, he possessed the concentration span of a gnat. The Wee Man could get bored too easily. He could put in a fabulous morning at training, impress everyone, and leave with a big smile on his face. 'See you later, boss,' he would laugh. Normally, I was at the office until around five o'clock, so Jinky was out of my vision for four hours or so. I couldn't exactly put an electronic tag on him, but it would have come in handy to monitor what he was getting up to.

I was heartened when he took to going long walks in the countryside or doing a bit of fishing on the Tay. I had introduced him to the use of the rod while we were at Celtic. We would take off for some quiet location in Perthshire or some such place just to sit by the banks and idle away a couple of hours or so. It was great for relaxation and, if you were extremely lucky, you might even catch a fish. Had Jinky turned over a new leaf? I hoped so, but I was still wary. The Wee Man was full of great intentions, but he had to be watched. He was a massive celebrity on Tayside and everyone wanted to mingle with him and to spend some time in his company to be regaled by some of his marvellous exploits on and off the field. He was a magnetic personality and that's what brought about his downfall in Dundee.

Jinky always found it difficult to say no. I realised that was a problem with George Best, too. Bestie would agree to give so much of his free time to spend on engagements or just meeting people and, like Jinky, rarely got a moment's peace. Could you have ever imagined either Jinky or Bestie sitting peacefully in an armchair, no distractions, feet up and absorbed in a good book? Me, neither.

It didn't take long for Jinky to start heading for the pub with some team-mates and some newly-acquired hangers-on after training. He would never have believed he was actually being a bad influence, but a lot of the younger players were in awe of him and were hanging on his every word. It wasn't the Wee Man's fault, but it was becoming the worst case scenario. I noticed he was settling into a routine and he was coming back to the hotel later and later.

I took him aside on a daily basis. 'Look, Jinky, screw the heid, will you?' I implored. 'We've got loads of dosh I want to give you, but you've got to earn it. Forget the bevvy and get on with taking care of business. Go crazy at the weekend with your pals in Uddingston, but watch what you're doing up here.' Rearrange the following into a well-known phrase or saying: Ears Words On Falling Deaf.

Jinky wouldn't have realised it, but he was pushing me to the absolute limit. I found the managerial side of football pretty exhausting. There were so many things to be taken care of and I was beginning to realise why most managers I met during my playing days were grumpy old bastards. You had to deal with the press, local and national. You had to take their phone calls and there was nothing like the weekly press calls these days where you could meet the newspaper, radio and TV guys all on the one afternoon and that was you pretty much left in peace for the next few days. Of course, you had to keep tabs on players who may became of interest and it was always handy to know what was going on in the opposition's camp before you faced them. There was training to arrange, team formations to be looked at, keeping updated on injuries and so on. There could be tiring journeys to watch games to check out teams and current form of their players. I didn't quite get round to counting the paper clips, but that's exactly what it felt like. In the midst of all this, my wee pal was giving me grief.

He wakened me up one morning by rattling on the door at around 1.30 in the morning. There was no point in taking him to task at that particular moment because reason had been washed away in a sea of alcohol. He swayed from side to side, looked at me, focused and mumbled, 'Hi, boss.' With that, he trundled off to his room. I was more frustrated than angry. The following morning I grabbed Jinky. Normally, I drove him to our training ground at Strathmartin Hospital where they had excellent facilities, including a lush playing surface. There were also a big hill. Guess where Jinky was heading that morning?

The Wee Man was still half-drunk and reeking of booze when I virtually threw him into my car. I knew Jinky could take a cargo, so I wondered what on earth he had been drinking to leave him in this condition. It would have to have been substantial, that's for sure. I've got a fair idea of what I'm talking about because I was known to quaff an ale or two with him and he possessed an exceptional tolerance level to booze. My heart sank. This just wasn't a convivial pint or two after training. This was a full-blown bevvy session. I got him to the training ground and said to Willie Wallace, 'Work that wee bastard to a standstill today. Put him through the wringer. I'm not letting him away with murder.' Wispy didn't hold back. After the players had gone through their normal routines, Jinky was called back for some extras.

Wispy handed him a medicine ball and told him to carry it up to the top of the hill and back again five times. Jinky took the ball and completed the chore before handing it back to his former team-mate. Wispy gave it back to him. 'Let's have another five, Jinky,' he ordered. The Wee Man groaned, but he knew what it was all about. I almost felt sorry for him. Almost. Somewhere in between those runs Jinky was violently sick. He was coughing and choking, but stuck to the task. After his session on the hill, he thought that it was over for the day. No chance. Wispy gave him the medicine ball again. 'We're going through another routine, I'm afraid, Wee Man. We need to get you fit.'

Jinky was told to run from the eighteen-yard line to the goal-line and back five times. He glowered at the wretched weight that was the medicine ball and did as he was told. He looked as though he was about to expire at the end of that routine. 'Now do it five times from the halfway-line to the goal-line and back,' smiled Wispy, who, if he hadn't made it in football, would have fitted in quite nicely to a role with the Gestapo.

Jinky must have been aching all over, but he said nothing. Off he went to complete that particular task. When he returned he looked at Wispy and asked, 'You want me to run the full length of the pitch now with this fuckin' thing, don't you?' 'Got it in one, Jinky,' replied my No.2. 'Off you go.' His lungs must have been burning and his legs must have been in terrible distress. He did as he was told, though. He must have been on the point of collapse when I told him to go and get a shower. Sounds drastic, I know, but I was absolutely desperate for the Wee Man not to let anyone down, especially himself.

He didn't utter a word in the car on our way back to Dens Park. I didn't even get a 'See you later, boss' as he left. I wasn't bit surprised to later learn that he bodyswerved the local hostelries that afternoon. He headed straight back to the hotel, didn't even have a quick one at the bar with the regulars, went to his room and crawled under the bed sheets. Lesson learned? Remember, it's Jimmy Johnstone we're talking about.

I thought it would be a good idea to pair Jinky with Gordon Strachan in training. Wee Gordy was another who appeared to be in awe of Jinky and I thought his natural enthusiasm would spark my pal. It appeared to be doing the trick for a few days, too, until Gordy injured a toe which became infected. A few days' rest was required. I think Jinky picked up a strain of some kind around the same time. Boredom kicked in big-style, unfortunately, with the Wee Man. He couldn't even get to training in the morning and there were many other distractions. Jinky had taken a liking to his new team-mate and it was reciprocated by a fresh-faced teenager.

I never had any doubts about Gordon's dedication and application. I also knew he was a youngster who kept his word. I was told Manchester United had offered him a trial before he actually signed any contract at Dundee. However, because he wouldn't go back on a promise, he rejected United and put pen to paper on schoolboy forms at Dundee, left school at fifteen and became an apprentice on the ground staff in 1972. Ironically, he was signed by John Prentice, the manager who gave me my international debut in 1966 against England at Hampden. That man could spot a player.

I also knew Hibs had missed out on him after a row between his father and Easter Road boss Eddie Turnbull over expenses that had already been agreed. Turnbull - known to everyone in football as Ned - thought chairman Tom Hart had been too generous and wanted to cut them. Gordon's dad wasn't having any of that and any possible move to his boyhood favourites ended there and then. Not one of Ned's best bits of business, that's for sure.

It must have been really hard work for Gordon as a young kid. He hailed from Muirhouse, a tough council housing scheme in Edinburgh, and was on the bus at 6.15 in the morning to take him to the city's Waverley Station and then onto Dundee. Rain, hail or shine, Gordon was on that train every day. He was never lonely on that journey because I think about half the Dundee squad came from the capital. Gordon would have travelling companions in George Stewart, Bobby Robinson, Bobby Ford, Ian Anderson, Alex Caldwell and George Mackie among others. Maybe it would have been better if we had held our training sessions in Edinburgh! Whereas his mates could travel back after the morning training session, Gordon, as the only apprentice in the group, had to remain behind to do all sorts of other menial duties around the ground. He couldn't have got home much before 7.30 in the evening. No-one ever heard him grumble.

Actually, I first saw him when I joined the club from Nottingham Forest in the summer of 1973. I got to the ground a couple of weeks ahead of the pre-season schedule and I spotted some kids having a five-a-sides game behind one of the goals. 'Can I join in?' I asked. 'Are you any good?' responded Strachan with a cheeky grin. 'I'll do my best,' I said. I was hugely impressed by him right away. He was just a wee boy, really, but he had so much ability. He was always looking for the ball, always wanting to be in the thick of the action. He was non-stop and that endeavour never left him at any stage in his career. From a raw kid to a veteran at Coventry City via Aberdeen, Manchester United and Leeds United, playing into his forties, he never lacked enthusiasm. Ron Atkinson, the manager who took him from Pittodrie to Old Trafford in 1984, once said, 'There's no-one fitter at his age - except, maybe, Raquel Welch.' Now that's a compliment.

So, I had nothing to worry about Gordon as far as his professionalism was concerned. And when I paired him with Jinky I genuinely believed they would feed off each other. I also told Gordon to push the Wee Man and I thought Jinky would respond. Well, it looked sound enough in theory. Things can often go slightly awry in practice, as we all know. Anyway, one day Jinky, with nothing to do, invited the injured and sidelined Gordon out for lunch at the Queen's Hotel in the city. Innocent enough and there was no way my young player would knock back such an invite from a true football legend. Jinky was always good company and had a steady line of anecdotes. Wee Gordy was hooked.

The drink was flowing by the time lunch was over and done with. Now, Gordy was no drinker. He was a lightweight and I was aware of that, but it's easy sometimes to lose inhibitions once radical thought is dismissed as the alcohol goes to work. Gordy would have been trying to keep pace with Jinky without even realising how much he was consuming. He always admitted he wasn't in the same league as Jinky as a footballer. He discovered that day he wasn't in the same league as Jinky as a drinker, either. Not too many were, in fact.

A barman at the Queen's later told me my two players had consumed four bottles of wine with their meal. The bright thing after that would have been to go home and have a bit of a kip. Indeed, I later found out that they went to Strachan's home, had a few more drinks and then fished out a ball and had an impromptu kickabout with some local kids in the street. That sight must have bewildered passers-by.

After that, it was off to the pub. And then another pub. They must have been fairly puggled by this stage because someone thought it would be a great idea to get a taxi to Errol and have a few more in the Central Hotel. Not a particularly good idea considering the hotel was only fifty yards across the road from the Commercial Hotel, where the proprietor, of course, was a certain Mr.T. Gemmell Esq. I noted Jinky hadn't returned, but wasn't overly concerned. He could have been fishing by the Tay for all I knew. That notion was knocked on the head when one of my regulars came in. 'Hey, Tommy, did you know two of your players are over at the Central trying to drink the place dry?' he asked. Not for the first time my heart sank. 'Jinky and who else?' I responded. 'Wee Gordon Strachan's with him. He's totally blootered. Wee Jinky's no' much better.'

I was fuming. How stupid could they be? It was bad enough going on a pub crawl, but to do it just across the road from their manager was unbelievable. I marched across the road, just in time to see a sloshed Strachan staggering through the door. He weaved unsteadily towards me without lifting his head.

'Where the fuck are you going?' I bellowed.

'Where the fuck am I going? I don't even know where the fuck I am,' slurred Strachan.

'Do you know who you're talking to?'

'I don't even know who I am.'

I wasn't sure if he was trying to be funny. Then he focused, blinked one eye, and managed to make out my image and burst into tears.

'Sorry, boss,' he uttered. 'Sorry, sorry, boss. I don't suppose you could get me a taxi?'

'Get over the road,' I ordered. 'I'll deal with you in a moment.' I then went into the bar to give Jinky a piece of my mind. The wee bugger had scarpered. The sixth sense that came to his aid so often on the football pitch worked just as well when he was blotto off it. 'You've just missed him, Tommy,' the barman informed me. 'He left a couple of minutes ago.' I caught up with Strachan and all the time he was crying, 'Sorry, boss, really, really sorry. Can you get me a taxi?'

There was little point in giving Strachan a dressing down. He was obviously out the game. I made sure he got home in one piece - he would now be his wife Lesley's problem - and I awaited with the greatest of interest when Jinky might grace my establishment with his presence. Eventually, there was a racket at the front door. It was about two o'clock in the morning. I opened the door and there was the Wee Man. Putting it mildly, he was the worse for wear. Before I could say a word, he looked up, bleary-eyed and muttered, 'Ach, we were only having a wee bit fun.' I got a hold of him and huckled him to his room and chucked him into his bed. As I closed the door behind me I heard a muffled, 'Ach, it was only a couple of fuckin' drinks.'

You can't keep things like that quiet for long in a hamlet such as Dundee. Ian Gellatly, the chairman, would have heard about it minutes afterwards. The following day, he asked me how we were going to deal with it. 'Leave it to me,' I said. To be honest, I wasn't interested in fining the pair or suspending them. Once they had properly sobered up, I had a good old-fashioned heart-to-heart with both. Gordon Strachan swore it would never happen again. As far as I am aware, that remained the case throughout his career. At least, Jinky did him a huge favour that day. My old team-mate was contrite, too. 'It just got a wee bit out of hand,' he said. 'I didn't see it coming. Sorry, Big Man.'

I am not one for holding grudges, so that was the end of it as far as I was concerned. The newspapers, of course, had been tipped off by some helpful local worthies and my phone was red hot for hours. I managed to fend off most of their enquiries and, whether they believed me or not, the matter never hit the headlines. Those were the days where you knew most of the reporters and you trusted them. Fraser Elder and Dick Donnelly, two doyens of the written word, were among the scribes who were in my office every day to pick up a tale or two. Discreetly, you could ask them to look the other way and you would sort them out with a good line in the near future. They would keep their end of the bargain and I would keep mine.

I have to be completely honest here and say I was heartbroken that things did not work out for Jimmy Johnstone at Dundee. It could have turned out to be a grand finale to a wonderful career. That would have been fitting after all Jinky had contributed to the game. He deserved sustained applause at the final curtain on what really wasn't a job of work but his vocation. Alas, it wasn't to be. He started only two games for us and made a substitute appearance in another. We knew it was all over after about three months. I had the secretary draw up a waiver stating that Jinky's contract with Dundee Football Club was being terminated with immediate effect. I promised to pay him the second part of his signing-on fee. I don't think he was even thinking about the money when he signed the form. We had been through so much together, going way back to the days when I trained to be an electrician at Burnbank Technical College and Jinky took a course in welding. That was in 1960. This was 1977. There had been a lifetime in between.

He signed the waiver, handed it back, looked at me, smiled and said, 'Thanks, anyway, Big Man.'

My heart plummeted like a stone. We had a wee cuddle and he was on his way. His taxi arrived at the front door of Dens Park and, with that trademark cheeky grin, he glanced back at me, smiled again and waved. I felt my eyes welling up. There was a strange feeling in the pit of my stomach. If an individual can't get emotional at a time like that then they should check and make sure they still have a pulse. As the vehicle took off, I couldn't help but wonder about the Wee Man's destination.

Would he get a chance at another league club? He had just turned thirty-three and I knew a focused Jimmy Johnstone could still play on for another couple of years. After turning out in nine games for Shelbourne in Ireland, he had a short spell in the Highlands with Elgin City and then spent six months with Junior side Blantyre Celtic. It was all over in 1979, two years after I had taken him to Dundee. Two dreadfully wasted years in the career of a footballing genius. Gordon Strachan must have seen the error of his ways that fateful day in Dundee. He was still playing first class football with Coventry City at the age of forty.

Football chairmen and directors often have the backbone of a banana. So, it is to the credit of the Dundee board that they afforded Jinky the opportunity to relive the glory days. A lot of boards, realising the Wee Man's wayward, carefree reputation, wouldn't have even considered it. If that jigsaw had come together - and Jinky had behaved himself - it could have been a marriage made in heaven. Football is loaded with fairy tales. Sadly, this wasn't one of them.

Over the years, thankfully, I didn't have too much hassle from my respective boards at Dundee or during my two stints at Albion Rovers. When I became a manager first time around at Dens Park, I made it clear I didn't want any interference in team matters. I wasn't one bit interested in anyone else's input. I had seen it, of course, at Celtic before Jock Stein arrived in 1965. Pre-Big Jock, chairman Robert Kelly selected the line-up and team boss Jimmy McGrory had no say in the matter. I wasn't having any of that. If I thought someone was butting in to a territory where they were most unwelcome, I would have a quiet word with them. Normally, it would go along these lines, 'You want to be in charge? That's fine. I'll just quit here and now. You can take the training. You can pick the team. And you can select the fuckin' tactics.' Remarkably, it did the trick every time. They backed off to where they belonged and I got on with my job without any silly suggestions from unwanted quarters.

My old mate Brian Clough was talking to me at a sporting function in Nottingham one evening when I was at Forest and he was manager of Derby County. He asked me, 'Are you interested in getting into management, young man?' I told him it was something that had a certain appeal and he warned me to always remain on my guard. He said, 'Most directors are shithouses and backstabbers who would have given Julius Caesar a good going over!' Then he laughed and added, 'The authorities often ask about football hooligans. Well, there are ninety-two chairman, for a start!'

In his autobiography, the great Len Shackleton, a goalscorer who attained legendary status at Newcastle and Sunderland in the forties and fifties, once devoted a chapter entitled 'What Directors Know About Football'. Under the heading, there was a blank page. Actually, there are guys who sit on boards up and down the country who do know a little about the game. But, as they say, a little knowledge is dangerous. I may not be in a dug-out these days, but I am still a firm believer that a manager must be allowed to manage. As simple as that. You are brought to a club for your expertise by owners, chairmen and directors who must believe you are the right man for the job in the first place. And then they want to do it for you. Doesn't make much sense, does it?

We all know it's a precarious job and we carry the can when things don't quite go according to plan. When did a chairman ever sack himself for getting it wrong? That would be a first. Some clubs change their managers with the frequency most people change their socks. Mind you, I don't think there will ever be a quicker sacking than that of former West Ham player Leroy Resenoir in May 2007. He lasted TEN MINUTES as manager of Torquay United. No sooner had he been unveiled as the team's new boss when he was told that the club had been bought by a business consortium and his services were no longer required. Everyone realises it's a results-driven business, but spare a thought for poor old Leroy - he didn't even get a chance to lose a game!

I went into the job with my eyes wide open. I was well aware of the pitfalls. For a start, the manager who had brought me to the club was Davie White and he had just been sacked. The team had missed out on a quickfire promotion back to the Premier League and the board had been ruthless. Remember, Davie White was a manager who had won the League Cup - with me as his captain - in December 1973 when we beat Celtic, of all clubs, 1-0 in the Final. It was the first major piece of silverware the club had picked up since the heady days of the 1963 title-winning team that contained such players as Alan Gilzean, Ian Ure, Alex Hamilton, Andy Penman, Gordon Smith and Bobby Cox. The club had been a decade in the wilderness until White arrived after being sacked as manager of Rangers. In 1973, the club also finished fifth in the Premier League and won a place in the UEFA Cup where, unfortunately, we failed to make an impact.

Three years later Dundee were relegated on goal difference after finishing with thirty-two points, the same total as Aberdeen and Dundee United. St.Johnstone had already lost the survival struggle weeks before the end of the season. It was as tight as that. But the directors made it fairly obvious that the team's stay in the second tier was to be a brief one. Their mantra was, 'We're a Premier Division team playing in the First Division.' Unfortunately, that made Dundee a target for other clubs round about them. A game against us was one of the biggest of the season and our opponents were well primed for those occasions. At the end of the campaign, in which I was playing in central defence after admittedly losing a yard or so of pace at the age of thirty-two, we finished third. We were eleven points behind a very good St.Mirren team, managed by a certain Alex Ferguson, and seven behind an extremely competent Clydebank.

I was on holiday in Majorca when I received the news that Davie White had been given the sack. It was a sad ending to an adventure that had promised so much only four years earlier. That's football, though. Just look at Manchester United. They won the European Cup in 1968 and were relegated in 1974. Now that's what I call a fall from grace. As I travelled back from my vacation, I had no thoughts about becoming manager of Dundee. Take it from me, there was no skullduggery behind Davie White's back. I liked the man and used to socialise with him and Willie Henderson on the odd occasion. As a matter of fact, Ian Gellatly, the Dundee chairman, asked me for a recommendation about who should become the club's new manager. I didn't have to think too long. I put forward the name of my good friend and former Celtic colleague Bertie Auld. There was no reason for doing so other than I knew Bertie was doing a marvellous job with no money to spend at Partick Thistle. I was asked to phone Bertie which I did.

Naturally, Bertie was interested in talking to Dundee to see what was on offer. I arranged to meet him at my hotel in Errol. Bertie asked me what to expect from the directors, their ambitions, their hopes, their plans and so on. When he had his interview with the board, he knew fully what to expect. Bertie went to meet the directors at the sprawling home of Gellatly. According to Bertie, the chairman asked him, 'What do we need to do to make you manager of Dundee, Mr.Auld?' Bertie replied, 'Buy me a house like this for starters!'

Bertie's move from Maryhill to the City of Discovery never materialised, of course, but his meeting with the board had massive consequences for me. Before he left Gellatly's palatial home, my pal said, 'I don't know why you are talking to anyone else when you have your next manager on your very own doorstep.' He was asked to identify the individual. 'Tommy Gemmell's your man. He's the guy you want.' Somehow the story leaked to the press that Bertie was wanted by Dundee. (My wee mate had plenty of pals in the media - that's all I'm saying.) Partick Thistle, alarmed at the prospect of their manager leaving them, immediately gave him a pay hike. Me? I got an interview and got the job. Now for the hard bit.

I had been told there was no money to spend, so, on that score, the board had been completely up front. There had been no false promises. They also wondered if I would combine playing with managing. I gave that some serious thought. After a couple of days I informed the board I believed it would be best all round if I concentrated one hundred per cent on management. To be honest, I thought I could have played on for another couple of years, at least, but I could see there would be huge problems in twinning the jobs. For a start, as a manager I could give someone a bollicking at half-time if I didn't think he was pulling his weight. How, though, could I criticise someone else if I was having a stinker myself? And who was going to give me a boot up the backside? No, it had to be one or the other and I had made my choice; I would be the manager.

The new season didn't seem that far away and, naturally enough, there had been a fair upheaval in my professional life since I had walked through the front doors at the end of the previous campaign and wished everyone, 'Happy holidays.' Now I was in charge. I had to try to turn things around as quickly as possible. I knew we needed new players, that much was obvious. However, we had no money. It was time to wheel and deal.

There were players I wanted out and there were others I wanted in. That's one of the occasions when you need your board to back you. I gave them a list of a few players I thought would be better moving to other clubs. Obviously, I didn't expect them to agree with every single one of those names because everybody had their favourites. However, the directors hadn't shared a dressing room with some of those guys. I knew those players' attitudes and I was aware of those who would go that extra yard for the club. And, just as importantly, those who wouldn't. Thankfully, the board accepted my proposals and that allowed me to get to work immediately.

Naturally, I knew the areas at the club that needed strengthened right away. I urgently required a new left-back. A phone call here and a phone call there and I was informed Hibs manager Eddie Turnbull might be persuaded to allow Erich Schaedler to leave the club. I was also told Turnbull was looking for a frontman to lead the attack. Immediately, I got in touch with the Easter Road gaffer. He was gruff even when he was in a good mood. I didn't waste much time. I told him I wanted Schaedler and I was willing to allow Bobby Hutchinson, who had scored fifteen goals the previous season, to go in a straight swap with no cash changing hands.

Actually, I was quite happy to see Hutchinson leave Dundee. Nothing personal, you understand. I knew he and his fellow-frontman Billy Pirie used to get the same train to Dundee every day. Billy lived in Aberdeen and Bobby in Montrose. The weren't daft enough to have a drink before they turned up for training, but I knew they were having a couple in the bar at the Dundee station on their way home. If the train was delayed for any length of time things could get a little out of hand. And there were enough people in the city who were only too swift to let me know what my players were getting up to. Inevitably, their two-man drinking club would have to be broken up.

So, when I got the news that Hibs were looking for a striker and were prepared to allow Schaedler to move in exchange, I acted in haste. Ned Turnbull seemed amiable enough when I motored through to Easter Road, but before we could shake hands on the deal he had some unwelcome news for me. 'Sorry, Tommy,' said Ned, 'but the board have just told me they want an extra £10,000 in cash.' I accepted I was a rookie manager and the far more experienced Turnbull might be pulling a fast one. I kept a straight face. 'Aye, Ned, that's a problem. I wouldn't mind Schaedler, but I won't be too upset to hold onto Hutchinson. He scored a lot of goals for us last season, after all. Maybe I'll have to look elsewhere. In any case, we don't have £10,000 to spare.' Ned's expression changed immediately. 'Oh, let's get the deal done,' he said. 'I'll settle it with the board afterwards.'

I soon found that managers liked to play their little games. I learned very quickly. Obviously, my Tayside counterpart Jim McLean, over Tannadice Street at Dundee United, was one of those guys to whom nothing was ever straightforward. Glum Jim made Ned Turnbull look like the Laughing Policeman. During my three years as manager of Dundee there were thirty-eight changes at the club, players leaving and players arriving. However, John Holt wasn't one of those who joined us. I noticed he hadn't played a first team game for Dundee United for about three months and I was looking for someone to put some steel into our midfield. I thought Holt would provide that.

I sounded out the player. Would he be prepared to switch from United to Dundee? The player was right up for it. He didn't hesitate. 'Sort it out, Tommy, and I'll be happy to sign for your club,' he told me. In fact, I got the impression he was desperate to move. Of course, it was an illegal approach, known as tapping. I didn't feel guilty because I knew it went on all over the place. So, armed with the knowledge that Holt wouldn't hesitate in crossing the city, I got in touch with the Tannadice gaffer. As ever, McLean was his evasive self. 'Naw, I'm no' sure we want him to leave,' he told me. 'He's a very good player, very important to my team.' When I pointed out that he hadn't actually been in the team for quite awhile I was met with, 'Aye, there'll be reasons for that.' There was a pause before Jim came back with, 'Let me think about it.' Everyone knew McLean made all the decisions at United. He didn't have to run anything past his board for their approval. Then he said, 'We could let him go for £30,000. I think my board would accept that.'

In these moments you realise it would be just as satisfying and rewarding to go out and have a reasonable conversation with the side of the building. I persisted, 'Look, Jim, you know we don't have that sort of money.' I'm not sure we could have gone as high as thirty quid never mind £30,000. At that moment I realised McLean had no intention of doing business with us. He would have hated for Holt to have switched clubs and then shown him up by doing us a right turn. Obviously, he was just trying to discourage us. I think John Holt would have been good for Dundee and I'm equally sure we would have been good for John Holt. It wasn't to be.

One guy who did a great job for the club, in my opinion, was goalkeeper Ally Donaldson. I realise there will be more than a few Dundee fans who might think I would go for Thomson Allan as my shotstopper in my dream team, but I'm picking Ally. He had everything a goalkeeper needed, as far as I was concerned. He was tall and athletic. Stripped to the waist, he would have given Tarzan a swing for his money. He was brave and had good hands. Another thing I really liked about Ally was his dedication. He was part-time, but he put in a full-timer's shift. He worked as a travelling rep, but he somehow always made it on time to turn up for training between 12.30 and 2pm. Then he would go out with wee Hughie Robertson, one of the coaches who had been a first-class winger at the club, and he would be put through a gruelling session for the full one-and-a-half hours. He would go through this routine every day without fail. Now that's what I call professional.

Thomson Allan was in goal when Dundee won the League Cup in 1973 and was a steady enough custodian. Like a lot of his kind, I have discovered they are pretty good at actually stopping the ball. That's what they do most often during training sessions. People bang in shots and they dive all over the place trying to get to the ball. But I haven't seen so many who are as confident when it comes to dealing with crossballs. Tommy Docherty might have been the first to come up with, 'Their goalkeeper is like Dracula. He's frightened of crosses.' Yes, I know it's been done to death, but that terrible pun does sum up quite succinctly the outlook of an awful lot of keepers. They are perfectly fine in dealing with direct efforts, but once the angles start to change their mindset goes a bit haywire. Thomson Allan was secure enough, but when Willie Ormond, then the manager of Hearts, offered me £7,000 for the keeper I didn't hesitate in taking it. So, I would give the No.1 shirt to Ally Donaldson, one of the most consistent of his ilk I ever met.

Bobby Wilson, at right-back, was a great club servant who was a first team regular for a decade. I played alongside him, of course, and I thought he was very steady. He rarely attempted something he knew he couldn't achieve. There were no frills with Bobby. He was sturdy, good in the tackle and could always be depended upon to give his all. Every team needs a player like this guy, so, without a second thought, I would give him the No.2 shirt.

I signed Stewart MacLaren from Motherwell a year after taking over from Davie White and I wished I had got him twelve months earlier. He was an exceptionally combative central defender, but he could also do a very good job in midfield. He was a robust guy and a winner, which, obviously, is very important. I paid something like £25,000 for him and I think Dundee more than got their money's worth. I also spent £15,000 bringing his former Fir Park team-mate Willie Watson to the club. If I moved MacLaren into the middle of the park I could always rely on Watson to do a steady job in his place in central defence. However, balancing this side is important, so I would put MacLaren in at centre-back.

Iain Phillip would be an excellent foil in the middle of the rearguard. He was a great user of the ball and rarely squandered a pass. He read the game well, too, which was just as well because he wasn't the fastest. Phillip was a clever player and you couldn't miss him because he was about 6ft 2in tall and had flowing locks and a Zapata moustache. He was always being tipped to get an international call-up, but, for whatever reason, it never materialised. The Dundee fans would often insist, 'If he played for Celtic or Rangers, he would never be out of the Scotland team.' I don't know about that, but Phillip was good enough for Crystal Palace boss Bert Head to shell out a six-figure fee to take him to Selhurst Park.

There was no problem choosing a left-back, either. It had to be Erich Schaedler. I would like to think I knew a little bit about playing in this position! Erich, apart from everything else, was a fitness fanatic. He would put in a pulverising shift at training, really put himself through it, and then go to a gym in Edinburgh and go through it all again. He embarked on this routine every day. Naturally, he was as strong as an ox and he could travel up and down that wing like nobody's business. He had a great attitude, too, and was one of those sort of guys who would have tackled the proverbial brick wall. He was afraid of nothing. I would rate him as one of my best bits of business in the transfer market.

Gordon Strachan, sober, of course, was a great man to have in your team. I could see why my predecessor, Davie White, had made him skipper of the club at the age of nineteen when I was injured and missed the run-in to the fateful 1976/77 season. Everything in the team seemed to go through Gordon and he was never afraid of accepting responsibility. He didn't take it as a slight when I gave the captaincy to Erich Schaedler and, in fact, might even have been relieved.

There were two reasons for me making that decision. One was I thought we needed more experience at that level and Schaedler had already played for Scotland, ironically against West Germany, the country of his father's birth. That explained the extra 'h' at the end of his Christian name. The other reason was the fact that I realised I would not be picking Gordon for every game in the First Division. The hammer-throwers in Scotland's second tier would have kicked lumps out of the Wee Man. I was well aware there were a few in that league who couldn't trap a medicine ball, but were quite adept at attempting to volley dangerous opponents over the stand. I wasn't going to put Gordon through that. He just wasn't ready to face that sort of onslaught. I explained that to him, too. I knew he wanted to play in every game and he confirmed that, but I couldn't take a risk of someone putting him on the sidelines for months with a serious injury.

As it turned out, I only had Gordon at the club for a few months before he left us for Aberdeen in November 1977. Of course, I didn't want him to go, but I realised it was the only course of action to save the club from going under. Chairman Ian Gellatly telephoned me early one Monday morning and didn't bother with his usual preamble. He got straight to the point. 'Tommy,' he said, 'we need to get £50,000 urgently or the bank will close the gates on Friday.' Just like that. Talk about being between a rock and a hard place! I knew my old Celtic buddy Billy McNeill had been sniffing around Gordon. Was he interested in putting his interest into hard cash? I put a call into the Aberdeen manager. I laid it on the line and was totally honest. 'We need £50,000 by the end of the week or there will be no more Dundee Football Club,' I said. I added swiftly, 'But don't think you can get Gordon Strachan for only £50,000 because you and I both know he is worth a lot more than that.' Billy asked for some time to talk to his board and he would get right back to me. Caesar was as good as his word. 'We'll pay the £50,000,' he said, 'but, sorry, we can't go higher than that.' I took a chance. 'Would you be willing to throw in a player, as well?' I enquired. Caesar answered, 'That's a possibility. Who are we talking about?' I had always liked the look of Jim Shirra, another wee left-sided terrier who could snap into the tackle. He was my type of player and I also knew he would be ideal in the First Division. No-one would bully this bloke.

'I'll get back to you, Tommy.' I reminded him that time was not an ally of Dundee Football Club and he promised to phone first thing on Wednesday morning. As usual, he was as good as his word. 'Right, Big Man, you've got a deal,' were the words that made me smile. We got the cash up front and the cheque cleared and Dundee would live to fight another day. It turned out to be a great deal for both clubs and the players benefited, too. We all know what happened to Gordon on his travels through football, but Jim Shirra, who was valued about £35,000, also enjoyed a good career at Dens Park where he was getting regular first team football.

However, complications are never far away in football and that deal might not have gone through if it hadn't been for another old Celtic mate, Mike Jackson. Mike was in charge of Queen of the South at the time and they had just hammered Dundee 6-0 in a League Cup-tie. We had lost, surprisingly, 3-1 at home in the first leg. I will never be known as a quitter, but I had to look sensibly at the situation as we prepared for the return game in Dumfries. I knew we were due to play Hearts in the league three days later and I realised only too well that the Tynecastle outfit were likely to become one of our main rivals in the race for promotion. I rested some of my top players with the Edinburgh test in mind. Mike's team simply took us apart that night. Strachan played that evening - in fact, it turned out to be his last game for the club - and I was proud of his determination throughout an embarrassingly one-sided encounter.

Mike Jackson told me later that he was phoned afterwards that night by his big buddy Billy McNeill. Mike told me, 'Billy wanted to know how Gordon had performed. I told him he was the only guy in the Dundee team that looked as though he was trying. I told Billy not to hesitate if he wanted the player. We may have won by a landslide, but Gordon was still racing around with the referee about to blow for full-time. To me, it showed great character.'

Beside Strachan I would place Jocky Scott. I bought him from Aberdeen for £15,000 in 1979 for his second stint at Dundee. However, if the previous gaffer, Davie White, had had his way Jocky would never have darkened the Dens Park doorstep again. Actually, it's difficult to disagree with White's thinking. Jocky and a few of his team-mates did something that was bang out of order on the evening of our celebrations at the Angus Hotel in Dundee after we had beaten Celtic 1-0 in the League Cup Final in 1973. The champagne corks were popping all over the place and everyone was having a great time. Let's face it, Dundee didn't win too many trophies, did they? So, when you had the opportunity to enjoy such a success then you were quite entitled to let your hair down.

As the evening was reaching its crescendo, it was noted that a few players were missing. A quick head count told us Jocky Scott and Gordon Wallace, the man who had scored the only goal at Hampden, weren't anywhere to be seen. I think Bobby Robinson and George Stewart were AWOL, too. Where on earth could they be? Amazingly, it was later discovered they had gone to the home of Dundee United manager Jim McLean in Monifieth to celebrate with him. It beggars belief, doesn't it? Wee Glum - sorry, Wee Jim - had been first team coach at Dundee the previous year before leaving for Tannadice.

Scott and his cronies must have felt they owed some debt of gratitude to McLean, but, clearly, they didn't think that one through. Personally, I would have taken it as a slap in the face if any player had done that to me if I been manager of a club that had just won a trophy. It's unthinkable. You have got to hope that McLean wouldn't have encouraged it, but the players should have known better. It was a crazy thing to do and no-one could have blamed White for being upset. This was Dundee's night to give it yahoo and had nothing at all to do with the manager of the city's rival club. I'm told Davie White was livid when he discovered where a chunk of his first team were that night. He took it personally and I, for one, would never have blamed him. Quietly, over the next couple of years, those players were shipped out, Jocky Scott among them. But, being the forgiving sort of guy that I am, I brought him back when he lost his place at Aberdeen to, of all people, Gordon Strachan. Jocky could play alright. He was stocky, good on the ball and could score a goal or two.

By the way, Scott and his pals must have discovered something that had eluded the rest of the universe - that Jim McLean was a fun guy to be around. I often thought his idea of happiness would be sitting in a swamp at midnight reading War and Peace. He always gave me the impression that he believed they were going to slap a tax on smiling. He wouldn't have been my first pick to get stuck in an elevator with. I have to admit I was surprised when he had to undergo heart surgery some time back. Surprised the surgeons found a heart!

Wee Jim's nickname, among others, was 'Beano'. Why Beano? It may have baffled some. At one stage he played in the same Dundee attack as a guy called George McLean, the former Rangers striker. His nickname was 'Dandy' after a fictional detective character called 'Dandy McLean' that used to appear in the Sunday Post. The Dandy and Beano were two of the most popular children's comics that were around at the time and, of course, they were both produced by Dundee-based DC Thomson, the giant publishing empire who, along with the Sunday Post, gave us the Weekly News and magazines such as the People's Friend. So we had a pairing of Beano and Dandy in the forward line. Bet you didn't realise Dundee was the epicentre of humour!

That leaves another place up for grabs in our midfield three and another fairly easy choice here is Bobby Robinson. He was known as Trigger to his team-mates and it had nothing at all to do with any resemblance to Roy Rogers' horse, I'm glad to say! No, he was so fast he was like a shot out of a gun. He was an athlete and ideal for a role in any midfield. He was a very popular lad and we were all delighted when he won his four Scottish international caps. He made his debut alongside Erich Schaedler in West Germany in 1974 where my old Celtic mate Davie Hay, still a pal to this day, skippered Scotland. Unfortunately, we lost 2-1, but, by all accounts, Willie Ormond's side gave the team that would go onto win the World Cup in their own country later that year more than a run for their money. Bobby Robinson wouldn't have looked out of place in that company.

Up front there would have to be a place for Eric Sinclair, a willing workhorse if ever there was one. He was a real, honest grafter who was totally unselfish. He was no Bobby Lennox when it came to jetting all over the place, but he had great enthusiasm and was never slow to chuck his weight around. He was also known to knock in a goal or two, as well, which helped. The fans loved him, too, and that was important. They identified with him and he became a cult hero with the support.

Billy Pirie joined from Arbroath and he certainly knew how to hit the ball into the net. He was also a lazy so-and-so. Bone bloody idle. Billy just didn't want to know about work outside the box. He was a goalscorer and he wasn't interested in the poor sods who had to go and win the ball, fetch it, bring it forward and then deliver it to his toes. Mind you, what a good job he made of tucking them away. He was a natural goalscorer and sometimes it was simply impossible to criticise him. He would do virtually bugger all in a game and we would win 1-0. And he would get the goal. He might have only one kick at the ball, but he was the player who made all the difference. I have to say I was impressed by the way he always worked the goalkeeper. He rarely missed the target and was one of those sort of players big defenders hated because he had a low centre of gravity. That allowed him to swivel and, a split-second after he had his back to goal, suddenly he was facing the keeper.

He was one of those sort of strikers who scored goals in bunches. At the start of the 1976/77 season he netted four goals in six League Cup-ties - and three came in one game, a 3-3 draw with Motherwell. Then he scored eighteen in fourteen league games. He hit zilch in the next six games before notching six in successive outings, four in an 8-0 win over Falkirk and two in a 3-2 triumph over Morton. He guaranteed you goals and, naturally enough, he was worth his weight in gold. But he was still a lazy beggar. The headline writers wouldn't have had too far to look for material with him. How about, BILLY IDLE?

I took an immediate shine to Ian Redford when I helped out with the Errol amateur side in 1976. As a player, I had some spare time and I thought I would do my bit for the locals and I'm glad I did because it brought £210,000 into Dundee's coffers in 1980. In between, we got four years' sterling service from a very clever left-sided player. I wasn't surprised to see Redford linked with a whole host of clubs and it was only a matter of time before we would receive a decent offer for him. It duly came from Rangers manager John Greig. Was I surprised about a bid from Ibrox? Not really when you consider I had previously been informed the player had been tapped by them! So, it was just a question of when that call would be made. My old adversary didn't disappoint. I was ready for him. The conversations went a bit like this:

GREIG, 'I like the look of your young lad Ian Redford.'

ME, 'I'm not surprised, John. There are a lot of teams who like the look of him. I don't blame them, he's a very good player.'

GREIG, 'What are you looking for him? How much will you be willing to accept?'

ME (getting ready for the transfer game to begin), 'Well, he's not for sale, John, but you know the policy at this club. We're fairly healthy at the bank at the moment, but we are always open to a reasonable bid for any of our players.' (I knew my chairman would bite the hand off Rangers if they offered anything close to six figures for a player.)

GREIG, 'We can go to £100,000. What do you think?'

ME, 'Nope. I wouldn't let him go for that. No chance.'

GREIG, 'Maybe we can take it up to £110,000. Does that sound reasonable?'

ME, 'I don't think my board would be interested in losing our best player for that sort of figure, to be honest, Greigy. If you want, I'll put it to the chairman and get back to you, but I wouldn't get your hopes up. I know the chairman is a big fan of the lad. He won't want him to leave.'

The Rangers manager agreed to give me a telephone call the following morning to get a progress report. Greigy didn't know it, of course, but I was comfortable in this game of bluff and double-bluff. For a start, they had contacted the player, so they had shown their hand. They had targeted him and I was going to push them all the way. I took a chance at this point that might have backfired. I didn't bother to tell Ian Gellatly of Rangers' interest or their £110,000 bid. The following day Greigy made the call.

GREIG, 'Have we got a deal, Tommy?'

ME, 'Sorry, old mate, it's a no from my board. They would prefer to keep the player. They accept they will have to let him go at some point as he keeps making progress, but not at £110,000.'

GREIG, 'I can take it up to £120,000, Tommy. Would that do it?'

ME, 'No, I don't think so. Maybe £150,000 might be of interest to the board. I can't promise, but that will get them listening.'

GREIG, 'I'll phone this afternoon. Okay? I'll go back to my board.'

At some point before five o'clock, as I was tidying up things to go back to the hotel, the telephone shrilled. I had a fair idea of the identity of the caller. On came the Rangers boss.

GREIG, 'My board will stretch to £150,000. I don't think we can go beyond that. Will you get back to me tomorrow?'

I said I would and now I was in a bit of a quandary. I realised only too well what Ian Gellatly would say if I told him Rangers were offering £150,000 for one of his players. I had to tell him, I couldn't leave him in the dark any more. I put a call into him. 'Take it!' was his expected response. 'Tommy, don't hesitate - take it!' I told him I thought we could still get more. Our chairman often smoked a pipe and I could just about hear the excited puffing coming down the line.

I duly telephoned Ibrox the following day. I was probably putting my job at risk, if not my entire career in total jeopardy. I took a chance.

ME, 'Greigy, sorry. but they're not interested at that price, either. Any chance you can add to it?'

The Rangers manager was obviously hell-bent on getting his man. Equally obviously, was the fact he had already had a pow-wow with his directors.

GREIG, 'We can offer £160,000. How about that?'

ME, 'Look, Greigy, this could be a right good player for you. I know that and so do you. How about £180,000?'

GREIG, 'Christ, Tommy, are you joking? I can't go to that. Look, you better deal with one of our directors. I'll let him take it on now. Okay?'

I said that was fine and he gave me the telephone number of Jack Gillespie. Actually, I knew Jack personally. He was a garage owner in Lenzie and our paths had crossed on several occasions. As you might anticipate, our chairman was eager to be kept in the loop. When I told him I had knocked back £160,000 he said, 'Good God! Do you know what you're doing, Tommy? That's a lot of money.' I could hear the furious puffing of the pipe in the background.

'Leave it with me,' I said with more confidence than I should have possessed. I just had a feeling Rangers were so keen on the player that I could push them that little bit further. I put a call into the Rangers director. I knew he had a vast personal fortune and was used to dealing in high figures. The game was still afoot, as Sherlock would have said.

GILLESPIE, 'What's happening, Tommy?'

ME, 'You want one of my players, Ian Redford, and we're willing to sell - but only at the right price.'

GILLESPIE, 'What's the right price, Tommy? John Greig mentioned something like £180,000. Is that the figure?'

ME, 'It's an offer I would put in front of the board, Jack, but I still can't promise anything.'

GILLESPIE, 'Okay, we'll bid £180,000. Will you get back to me?'

Just like that. In a space of a few days and several phone calls, I had managed to get Rangers to add £80,000 to their original offer. Deep down, though, I was convinced there was more to come. 'Take it!' said Ian Gellatly. 'Take it! We'll not get any better than that. Take it!' Once more I got the impression the frantic smoke signals must have been engulfing the entire Gellatly household. 'Leave it with me, chairman,' I said. I was on a roll and I believed Jack Gillespie wouldn't want to be seen to be backing down in this situation.

ME, 'Sorry, Jack, they've said no again.' (Okay, I lied there.) 'They're looking at all the big dosh that is being paid down south at the moment and they believe it's only a matter of time before they get a massive bid from England for Redford.'

GILLESPIE, 'I'll go to £200,000, then. Will you put that to your board and get back to me?'

ME, 'No problem. I'll talk to them tonight.'

'Take it!' was the predictable echo of a response from my chairman. In his mind the money had already been banked. 'Take it!' I got the impression, with all that manic puffing of his pipe, that the Gellatly spread now resembled a scene from Victorian London. The following day the Redford Saga was about to come to a halt. I telephoned Gillespie.

ME, 'You'll not believe this, Jack, but they want more.' (Okay, I was being extremely economical with the truth at this point.)

GILLESPIE, 'How much more? What are we talking about now?'

ME, 'I think they'll settle for £210,000. I'm pretty sure that will get the deal done. I don't see them knocking that back.'

GILLESPIE, 'Okay, we'll go to £210,000, Tommy, but that's the end of it. There's no point in asking for more. This is our final bid. Absolutely final.'

I duly got in touch with my ecstatic chairman. He cried, 'What? They went to £210,000? Well done, Tommy. Great job. I never doubted you.' There wasn't such puffing activity on this occasion as his heartbeat obviously got back to normal. There were no instalments or anything like that. The money went in as a lump sum. Mind you, I never saw a penny of that cash. A couple of quid would have helped me bring in some new players to freshen up the squad, but, as I had already guessed, that money was heading straight into the bank account of Dundee Football Club. Such is life.

I was grateful for Dundee giving me the opportunity to manage their club. Sitting behind the manager's desk certainly added to my football education. I was also fortunate that the Tayside club only had three directors. There was Ian Gellatly, Graham Thomson, the Managing Director of Timex, and Willie Lyburn, a farmer from Blairgowrie. It helped if you needed a swift decision from the board. It wasn't a Cecil B De Mille job with a cast of thousands. It was three guys who could make a few phone calls and get things done in jig-time. There was no animosity when I was relieved of my duties after three years in 1980. We were relegated from the Premier League after starting off with two seasons in the First Division. It was all a massive learning curve. Words from Cloughie came back to me. He said, 'Rome wasn't built in a day, young man. But, then, I wasn't on that particular job!'

The first year in charge was all about transition. We had to build again for the future and it was great to get promotion in that second campaign. The Premier League proved a hurdle too far. I'm not one for making excuses, but I had no money to spend. That might have made a difference. Not achieving something at this level will always be one of my biggest regrets. Remarkably, we were good enough to beat Celtic, then challenging for the championship, 5-1 at Dens Park after gifting them a goal of a start. There was an intriguing photograph in one of the Sunday newspapers the following day. It showed me and Willie Wallace in one dug-out and Billy McNeill and John Clark in the other. Four Lisbon Lions within yards of each other, but miles apart in our emotions.

Sadly, other results that season swamped that achievement. We dropped far too many points against opponents we should have overcome and when you continue in that theme one thing is inevitable - relegation. Of course, I was far from happy to lose my job, but there was little point in making a fuss. I had done my best with, admittedly, meagre financial resources. Willie Wallace and I would scour Britain for possible signings, but even if we found someone we thought was suitable, the board could put the kybosh on any proposed deal. If, say, we agreed a signing-on fee of £3,000, the directors would want to spread it over a three-year contract.

A lot of signing targets simply said, 'Thanks, but no thanks' and got a better deal elsewhere. Disappointed, yes, but not bitter. Far from it. Regrets? Of course, as Old Blue Eyes would say, 'I've had a few.' I can look back and wish with all my heart a wee pal of mine had made a success of it at Dens Park. I would have loved Jimmy Johnstone to have shown his genius for a couple of extra years, at least. At his best, he could have walked into any team in the world. Any club. Any country. You better believe it.

But there were great times, too, and I've enjoyed looking back at my time at Dens Park to come up with my all-time eleven from heaven. Here is the line-up again, (in a 4-3-3 formation): Ally Donaldson; Bobby Wilson, Stewart MacLaren, Iain Phillip and Erich Schaedler; Gordon Strachan, Jocky Scott and Bobby Robinson; Eric Sinclair, Billy Pirie and Ian Redford. Fabulous team. And fabulous lads, too.

One name is missing, though.

CHAPTER TEN
VODKA VIC AND THE WILD ROVERS

One of the strangest complaints I ever received in all my years in football came at Albion Rovers. Nothing really surprised me at Cliftonhill, but this came pretty damn close. Apparently, director David Forrester was a bit upset that my team were winning too many games.

He sidled up to me one day, looking more than a little worried. I wondered what the problem could be because the team were doing quite well. 'Tommy, I've just had a word from the bank,' he said in hushed tones. 'They've informed me we are paying out too much in bonus money.' I looked at the chairman and remembered he was a chartered accountant. He didn't joke about money.

Actually, he was obviously quite alarmed at the prospect of his club continuing their unbeaten run. You could probably guess at my first reaction. Once the incredulity subsided, I said, 'What a fuckin' shame. Those players signed those contracts in the summer and we agreed the money for a win and a draw. It's there in black and white and, as far as I am concerned, it's legal and binding. They are playing out of their skin for this club. Do you want to ask them to tear up those deals and accept lesser ones? Certainly, I don't.'

Forrester spluttered something before skulking off. Actually, what we did to cover the hitherto unheard-of stream of expenses was to find other ways of bringing money into the club and not just not through the gate. We moved into the world of corporate hospitality and made a fuss of the local businessmen who were well treated on matchday for shelling out a little extra and bringing along their guests. The board explored a few financial avenues no-one had bothered to look at before. Do you know there was no such thing as an Albion Rovers replica shirt back then? Okay, they didn't sell thousands, but every penny counted at this club.

The players' contracts were honoured and the Wee Rovers, as they are still affectionately known, reached eighth place in a fourteen-club division in my first full season in 1986/87. That was the club's best finish since 1978/79, so, at least, progress was being made. Slowly, but surely. My old Celtic mate Mike Jackson renamed Cliftonhill 'The Stadium of Light' after Benfica's famous stadium, a name that was later copied by Sunderland. When Mike was asked why, he replied, 'Everywhere you look there is a fuckin' hole in the wall, a fuckin' hole in the ceiling, fucking' holes in the windows, fuckin' holes everywhere.'

I have to say I had an open mind when I was contacted by Tam Fagan, who was then the chairman, about the possibility of becoming the club's manager. It was early in the new year of 1986 when Tam made the phone call. Tam was cutting it a little fine before I gave him my answer. It was a Friday tea-time when he got in touch and Rovers were due to play Queen's Park in the Scottish Cup at Hampden the following day.

Tam was a bit eccentric and I liked him. I got to know him when I was at Celtic and he used to go to the Vesuvio restaurant in St.Vincent Street in Glasgow, an eaterie frequented regularly by myself and my Parkhead colleagues. He was Mr.Albion Rovers and seemed to revel in the title. He was the major shareholder at the club and what he said was law. He also owned a nightclub about four football pitches away from Cliftonhill. Yes, I was surprised by that - a nightclub in Coatbridge! I was living in Uddingston at the time and Tam's house was about a five-minute drive away. After taking his call, I jumped in the car and pulled up at his place. It looked quite grand from the outside, but, once I was through those main doors, I could see that the interior hadn't been treated to a makeover for some considerable time.

There was Tam sitting in his well-worn armchair puffing away at a cigarette. There was an ashtray in front of him that must have had the collection of at least a week's worth of stubs. If there had been a puff of wind through an open window we could have had something akin to an Icelandic ash cloud over Coatbridge. I noticed he was wearing an old grey woolly jersey which had a massive hole in the right sleeve at the elbow. It had singe marks around it. There was an electric fire situated to Tam's right, dangerously close to the elbow, and I wondered if this was a new mark. Or had it been there for years? I decided on the latter. Now I realised Rovers didn't have money to throw around, but I wondered about joining a club where the chairman couldn't afford to invest in a new sweater. Tam was completely oblivious to the fact my gaze kept falling on this great hole in his elbow. After a wee bit of chit-chat, we did eventually get round to talking about finances. 'Does the club have any money to spend?' I asked, already knowing the answer. Tam shook his head solemnly. He answered, 'No.' If he had said anything else, I would probably have pitched forward head-first in shock into that electric fire.

Okay, I had to know what was in it for me. I liked Tam, but I wasn't going to work for free. I hoped he didn't think that was a possibility. He hummed and hawed and gave me all the usual spiel. 'We're just a wee club, Tommy, and we don't know where our next penny is coming from.' This went on for awhile. I looked at my watch. 'Tam, do you know you've got a kick-off at Hampden in about sixteen hours' time?' That helped him focus. We settled on £50-per-week plus expenses.

I've been asked many times why a Lisbon Lion would even consider such a job. Maybe some people thought I was demeaning myself, but I didn't see it that way. Cliftonhill was about ten minutes up the road from my home and that suited me perfectly. If I had been offered a job at a bigger club that entailed a lot of travelling I would have knocked it back. I wouldn't have been prepared to give up so much of my time on the road. I was happy enough working in the financial sector and gave little thought to returning to full-time football management. Expectation levels weren't high at the club, either. So I was hardly going to be put under pressure. Of course, I wanted to do well for myself and for Rovers, but we had to look at these things realistically. I had my professional pride, but I knew sell-out European nights at Cliftonhill weren't going to happen. I had got myself a hobby and I would give it my best shot in the trying and unusual circumstances.

I was greeted at the ground the following day by Joe Baker, who would be my assistant. Joe was a legend in his own right. He was selected for the England international team while he was playing for Hibs in the Scottish League. I think that made him unique at the time. I recall him playing against Scotland at Hampden in a 1-1 draw in 1960 when he tried to barge my future Celtic goalkeeping team-mate Frank Haffey over the goal-line. He went to Italy to play alongside Denis Law in Turin, but returned after about a year to join Arsenal. He later played for Nottingham Forest and then Sunderland before he returned to the Easter Road side. He completed his career at Raith Rovers with 301 goals in total for club and country.

Joe, who was born in Liverpool but spent almost his entire childhood in Wishaw, had always been a bit of a Celtic fan, but the Parkhead side never made a move for him. There's no doubt he would have done a job for the club in the early sixties. I immediately took to Joe. He really was a genuinely nice lad and he was happy to be No.2 at Rovers. He never wanted the main job. He told me he didn't need the pressure. For God's sake, this was a guy who played alongside Denis Law in the demanding atmosphere of Italian football and he was talking about too much strain at Cliftonhill! Anyway, Joe was quite content to back each team boss who came in and Rovers did have something in the region of thirty managerial changes in sixty-six years. Obviously, it wasn't a job for life.

I didn't get off to a winning start, unfortunately, as we lost 2-1 to Queen's Park. I thought we had played reasonably well, could see where we could strengthen some things. The players looked fit enough, but were certainly tactically naive. I liked their enthusiasm, though, and thought at least I had something to work with. The attitude of the Rovers directors was a delightful surprise, too. They seemed fairly satisfied their team had only lost by a solitary goal. No-one was screaming for the manager's head after only ninety minutes. I thought it best not to ruin their day by awakening them to the fact that if they had managed to win through there might have been the possibility of a money-spinning draw against either of the Old Firm in the next round. That notion hadn't seemed to occur to any of them as they guzzled their gin and tonics in the Hampden boardroom.

It would be one of life's marvellous understatements to say things were quaint at Rovers. I had once played there in a closed-door game with Celtic and, although the pitch was fine, the other facilities were Spartan, to be kind. Nails were hanging out of walls in the dressing room to be used as coat hooks. The entire place was rundown. Stadium of Light? Aye, I can see why Mike called it that. Fifteen or so years later I had returned and it was still looking a bit threadbare. Not a lot had happened in the intervening years. The Health and Safety people would have had a field day if they had ever inspected the ground. Apoplexy all round, methinks.

The kitchen was falling apart, for a start. Luckily, my mother-in-law was having a new kitchen fitted, so I asked her for her old one. By that stage, David Forrester had replaced Tam Fagan as chairman with the sad passing of my old Vesuvio friend, surrendering to ill health after a brave fight. Anyway, I went to Forrester and told him that there was a kitchen up for grabs if he wanted it and, excitedly, he said, 'Yes', adding needlessly, 'But we can't pay too much.' His eyes lit up when I told him he could get it for nothing if they picked it up from my mother-in-law's home in Carntyne.

After awhile it was duly lifted and ferried over to Cliftonhill where it lay for weeks. I asked a director, 'When are you going to install the kitchen?' A frown came over his face. 'Oh, we can't afford a joiner, Tommy,' I was told. 'We're waiting for a supporter to do it for free.' Someone did step forward to take on the task and the old kitchen just disintegrated into a pile of sawdust when it was removed. One thing the directors did not skimp on, though, was booze. They had a drinks cabinet that could have served the entire population of Coatbridge on any given weekend. My wife Mary came over to the ground with me one evening when we were having a meeting with the board. One of the directors opened this cupboard that had every sort of glass container known to mankind. There were no two glasses that matched.

Mary then went to make a pot of tea and couldn't believe that she could not find a cup without a chip in it. I once asked them for £200 for a signing-on fee for an amateur centre-half who had shown up quite well in a trial. They knocked me back. I lost the plot. 'You've got every fuckin' drink in the world in that cabinet and I can't get £200 for a player!' Obviously, they had their priorities sorted out. Booze or bonuses? No contest.

Strange things happened around this wonderful wee club. On one occasion in January 1994, during my second stint, some supporters were finding difficulty in arranging a bus to take them to Huntly for a game on a Saturday. The solution was simple. They telephoned the club to tell them of their predicament. Imagine their surprise when they were immediately invited onto the team coach travelling to the Highlands. A party of about twelve fans got a hurl there and back for free. Nice touch and typical of the club/supporter relationship at this level. Pity we were gubbed 5-3!

The players were all earnest enough individuals who wanted to better themselves. Of course, we were a part-time outfit and that could lead to all sorts of problems. We trained on Tuesday and Thursday evenings and there was little I could do when a player phoned in to say he had the chance of some overtime or the boss was getting on his back to work late on one of those nights. They were getting something like £10 at Rovers, so they had to take care of their real profession. I had to excuse them.

Here's an example of what I had to expect at the club. Defender Des McKeown had been playing very well and had been an ever-present, playing thirty-one games on the bounce, but I had to leave him out of important games against Meadowbank Thistle and East Fife. Why? His

234

full-time job was in sales and he had just won a fortnight's holiday in Tenerife for himself and his wife and, as no-one on the board at Cliftonhill had a private jet at their disposal to ferry him to and fro on matchdays, we had to forego his services for those two games. I could hardly stand in his way, could I?

We had a collection of joiners, labourers, lorry drivers, electricians, car mechanics, painters, oh, you name it, we had them. I think we missed out on candlestick makers. If someone came up with an excuse to miss training and I smelled a rat I would have a word with them. I would soon know whether he was flannelling me or not. Remember, I used to be a player under Jock Stein's wary eye, so I swiftly realised when someone was at the madam. They would just have to work harder at the next training session and, you better believe it, I made sure that was the case. There was little point in suspending a player because, at best, we only had about sixteen men in our squad to begin with. So, it would have been daft to have taken that action then someone picked up an injury a day or two before a game. In the main, though, there was a lot of honesty among the characters at Cliftonhill.

There is always one, though, who is a pain in the backside. Vic Kasule was that annoying and infuriating individual. I think he believed he was Coatbridge's answer to George Best. Or, at least, a wild Rover. He was a bit of a rarity at the time because he was a black footballer and stood out in any game. I hope I am not being politically incorrect in making that statement. To be honest, I thought he had ability, but possibly not as much as he believed he possessed.

I have to also admit I came very close to banjoing him once in the tunnel. We were playing Arbroath up at Gayfield and we were winning quite comfortably (words no Albion Rovers manager would get used to saying). It was getting near the end and we had used our two substitutes. I was watching Kasule out on the wing taking on a home defender. He skinned him. Stopped the ball and went back to beat the guy again. When he did it a third time I just exploded. I turned to Joe Baker and yelled, 'Get him off that fuckin' pitch!' My assistant answered reasonably, 'Tommy, we don't have anyone else to put on in his place.'

'I don't fuckin' care. Get him off!' I shouted again.

Kasule looked bewildered when he was given the hook. In that lackadaisical manner of his, he shrugged his shoulders and started to go up the tunnel. I raced after him. I hadn't moved so fast since the days when I had to face the likes of George Best or Willie Henderson. I caught him before he could get into the dressing room. I pinned him to the wall, holding him by the neck while I pulled back my fist. 'Listen, you bastard, don't you ever take the piss out of a fellow-professional again,' I growled. His eyes looked as though they were going to explode out of his face. They seemed to be getting wider and wider as I waved my fist around. They were like two full moons. 'Am I getting fuckin' through to you? Never do that again while I'm your fuckin' manager.' Joe arrived just in time to grab my hand. I had lost it, I'm ashamed to admit. But making a fool of a fellow-player would never be tolerated by me. I think I got the message through to Kasule.

There was another time when the players were rolling into Cliftonhill to get prepared for a game. They were steadily arriving within the pre-arranged time schedule. With one exception. You've guessed it. There was no sign of Vic Kasule. With just over an hour to go one of our fans came in to tell us Kasule was in a pub just down the road from the ground. Maybe he was Coatbridge's answer to Bestie, after all! I couldn't believe it. I despatched someone to the bar to fetch Kasule and frogmarch him to the dressing room. He came in and looked at me innocently, 'What's the matter, boss? I was just having a couple of orange juices.' Now, remember, Kasule rejoiced in the nickname 'Vodka Vic' and I couldn't prove if there had been an added ingredient in his orange juices. I said, 'For fuck's sake, we've got a game in an hour and you're in the pub with the fans. Are you off your fuckin' head?' I knew the answer to that one, of course.

Bizarrely, Kasule's parents were two professional people. His father was a neurosurgeon and his mother was a psychiatrist or something in that field. She might have put in a bit of overtime at home with her son! Vodka Vic must have jumped a generation, I think, because he didn't seem to inherit too many of the smart genes. If he is reading this, I'm sure this will more than surprise him - I would select him in my favourite Albion Rovers team. As I said, he had talent, but he squandered those gifts. Had he applied himself, I have no doubt he could have gone on to bigger and better things. One comes before the other, though. Vic will know that now. He was only twenty-one years old when he left Rovers for Meadowbank Thistle at the end of my first season. No surprise there, I suppose. Possibly he preferred a boss who wouldn't threaten to put his head through a wall!

He lasted only a year with them and then had a two-season stint at Shrewsbury Town before returning for a year at Hamilton. Then he had spells in Ireland and Malta before playing one game for Montrose and coming off the radar altogether. He was twenty-seven years old when his career was virtually over. Coincidentally, that is around the same age Bestie chucked it at Manchester United. Spooky or what?

I would play Vodka Vic on the right wing of a 4-3-3 formation. Goalkeeper? It has got to be Allen McKnight. I managed to persuade him to swop Celtic for Cliftonhill in a loan deal in 1987 and, no, I didn't have to hypnotise the Irishman to get him to agree to the switch. He wasn't getting much of a look-in at Parkhead because of the consistency of Pat Bonner and I reasoned he would at least get some first team football at Rovers. My pal Caesar, Billy McNeill, the Celtic manager at the time, played his part in the move and urged McKnight to take the opportunity to show what he could do at a team where he was bound to be kept busy on a consistent basis. Caesar got that right.

I wasn't surprised McKnight got a good move to West Ham a couple of years after his spell with us. In fact, he went onto to play ten times for the Northern Ireland international team. He would have been nothing if it hadn't been for Albion Rovers!

My back four of Tom McDonald, Tony Gallagher, Jim Lennon and Des McKeown may not mean an awful lot to even the most avid neutral football fan and I mean no disrespect in making that statement. Let's face it, not too many Rovers games were televised and we didn't pack them in through the turnstiles back then. Or now, for that matter. What

I would say about these guys is that football would have been a lot poorer if they hadn't been around. There are a lot of gems to be found in the lower leagues. My fellow-Lisbon Lions Ronnie Simpson and Willie Wallace kicked off their careers at Queen's Park and Stenhousemuir respectively. Stevie Chalmers, our matchwinner against Inter Milan, played for three Junior clubs, Kirkintilloch Rob Roy, Newmarket Town and Ashfield, before signing for Celtic at the age of twenty-three.

It was the same in England. Bill Shankly spent a lot of money as Liverpool manager, but he also raided the likes of Scunthorpe for players such as Kevin Keegan and Ray Clemence and paid peanuts for them. Changed days now, of course, when you read about some clubs getting ten year olds on contracts. That's ridiculous. Soon they'll be signing them when they are still in the womb! But, even today, there are still some blokes in lower leagues who just need to be in the right place at the right time to get the opportunity at a higher level.

Tom McDonald was actually quite tall for a full-back - around the six foot mark - and you always knew what you would get from him. He had a reasonable turn of speed and was decent in the tackle. Tony Gallagher, in the heart of the defence, was an old-fashioned centre-half who was good in the air. He was fairly consistent, too. Beside him I would put Jim Lennon who was the perfect foil for Gallagher. He swept up around him much in the same way John Clark did with Billy McNeill, but not on the same level, of course. At left-back I would choose Des McKeown. He had a sweet left foot and liked to attack at every opportunity. I gave him a few hints, of course! He was another who was as honest as the day was long and another you could rely upon to put in a good shift.

In midfield, I would pick Alan Rodgers, Sammy Conn and John Greene. You will have to take my word for it, but there is a good balance among that trio. Rodgers may not have been in the class of an Archie Gemmill or an Asa Hartford, but he had the same work ethic. He was an industrious player who covered a helluva lot of ground during a game. Conn was another dynamo. He also possessed a great left peg and wasn't frightened to have a go at goal. If we got a direct free-kick about twenty-five yards out, he was the man for the job. He was a fabulous leader, too. He really enjoyed captaining the club on the occasions he got the nod.

Greene completes the threesome and, like his colleagues in the engine room, he put himself about. He had bags of energy and was a real ninety-minute man. I used to watch some of these players during a match and wonder what they would have been like if they had proper full-time training and the correct facilities. If anyone witnessed Rodgers, Conn and Greene buzzing around that pitch virtually non-stop for an hour-and-a-half they might have been calling for drug tests afterwards. Or, at least, asking them for some of what they were on!

Kasule (aka Vodka Vic) would be on the right, of course, and I would play Brian Black up front through the middle. He was a powerful, direct targetman who never gave up on lost causes. Paul Teavan is a must for the outside-left position. If I remember correctly, I picked him up from Bellshill Athletic and he was another who never let the team down. He was a tricky wee winger, very direct and had a lot of pace.

Looking back, that's not a bad line-up. If I had them all available for selection at the same time covering my two spells at Albion Rovers I'm sure we would have made a more than reasonable impact. Dream on, Rovers fans!

CHAPTER ELEVEN
ALL THE BEST

FAVOURITE PLAYER PLAYED WITH: Jimmy Johnstone

FAVOURITE PLAYER PLAYED AGAINST: Stanley Matthews

FAVOURITE OTHER TEAM: Motherwell

MOST DIFFICULT OPPONENT: George Best

MOST MEMORABLE MATCH: 1967 European Cup Final: Celtic 2, Inter Milan 1

BIGGEST THRILL: Signing for Celtic

BIGGEST DISAPPOINMENT: Losing 2-1 to Feyenoord in the 1970 European Cup Final

BEST COUNTRIES VISITED: Australia, New Zealand, America, Canada

FAVOURITE FOOD: Lamb chops and vegetables

MISCELLANEOUS LIKES: Cooking, theatre, reading

MISCELLANEOUS DISLIKES: Ignorant people

FAVOURITE TV SHOWS: Nature programmes, cooking, sport

FAVOURITE MOVIES: Dr Zhivago, The Quiet Man

FAVOURITE ACTOR: Richard Burton

FAVOURITE ACTRESS: Maureen O'Hara

FAVOURITE SINGER: Frank Sinatra

FAVOURITE BANDS: The Beatles, Rolling Stones

FAVOURITE COMEDIAN: Billy Connolly

BEST FRIEND: My wife Mary

BIGGEST INFLUENCE: My parents (in life) and Jock Stein (in football)

IF YOU HADN'T BEEN A FOOTBALLER, WHAT WOULD YOU HAVE
BEEN: An electrician

FAVOURITE SPORTSMAN: Muhammad Ali

CELTIC QUICK NEWS
QUESTIONS AND ANSWERS

On Wednesday 12 February 2014, the leading Celtic supporters website – www.celticquicknews.co.uk - published a blog post written by Celtic legend and Lisbon Lion Tommy Gemmell. The contributors to the site thereafter posted questions for Tommy to answer and both these questions and Tommy's answers are included in this chapter of All The Best. The affection, admiration and awe that the support have for Tommy is easily spotted in these heart-warming exchanges. Tommy Gemmell is a Celtic legend.

QUESTIONS FROM BOBBY MURDOCH'S CURLED UP WINKLEPICKERS

When you chased that German to boot him up the bahoochie, was it the fastest you had ever run and the hardest you had ever kicked? And was it the first time you completely missed the ball? By the way Tommy. We all appreciate your efforts over the years and I for one will make no more reference to the incidents mentioned previously. Otherwise, you'd be as well to call the book 'Tommy Gemmell Kicks Ass!'

That was the angriest I have ever been on a football pitch. Helmut Haller deliberately tripped me just as I was about to shoot from my favourite distance – about 30 yards out – and I just saw red. There was a minute to go and Scotland were losing 3-2 to West Germany in Hamburg in a vital qualifier for the World Cup Finals in Mexico in 1970. It was bad enough being fouled, but what really got me going was the fact the referee didn't even award Scotland a free-kick. When I turned round I could see Haller running for cover, but I just made a beeline for him. Was it the hardest I had ever kicked? My shots were measured at around 80-miles-per-hour and I think he got the motherload! And, yes, it was the first time I had meant to miss the ball.

QUESTIONS FROM BAWSMAN

Big Tam, your free-kick goal against Benfica is etched on the memory, as is his arse-kicking in the World Club Championship debacle. Can you tell me something about these two incidents in your career?

First up, the goal against Benfica wasn't a free-kick. Wee Bertie took the deadball effort and rolled the ball in front of me about 25 yards out. I just gave it a mighty whack with my right foot and was delighted to see the ball soar into the far corner. That European Cup-tie came shortly after I had been dropped by Jock Stein for the 1969 League Cup Final against St.Johnstone. He wasn't happy that I had been sent off in the midweek game against West Germany. But I was brought back against the Portuguese giants and was happy to play my part in a 3-0 victory. I wasn't proud of kicking the Racing Club player where the sun don't shine, but I'm afraid I had just had enough of the Argentines spitting, kicking and elbowing me during our three games against them. I just exploded. I'm only human, after all.

QUESTIONS FROM GAZCFC

Tommy, how long did you play for Meadow Thistle and did you ever bring the Big Cup back to Craigneuk or is that simply Craigneuk folklore?

What a good memory! No-one ever asks me about my career with Meadow Thistle! I played for them when I was 14-years-old and we had a reasonable team. I recall a player by the name of Tom Duddy who joined Celtic. He never played a first team game, but went onto sign for Cowdenbeath and then Airdrie. And there was a bloke called Eddie King who joined Hibs. I played in the morning for my school team and turned out for Meadow Thistle in the afternoon. Happy days! And, yes, I did take the European Cup trophy to Craigneuk to show it off to our neighbours. My parents were at Celtic Park when we returned from Lisbon the day after the Inter Milan game. Following all the celebrations at the park, I took a 'loan' of the silverware for the rest of the evening. Incredible! Could you imagine that happening today? I simply lifted the Big Cup and took it over to where I stayed with my parents in Craigneuk. There seemed to be about 300 people there to welcome me home. It was just fabulous. My parents' home was a second floor apartment and I think everyone – and I mean EVERYONE – crammed into their wee place that night.

QUESTIONS FROM GER57

Big Tam, I think you kicked that bassa from Racing Club harder in Montevideo! Hardly anyone in the stadium saw it except for the TV cameraman. Belter! Can you tell me why you kicked him?

The guy's name was Norberto Raffo. He had been at it against us in the games in Glasgow and Buenos Aires. He was a streetwise guy. He would spit on you, tap you on the ankles and give you a dig in the ribs. But when you tried to give him a dull one, he was alert and sneaky enough to get out of the way. He would jump out of tackles and leave you frustrated. When there was yet another lull in play he was standing there, just smirking. I lost it. That's when I decided to mete out some justice on behalf of myself and my team-mates. I'm not proud of it, but he had it coming.

QUESTIONS FROM 79CAPS

When you kicked that German player in the Germany-Scotland game (3-2 defeat) was it frustration because Muller fouled in

the build-up to the German goal or did that particular player do something to annoy you?

No, it wasn't Gerd Muller who fouled me. As I have answered elsewhere, it was Haller. Gerd was great at sticking his backside into defenders and making it virtually impossible for them to get in a tackle, but, on this occasion, it was their midfield player Haller who did the dirty. By the way, I didn't realise he could move so fast!

QUESTIONS FROM PHYLLIS DIETRICHSON

Welcome, Tommy, and thanks for many of my finest memories. My questions are. 'What was in your mind when you stepped up to take a penalty-kick? And did those thoughts change the more penalties you took?'

My main thought when I was taking a penalty was to get the ball on target. Obviously, that was a must! And I wanted to hit it as hard as possible. With that combination, I reckoned I stood a good chance of scoring a goal. I made my mind up very early in my career that was the way to take them. I rarely changed my mind when we got an award. Get it bang on the button and leave the problem with the goalie!

QUESTIONS FOR TINYTIM

Can you recall the most motivational team talk that you heard from a manager? And if so, can you tell us a bit about it?

Not a lot of people know this, but most of Jock Stein's team talks were done well before a game. He would go through everything in meticulous detail when we were at our training HQ at Seamill. He would drum things into us and, come the day of the game, he would go round us all individually and say, 'Now remember what we spoke about. You know how this guy plays, don't forget what I told you.' And so on. Yes, he had the ability to change things if it wasn't going to plan, but, thankfully, most times it did. But it was Seamill where the real hard work was done regarding tactics and suchlike.

QUESTIONS FROM SETTING FREE THE BEARS

'Simpson, Craig and Yours Truly.'

What a wonderful way to describe yourself.

John Clark can boast, ' Murdoch. McNeil and me.'

Bobby Lennox can leave out the last name of, 'Johnstone, Wallace, Chalmers, Auld and…' and just point to himself.

What a wonderful way to live life. Anyway, my questions for Big Tam are:

Who would come second in a world arse-kicking contest? Could Peter Lorimer kick the ball harder than you? Celtic Wiki says some foreign football journalists voted you the best 'right-back' in the world. Which side did you prefer?

World arse-kicking contest? Is that an Olympic event? If not, it should be! Not sure how I can answer that without lawyers being called in. As for right or left-back, I was comfortable in both positions. I was two-footed, although I would say my right was just a little stronger. When I played on the right, I went down the line most of the time to clip over crosses. On the left, I liked to cut in and give the ball a dunt with my right peg. But I was happy in both positions. Peter Lorimer could kick the ball as hard as me…in his dreams! Seriously, the Leeds United player who was known as 'The Lash' could belt the ball at a ferocious pace, so it would be a close-run thing.

QUESTIONS FROM MONTEBLANCO

Are you still on Ayala from Racing Club's Christmas card list? On current matters at Celtic, would you bring back the Green Brigade?

The name Ayala keeps cropping up, but I don't know if such a player actually played for Racing Club. Possibly people are getting him mixed up with Ruben Ayala, an Argentinian international winger who played for Atletico Madrid and was one of their three players sent off in that infamous brawl at Celtic Park in 1973. Either way, no, I've never had a Christmas card from the guy. Can't think why I've been left off his list.

The Green Brigade create a fabulous atmosphere at the ground and they bring a splash of colour. But, for me, two things to keep away from sport are politics and religion. If the Green Brigade turn up to purely support their team and give the players their wholehearted backing, then they should be welcomed anywhere.

QUESTIONS FROM PIGALLE

What were your feelings about the non-PC chant about you coined by the fans of yon Glasgow team no longer in existence?

Aye, I used to get it in the neck from the Rangers support – presumably it's the Ibrox club to which you refer! – but it didn't bother me one little bit. If they were giving me stick, then they were leaving someone else alone. And, by the way, I do have a birth certificate to prove I wasn't born out of wedlock.

QUESTIONS FROM NEAUSTADT-BRAW

Hi, Tommy. The Big Shot was my first Celtic book – 'that's me in the middle' comment about the Front cover picture, had my brother confused...braw ....do you still shoot? And what is the name o yer dug?

Yes, I used to go shooting, mainly for pheasant, duck or geese. But, no, I don't indulge these days which is good news for the wildlife in Perthshire! I still enjoy a spot of fishing, though. My dog's name was 'Jock'! Honestly, it was good to be able to order 'Jock' around for a change.

QUESTIONS FROM ZIGGYDOC1

Tommy, did you meet Danny Kaye when he stayed at the Central Hotel? And can you rank in order these three footballing greats: Jinky, Dalglish and Best?

Sadly, I never did get to meet Danny Kaye. Do you know people in the States used to say to him all the time, 'You look a helluva lot like Tommy Gemmell'? I don't know about his ability as a footballer, but I reckon I

250

was a better singer than him. And better looking. As far as Jinky, Bestie and Kenny, that's a very difficult question. For a start, they were three entirely different types of players. Jinky was a real box of tricks with fabulous dribbling skills and unbelievable close control whereas Bestie was a lot more direct when he was taking on an opponent. Kenny was obviously more of a goal threat than the other two and he was very accomplished at holding up the ball and bringing other players into the game. For me, they were all world class. However, if you twist my arm, I would put them in this order: 1: Jinky; 2: Bestie; 3: Kenny.

QUESTION FROM GG

Best of health, Tommy. Great to know you've recovered and are back to form. My question is, 'Why didn't you lift the Torrey Canyon?' It was a pleasure seeing you play over the years and meeting you a couple of times in Kearny and Manhattan.

Torrey Canyon? Are you referring to me being well-oiled? Thank you for the kind thoughts and you can buy me a glass of cold white wine the next time we meet!

QUESTIONS FROM LAWRENZO

How did you feel when you won the Scottish League Cup for Dundee against the Hoops back in 1973? I imagine it was a combination of professionalism, sadness and delight? But would like your thoughts? All the best Big Man, you were my wee maw's favourite player.

Embarrassed was my main emotion after the League Cup win. I was captain of Dundee and I had to go up those stairs to be presented with the silverware. Actually, I felt a bit like an imposter because of my ties with Celtic. However, I had a job to do with Dundee and I remember Gordon Wallace's goal that wet, windy and muddy afternoon at Hampden. I always thought Gordon was hugely under-rated and deserved his 15 minutes of fame. By the way, your wee maw's got great taste!

QUESTIONS FROM TRADITONALIST88

What were your favourite moments against Rangers as both a player and a supporter?

Any win against our old rivals was always welcome. Remember, I came into the Celtic team in the early sixties when we were getting regularly turned over by the Ibrox side. So, it was great to be around when things changed so dramatically. One game that sticks out is the League Cup Final win over them in October 1965. We had won the Scottish Cup by beating Dunfermline 3-2 the previous April. For the first time as far as I could remember, the bookies actually made us favourites to win the trophy that day. Thankfully, they didn't get it wrong and Big Yogi, John Hughes, had his shooting boots on as he smacked two penalty-kicks behind Billy Ritchie and we went on to win 2-1. I couldn't have done better myself! As a supporter, my boyhood team was my local side Motherwell. Believe it or not, I never saw them play Rangers.

QUESTIONS FROM TALLYBHOY

Paolo Maldini was a great left back, but only number 2 in the all-time list after yourself...and he never scored as many goals as you did! Are you proud to be recognised as the best-ever left-back?

Thank you very much for the compliment. Actually, I knew Big Jock rated me as the best in the world, but he never told me. He was talking to his good friend Tony Queen, a well-known bookie, when he made the observation. Tony pledged me to secrecy when he told me later. Maldini was a fantastic defender. Of course, he settled into a more central role with AC Milan in later years, but he was wonderful at left-back. He didn't attack too much, saving himself for set-plays.

QUESTIONS FROM I'M NEIL LENNON (TAMRABAM)

Tommy, I had the pleasure and privilege of meeting you in Dubai around 10 years ago along with Billy McNeil. Anyway, my questions relate to the rise of the modern 'super teams' like Barca and Real Madrid with seemingly unlimited finances who can sign the best

players from all over the world and who can compete at the highest level year after year by buying the best players from every country. My first question is, 'In 1967 and 1970 teams were still largely dominated by home-based players. How would the Lisbon Lions have fared in the current Champions League against these modern teams with unlimited cash to spend and the ability to assemble the world's best players in one team?' My second question is, 'If not all of them, which of the Lions would today's Barcas and Madrids try to sign?' And my third question is, 'Do you think you ever scored a better goal than your brother Archie did against Holland?' (Okay, I'm chancing my arm with that one! But I know you like a laugh!)

I'll need to go and lie in a darkened room after I've answered all these. Maybe we should just do our own 'Question and Answer' book. Okay, to answer your first question I would say you could spend as much money as you like, but it doesn't guarantee success. It helps, of course, but splashing wads of dosh won't, in itself, mean trophies piling up in the boardroom. The Lisbon Lions cost exactly £42,000 to assemble - £30,000 to Hearts for Willie Wallace and £12,000 to Birmingham City for Bertie Auld. Ronnie Simpson was bought from Hibs, but the fee was so small apparently that no-one took a record of it. What a bargain! We had wonderful team spirit, though, and an unbeatable camaraderie throughout the team. Money couldn't have bought those qualities. So, I firmly believe any team with that attitude and outlook would be successful anywhere in any era. Secondly, the Barcas and the Madrids might have wanted to buy all of the Lions, but we came as a package. It would be difficult to envisage Bobby Murdoch playing without his little sidekick Bertie on his left, for instance. Or Big Billy without John Clark. Thirdly, Archie's goal against Holland in the 1978 World Cup Finals was a thing of beauty, no doubt about that. It wasn't the type of goal I could have scored, but, then, I don't remember Archie crashing in 30-yarders in his career. By the way, you do realise the spelling of his surname is Gemmill and not Gemmell, don't you? We're not related and, unfortunately, played only once together in an international. It was against Belgium in Liege in 1971 and we lost 3-0, so maybe the combination didn't work!

QUESTIONS FROM EXPAT CELT

You speak of the Lisbon Lions and their different strengths and how the team gelled to make it magic. Has there ever been another team you have seen or played against that struck you as having similar qualities to those of the Lions?

The Real Madrid side that swept all before them in the early sixties immediately comes to mind. They were a beautiful team to watch, a real combination of skill and, when it was required, steel. They had so many graceful players such as Alfredo di Stefano, Ferenc Puskas and Francisco Gento. No-one who witnessed it, will ever forget their 7-3 European Cup Final win over Eintracht Frankfurt at Hampden in 1960. What a spectacle that was. By the way, how's this for a thought? Eintracht took 12 goals off Rangers as they won home and away in their sem-final. And Real took seven off them. Makes you wonder what the final score at Hampden might have been that day had Rangers got through. Lucky escape methinks!

QUESTION FROM AN TEARMANN

Tommy Gemmell. Scorer in Lisbon in a European Cup Final for Celtic. Tommy Gemmell. Scorer in Milan in a European Cup Final for Celtic. Humbly put Tam, I only dream of dreaming of those heights with Celtic. Do you know just how much you mean to the Celtic family?

Yes and I'm very grateful, too. I've had a lot of respect from the Celtic family almost from day one. The supporters were great to me very early in my career and I'm delighted I may have been able to pay them back in some manner. I think I was fairly consistent throughout my Celtic career and I was also lucky enough to score a few spectacular goals. If I gave you and fellow-Celtic fans a happy memory or two, then I did my job.

QUESTIONS FROM TOJO

Can you give us some comparison on the current Celtic players

versus the Lisbon Lions? Do present-day Celtic supporters get better value for money now or in your day?

I believe the Lisbon Lions are incomparable and I hope I don't sound conceited in saying that. The Lions simply gelled and, when we sparked, I believe we were the best club side in the world. As regards value for money, I think it was more exciting and entertaining in my day. But it is also fair to say that players such as Wee Jinky, Bertie, Bobby Murdoch, Caesar and Faither in goal only come along once in a lifetime. It was a happy coincidence we were all at Celtic at the same time.

QUESTIONS FROM TALLYBHOY

Big Tam, you scored 63 goals in 418 games for Celtic. That's a better ratio than some of current strikers! Could you have played centre-forward?

The quick answer is 'No'. A huge percentage of my goals came from long distance when I backed up the forwards. So, although I scored a few goals, they weren't the type of strikes you would associate with guys such as Stevie Chalmers, Bobby Lennox, Willie Wallace or Joe McBride. They did their best work in and around the penalty box. I was happy to leave the goalscoring to the guys who knew what they were doing.

QUESTIONS FROM THE SPIRIT OF ARTHUR LEE

King Lud or Era Bar?

Great question! Two pubs in Craigneuk when I was growing up. I didn't have a favourite – I was far too young to drink! However, I do recall collecting empty beer bottles and returning them to the pubs. I think you got a penny on the empties. I made an absolute fortune in that area!

QUESTIONS FROM TRADITIONALIST88

How do you see the future of Celtic and Scottish football generally and what action can be taken to ensure a fairer distribution of TV revenues are received by Scottish clubs?

That's up to the authorities to decide. The SFA and the League need to negotiate the best deals for our football clubs in general. There's a lot to be considered, crowd money, TV deals, sponsorship and so on. As for Celtic's future, it would be highly intriguing if they ever got the opportunity to play in England. That's the million-dollar question, isn't it? At the moment, though, I think we should concentrate on building a team that will rule domestically and perform consistently well in Europe. Just like the good old days!

QUESTION FROM LYMMBHOY

Uncle Tommy, can you tell is about your party piece? The German Song? Adam, Luke, Milly & Chloe.

Oh, you mean, 'Fritz a Grand Old Team To Play For'? Yes, I have been known to belt that out at parties. Normally, I start off with a bit of Sinatra, but it's not long before the 'German Song' gets an airing!

QUESTION FROM GG

Serious question this time. Wee Deedle Henderson claims you cheated when playing against him. Is it true you breathed on his contact lens before and during the game to restrict his vision?

Yes, of course, I did – anything to give Celtic an advantage over the old enemy! Seriously, though, Wee Willie was a marvellous winger and we had some memorable jousts. He was lightning quick and he never gave me a minute's peace when we were facing each other. I think Wee Willie would be the first to admit that I played him hard, but fair. Do you know we are still pals to this day? He was at my 70th birthday party last year.

QUESTION FROM TALLYBHOY

What's the story with Jinky's night out with a young Gordon Strachan while they were both at Dundee and you were the manager? I think Wee Gordon became teetotal after that night!

Actually, I've talked about this impromptu drinking double-act in the book. Yes, I had to give the current Scotland manager a bollicking. I told him, 'Don't go near that little bugger again!' For the sake of his liver, I don't think he ever did. Jinky? What could I say to my wee mate? He would just smile back and that was the end of the matter.

QUESTION FROM CARRIGAN

What is your opinion of the present Celtic team and how does the club get the fans back onside after a season full of conflict between the fans and the club?

The present Celtic team certainly has its merits and Neil Lennon has done an exceptional job in keeping them focused in the absence of their oldest rivals. People will look at the Premiership and believe it is a one-horse race. In such circumstances, the players may just relax a little. Possibly, not intentionally, but subconciously. I'm certainly not in full possession of the facts about any conflict between the fans and the club. One thing is certain – they need each other. In my day, there were few politics in the game as we left that to the guys who made their living in parliament. But Celtic and its support have always dovetailed together and I don't see that ever changing.

QUESTION FROM JOHN O'NEIL

Tommy and the Lions gave the Celts more pleasure than all the tea in China ever could. No need for alcohol, drugs, cigarettes or anything else. Just watch that game. Happy days. How lucky the older generation were to have that team to watch. What was your most memorable match domestically as a Celt?

There is little doubt the 3-2 success over Dunfermline in the 1965 Scottish Cup Final was a major turning point in Celtic's history. Before that game, the last trophy the club had won was the League Cup when we beat Rangers 7-1 in season 1957/58. That was quite a gap that had to be filled. We did that against a very good Fifers team in that Final. The victory gave us confidence and kicked off a very enjoyable winning habit. That was a big win for Celtic and the support.

QUESTION FROM MICK TT

Mr Gemmell, what was the feeling of the Celtic team of that era regarding the lack of International recognition of Celtic players? Did they care or was it just accepted as typical of the regime and their referees!

We always had the feeling back then that the SFA was very definitely Rangers orientated. And I mean that as no disrespect to the Rangers players who were chosen to represent their country – they weren't the ones doing the selecting, after all. However, it got to such a situation that the SFA couldn't ignore what we were achieving at Celtic. They HAD to bring our players into their squads and teams. All of the Lisbon Lions won full caps with the curious exception of Wee Bertie. That still amazes me to this day. My little chum was undoubtedly one of the finest left-sided midfielders of my era and, on his day, was simply mesmerising. But Bertie, of course, was never slow to speak his mind and maybe the blazers at Park Gardens thought they had enough on their plate dealing with Wee Jinky!

QUESTION FROM MOONBEAMS

Obviously, in hindsight, Big Jock cannot be criticised for his team selection on that day in 1967, but on the day prior to kick-off when the team was announced, was there a player who's exclusion from the line-up raised eyebrows in the dressing room amongst his fellow team-mates and you?

The outcome of the European Cup Final tells you Big Jock got his team selection spot on. Remember, this was the same line-up that had earned the goalless draw against Dukla Prague in Czecholsovakia to get us to Lisbon. Also, it was the same selection that had beaten Aberdeen 2-0 in the Scottish Cup Final only a few days after Prague. So, it was a fairly settled formation. Players such as John Hughes, in particular, Willie O'Neill, Charlie Gallagher and Joe McBride made solid contributions earlier in the competition, but the team that beat Inter Milan was obviously the right one for the occasion.

QUESTION FROM ROCK TREE BHOY

Henrik Larsson at his peak, would he have got into the starting line-up for Lisbon 1967?

You only need to read this book to discover how highly I rated Henrik. But, no, I wouldn't have had dropped anyone to get him into the Lisbon team. Here's a good wee story, though. Jim Craig was working for Celtic TV at the time and he was interviewing Wee Bertie. He asked Bertie the same question. He thought for a moment and said, 'Let's see now. I think I would have chosen Simpson, Larsson and Gemmell.' Not sure if Cairney saw the funny side!

QUESTIONS FROM JOHN O'NEIL

Tommy, who were the biggest cheats that you played against? Also, how good was that Benfica side which we demolished 3-0?

Easy answer to the first question – Racing Club of Buenos Aires by a mile. I talk about these poor excuses for sportsmen elsewhere, but all I would add is Sir Alf Ramsey got it right after England had played Argentina in the World Cup quarter-final in 1966. Alf didn't hold back when he was asked about the performances of his country's opponents that day. He branded them 'animals'. Which is a bit of an insult to the wild life out there. On the second question, that Benfica team was one of the best we had ever played. Any line-up with Eusebio in it is bound to be handy. We were brilliant the night we beat them 3-0 and my goal, as you will undoubtedly know by now, is still one of my all-time favourites. They gave us a bit of a doing in Lisbon, though. They really went at us and it was 2-0 with only a minute to go when they tied the game 3-3 on aggregate. We managed to get through a fairly hectic thirty minutes in extra-time before Caesar called it right when it came to the toss of the coin. Thank goodness!

QUESTIONS FROM 31003

Question for Tommy, straight from the hip. A relative of mine travelled on the team plane to the Feynoord Final. He told me all was

259

not well on the flight over and that he thought you and Jinky at one stage threatened not to play until a bonus dispute was resolved. Is that true? And, if so, could it have affected performances in the Final?

Absolutely not true! Someone's definitely got their wires crossed. Does your relative enjoy Duty Free before flights! There's no truth in that whatsoever. Jinky and I refusing to play in Milan? Are you kidding? If that had been the case, Big Jock would have booted us off the plane while we were a few thousand feet up in the air. Yes, I've heard so many stories about a bonuses row before the game, but if it happened I wasn't aware of it. We never knew what sort of extra payment we would get from the club. That was left with the directors. For instance, if we won the Scottish Cup we would probably find an extra £250 in our wage packet the following week. Pay advice would tell you what the extra money was for. We were beaten by a very good Feyenoord side in that Final. Give them credit for the performance of a lifetime. They caught us totally unawares and were a far superior team than we expected. End of story.

QUESTIONS FROM CELTIC QUICK NEWS

Tommy, how did the team prepare for the Final in Milan and how did this compare to the preparation for Lisbon? In particular, how did both the players and manager's approach differ regarding the build-up to these two Finals?

Sadly, I have to say it was night and day. We were well primed for the 1967 game against Inter Milan. Big Jock left absolutely nothing to chance. Three years later it was a different story. Possibly, we thought we were as good as European champions after our home-and-away wins against the seemingly 'invincible' Leeds United in the semi-final. I wouldn't say we were complacent against Feyenoord, but we might just have been a bit over-confident. The pre-match planning just wasn't the same and it was most unlike Big Jock to under-rate opponents. On this occasion, alas, that's exactly what he did. And that got through to the players. Don't forget the calibre of the Dutch side on the night.

Don't take anything away from them and a lot of people wouldn't have realised this, but they actually won the Intercontinental Cup – aka World Club Championship – when they beat Argentina's Estudiantes 3-2 on aggregate later that year. They won 1-0 in Rotterdam and drew 2-2 in La Plata. Actually, they came from two goals down in that game to force the draw, so that surely underlines how good they were. Take my word for it, though, we would still have beaten them in a replay.

QUESTION FROM TALLYBHOY

Do you still pop into the 'Horseshoe' for a refreshment?

Yes, I have been known to partake of a small libation in this very excellent wee Glasgow howf. It was a great meeting place for the players and we were always well looked after by the staff. It's what is probably known as 'a wee man's pub' because you rarely see females in there. But, yes, when I'm in Glasgow with friends I always try to pop in for a refreshment.

QUESTION FROM JOHN O'NEIL

One last question, Tommy. Do you think that the Lisbon achievement helped the wider Scottish public accept Celtic and its supporters more than was previously the case?

Definitely. I knew Rangers supporters who applauded our European victory. Privately, of course. Their players, too, talked about our achievement. Scottish football benfited greatly from Celtic's presence. We showed the world we could play in a sporting and praiseworthy manner. We were good for Scotland and, of course, our supporters are now, rightly, recognised as among the best in the world – if not THE best.

QUESTION FROM PHELIM BRADY

Immediately after the European Cup Final, I took to the streets with my pals to play football. I was doing one of those commentating while I played routines. 'And Gemmell shoots' I shouted as I didn't quite connect with the ball, kicked the ground and ripped the sole off my school shoes. My mother blames you to this day. My

question is, do you think 47 years is long enough to hold a grudge?

I think 47 years is long enough to take your shoes to the cobblers. And, by the way, did you just say, 'And Gemmell shoots'? Shouldn't it have been, 'Gemmell shoots…and Gemmell scores'?.

QUESTION FROM ASONOFDAN

A question for Tommy, my favourite Lisbon Lion! Do you still think the incident with Haller was the beginning of the end as far as your Celtic playing career?

No, not all. Celtic frowned on one of their players being sent off while on international duty, of course, and I was punished by being dropped for the League Cup Final against St.Johnstone. Remember, I was still good enough to be selected for the European Cup Final against Feyenoord in 1970. It was December 1971 when I finally left the club I loved, so there was a lot of football played with Celtic between the Haller incident on October 1969 and when I moved to Nottingham Forest.

QUESTIONS FROM THE HONEST COVER UP

Tommy, I'm too young to have seen you play in the flesh, but when I hear your name the first thing that comes to mind (as well as that goal in Lisbon) is thundering long-range shots. Is that something you could always do or was it a case of mastering the technique? Also, is there anyone else in your day or the modern game who you think could strike the ball harder? Thanks, looking forward to reading the book!

It was a question of practice, hopefully, making perfect. I spent around 25 to 30 minutes after the usual training sessions at Barrowfield bombarding Ronnie Simpson or John Fallon with long-range drives. I worked on the technique throughout my career. I don't know about anyone being able to strike the ball harder. It's a lighter ball, for a start.

QUESTION FROM TAMTIM

Which player in your professional career was the toughest

opponent to play against?

Jinky in training! Seriously, Bestie was always a handful. I played against him in internationals and in friendless and he was always a real threat. Like Jinky, he had the heart of a lion. There's no way the Manchester United legend was ever intimidated. A smashing wee guy on and off the pitch. And I can't forget Wee Willie Henderson. The Rangers winger was one of the top players in his heyday

QUESTION FROM THE TOKEN TIM

Question for The legend who is Big Tam. I wasn't lucky enough to have seen the Lions in the flesh (just a few short years ahead of my time), but it annoys me when I hear talk of Rinus Michels and Ajax being the founders of Total Football. I can only speak of the games I've seen on TV, but from the Final in Lisbon alone, I'd have to say Big Jock and you and your team-mates were the originators of Total Football. In the big scheme of things it's not a massive headache, but have you any thoughts on this and outside of Scotland do you think that performance in Lisbon has not been given the weight in history that it should have done?

The Dutch got the credit for Total Football, but, you're right, we were doing something similar at Celtic from the early days of Big Jock. He wanted players to play to their strengths and be comfortable when they were on the ball. I could have been an outside-left if you look at the way we played. Bobby Murdoch was a genuine two-footed player who could easily have adapted to life on the left. John Hughes could perform on either flank as well as centre-forward. Willie Wallace, Stevie Chalmers and Bobby Lennox could also operate in wide areas. And Wee Bertie kicked off his career as a left-winger before moving inside as a midfielder. So, yes, there was a lot of versatility in the team. Jim Craig didn't score a lot of goals, but he did an awful lot of unselfish running up and down the right wing. And what can I say about Wee Jinky? He could roam all over the place and look the part anywhere. He might have struggled at centre-half, though! I think Celtic got a lot of deserved praise throughout Europe for the way we performed in Lisbon. The name of the club may

263

not have had the glamour of Real Madrid or Barcelona, but I think we proved once and for all on that unforgettable day that we were not a collection of country bumpkins from Scotland. We were a team of class and substance.

QUESTION FROM LEFTCLICKTIC

Question to Mr Gemmell in my best Jim White voice, 'How come you're so good?' Thank you, Tommy, for nearly a full lifetime of pointing to the Big Cup and saying to Them, 'Look what we won!' Thank you, thank you and thank you again!

Thank you, too! Why was I so good? Very kind of you to say so. Personal accolades are all well and good, but I never lost sight of what I had to do in the Celtic team. I was part of a unit.I may have hit the headlines with the odd howitzer, but John Clark could have played as big a part in any victory in his quiet manner in the heart of our defence. He rarely got the headlines, but all the players knew what he provided on an exceptional and consistent basis.

QUESTION FROM TRADITIONALIST88

Why can our manager not attend a match as a neutral to perform scouting duties without being attacked?

It's outrageous and completely out of order that Neil Lennon has to take dog's abuse from absolute morons who have no place in society never mind sport. The sooner we get to grips with this curse, the better. Stringent action must be taken against pests who blight our game.

QUESTION FROM TALLYBHOY

Tommy, in his autobiography, Bertie Auld said he loved playing with you. Was he any good?

No, I believe he was well over-rated! No-one would have ever heard of him if it wasn't for me doing all his work on the left-hand side of the pitch. Only joking, Bertie! What a player and what a left peg. He and Bobby Murdoch were the best midfielders I ever played with. Wee Bertie was the finished article – he could tackle, pass and shoot. Not bad for a guy with only one foot!

QUESTION FROM VMHAN

I was at the 3-0 Benfica game as an 11 year old when you scored that belter. My question is, 'What was the feeling after that game, was it that we were comfortably through or did you expect a tough return leg?'

We knew it would be difficult in the Stadium of Light. Okay, we were three goals ahead, but Benfica were an attacking team who scored goals for fun in their national league. And no team with a player such as the great Eusebio could ever be written off. That was a hard night in Lsbon, but, thankfully I've got better memories of the Portuguese capital.

QUESTIONS FROM JUSTAFAN

Hi, Tommy! Will chance my arm and ask two questions! You are one of the most successful Celts of all time, but, of course, the start of your career was a time of failure for Celtic. Even as late as 1964 Celtic seemed destined for continued mediocrity. As a professional in the early, early part of your career, what were your thoughts AT THE TIME about the club, the management and your own and Celtic's future? Also, you often played behind John Hughes in your career. Big Yogi was another of my all-time favourites, but he struggled for consistency. At his best, one of the most exciting players I've ever seen, when off form, though… Anyway, can you recall any specific occasion when John made you go WOW? (In a good way lol).

First up, I was chuffed when Celtic signed me. I always dreamed of playing for Motherwell, but thank goodness that never happened. Celtic may have been in a bit of turmoil at the time, but they were still a massive club. People kept referring to them as 'a sleeping giant' and I just wanted to play my part in helping to bring them out of their slumber! I always saw my future at Celtic. I never hankered after a move and was only too willing to do what was necessary to get the club back to its rightful place at the top. Big Jock gave the place a real shake when he arrived and deserves great credit for that. There was no longer any interfering from above in team matters. It's was Jock's way or no way. Yogi could be exciting and exasperating, but what a player when he was on form. To be fair, he was more often brilliant than not. He caused defences no end of hassle when he was on song. At times he was unstoppable. I recall his one-man show against Rangers in January 1966 when we were trailing 1-0 at the interval. Yogi ran amok in the second-half, shredded the right side of their rearguard and they fell apart. Stevie Chalmers, with a hat-trick, Charlie Gallagher and Bobby Murdoch scored in a fabulous 5-1 win. Inconsistent? Name me a player who was 100 per cent consistent.

QUESTION FROM PARKHEADCUMSALFORD

Tommy, it is great to see you are putting pen to paper. How I loved your contribution to Celtic! Can you tell us about your earlier books about your career?

My first book, The Big Shot, was not actually an autobiography. There weren't even 100 pages in it! I was 25 at the time and there was a lot more to come. However, back in 1968, a Glasgow journalist persuaded me it would be a good idea to get some of my thoughts down in print so I went ahead with it. The second, Lionheart', was done over a decade ago and is a lot more rounded. But, as you can see, there's a whole load of fresh stuff in 'All The Best'. There was just so much material left over that I decided to get everything into print with this book. I've got no plans for a fourth – unless, of course, there is a public demand!

QUESTIONS FROM DONTBRATTBAKKINANGER

I have two questions for Mr Gemmell. Do you think that Celtic will ever appear in another European Final? And even mediocre, modern-day players make far more money than you did in your prime, do you resent this?

I'm assuming you mean the Champions League Final. That's the big one and that's where Celtic deserve to be although, of course, the UEFA Cup Final in Seville will always be a great memory and an incredible feat in reaching that stage. What a pity we lost! I would like to think it is possible for Celtic to grace another Final in the top-flight competition, but, obviously, it would be an extremely difficult task. I can always hope and dream. As regards the cash flying around football at the moment, I have to say I don't resent the current players their good fortune to be operating in an era when satellite TV is pouring millions into the game. Good luck to them. When I was playing, we were earning more than the working man. Mind you, I wasn't looking for untold riches when I kicked off. I think I started with £7 and that rose to £12, then £18 and up to £25 before the basic wage was pegged at £40 while I was still a young player. Remember, too, there were bonuses on top plus appearance money. And, thankfully, we started getting a lot of win bonuses from 1965 on!

NO QUESTION FROM FRANK RYAN'S WHISKEY

Hi, Tommy. No questions from me just a big thank you.

YNWA.

Thank you very much, also. If I ever put a smile on your face or your fellow-Celtic followers, then I'll consider it all worthwhile.

QUESTIONS FROM GOOGYBHOY

Regarding your goal against Feyenoord in the Final in Milan. Was that one you had worked on in training? Was it knocked back to you to give you more room to score? I am surprised more teams do not use this as a way of getting more room to get the ball up and over a wall or through it as your shot did? Or were you just aiming for the referee's backside?

We worked on that routine in training every day. When we were awarded that free-kick and Bobby Murdoch stepped up to take it, I knew exactly what he was going to do. No, I didn't aim for Italian referee Concetto Lo Bello's rear end, but I have to say it was a very strange place for him to stand behind the Feyenoord wall. I've never seen a referee adopt that position since. He did a good job of getting out of the way of my shot, didn't he?

QUESTIONS FROM JIMBO67

Wow! Willie Wallace and now Tommy Gemmell! Anybody who saw these Celts play must smile at the memory. Why has left-back been such a weak position since you left us? Jimmy Quinn, Andy Lynch and, especially, Tom Boyd were fine and Izzy can be great, but other than that there have been some real disappointments. Oh and Big Man, thanks for scoring the first goal I ever saw Celtic – a penalty at Brockville in 1968. Do you remember it?

Naturally left-footed players aren't exactly thick on the ground, so that may be part of the answer. I could kick with either foot, of course, which came in useful. It's a specialised position and players at full-back these days are asked to do an awful lot of work going up and down the flank. I was built for it and I believe I was fairly consistent. I hope you agree. I'm not being big-headed, but I was fairly happy with my performances in the green and white hoops. Believe it or not, I do remember that penalty-kick against Falkirk in 1968. Like every other Celtic player I hated playing at Brockville. Games on that horrible pitch at that equally-horrible ground are embedded in my memory bank for all time. It was goalless when we were awarded the spot-kick and I simply thrashed it into the net. Willie Wallace and Bobby Lennox got the others as we won 3-0.

QUESTIONS FROM THE LONG WAIT IS OVER

Just great to see a true legend on Celtic Quick News. I had the pleasure of TG's company at a corporate table at a Scottish Cup Final a number of years ago (we lost, but I don't blame Tommy!) What brilliant company and a true gent, giving unlimited time to anyone who approached him, which was pretty much constantly. Can any football club owe as much of a debt or identify so uniquely with one manager and team of players as Celtic does with Jock Stein and the Lisbon lions? Football, even to the most fanatical of us, is not more than life or death, but, in a sporting context, truly never was so much owed by so many to so few! All the best, Tommy.

I take it you're a big fan of Winston Churchill! All the best to you, too, and thank you for the comments. Much appreciated.

QUESTIONS FROM LIVIBHOY

What importance did Jock Stein put on trophies? Did he set out to win them all or was there a slide rule of trophies that Celtic would play for? Outwith European success, which trophy win or match gave you the most satisfaction as a player? Many thanks for taking the time to answer some questions. It's a pleasure to have a Lisbon Lion even reading our comments. My auld man met you once at a Player of the Year dance in Newcastle. He had somehow blagged his way into the function and was giving you stick about your nose and you said to him, 'I might have a big nose, but you have a big mouth!' Still tells that story to this day. I think he took great pleasure in a Lisbon Lion having the banter with him. The Lisbon Lions are not heroes to him they are gods!

Big Jock sent us out to win EVERY game. It didn't matter if it was a Cup Final or a friendly, he expected his team to be victorious in them all. So, he didn't pick and choose – he wanted EVERY trophy EVERY year. As I have stated elsewhere, the 1965 Scottish Cup win over Dunfermline gave the players a lot of confidence and got the club back on the trophy-winning trail after being in the wilderness for far too long. Yes, that 'you've got a big mouth' was my normal reponse to the cheeky buggers who had a go at my hooter!

QUESTIONS FROM TALLYBHOY

Tommy, I've just come across a photograph taken shortly after Celtic had beaten Hibs 6-2 in the 1969 League Cup Final. You are holding a bottle of beer and sporting a moustache! Can you tell us about that game and that moustache?

I didn't have that moustache for too long. I grew it as a sort of experiment. It had as many colours as an average rainbow! The game against Hibs was fairly memorable – Jim Craig scored one of his rare goals for the club that afternoon. Bobby Lennox hammered in a hat-trick and Willie

Wallace and Bertie Auld got the others. We were leading 6-0 with about 10 minutes to play when Hibs got their consolation goals. That was a very good win for us because the Edinburgh outfit were really strong at the time. They had players such as Pat Stanton, John Blackley, Peter Marinello, Peter Cormack, Jimmy O'Rourke and Eric Stevenston in their line-up. They were a nice team to watch, but they had no answer to Celtic that afternoon.

QUESTION FROM CLIFTONVILLE CELT FROM BELFAST

Tommy Gemmell! WOW! Just WOW! I wish I could think of a question worthy of the man! Have you ever been star struck, Tommy?

Yes, when I was a kid I used to watch Motherwell train. They were known as 'The Ancell Babes' after manager Bobby Ancell. I would rush from my house down to Fir Park to snatch a glimpse of my heroes. The club let the local youngsters in to see the players going through their routines. What struck me was the lack of ball work. It seemed all the players were asked to do was run round the pitch about one hundred times without stopping! They had stars such as Ian St.John, who joined Liverpool in 1961, Pat Quinn, Andy Weir, Andy Paton, Archie Shaw and Willie Hunter. I was in total awe of those guys.

QUESTIONS FROM CADIZZY

My question for the Big Fella is this. 'When you chased that German to boot him up the bahoochie, was it the fastest you had ever run and the hardest you had ever kicked?' And was it the fastest Haller had ever run?

I don't know if it was the quickest Haller had ever run, but it was certainly the loudest he ever squealed! I would have chased him out of the stadium and into Hamburg city centre to give him that boot up the backside. Don't think it was the hardest I ever kicked, but it must have come close!

QUESTIONS FROM WILLIEBHOY

We hear much moaning about honest mistakes from Scottish referees in recent years. But I am sure there were plenty of the same in your era. Any specific incidents of this nature stick in your mind? Also who was the best goalkeeper you faced? Thanks for the many great memories Tam. We even forgive you for leading Dundee to League Cup glory against us...well, almost.)

Bobby Davidson's display in our 3-1 defeat from Aberdeen in the 1970 Scottish Cup Final was the worst I have ever seen. That's not sour grapes and it's not just my opinion. Every Celtic player in the Hampden dressing room that day could hardly believe that performance from the match official. There was talk he wasn't particularly fond of Big Jock. Or Celtic, for that matter. He proved it that afternoon! It was a game in which you knew you would be punished for anything. The slightest show of dissent and you would have been in the book. You wouldn't have to be an expert in lip-reading if you saw my reaction to his award of a penalty-kick for the Dons after the ball hit Bobby Murdoch in the midriff. Presumably, he didn't hear me or I might have been off the pitch! Mainly, though, most referees were consistent and I thought the majority were fair. Tiny Wharton was a good match official and he had a bit of inter-action with the players. He would jog past you and say, 'Now, now Mr.Gemmell, I saw that late tackle. Don't do it again or you know what will happen.' He always addressed players as Mister. In return, I called him Mr.Wharton. Tiny's real Christian name was Tom, but he was 6ft 4in, so, of course, he had to be nicknamed Tiny. Apart from Faither in training, the best goalkeeper I've ever faced has got to be Giuliano Sarti, of Inter Milan. His performance in Lisbon was simply awesome. We were beginning to wonder if we would ever get the ball behind him. Thankfully, I managed it and Stevie did it, too. But Sarti was immense that day. He didn't deserve to be in a losing team. Thank God he was, though.

QUESTIONS FROM THE LONG WAIT IS OVER

If, instead of scoring with that thunderbolt, your shot had bounced off the post and Inter had broken away and scored a second, what would Jock have done? Also, could we have come back from 2-0 if that had happened?

Jock would have booted my backside all the way back to Glasgow! The golden rule was that if I was up in attack Jim Craig remained in our half and vice-versa. So, when Cairney slid that ball across their penalty area the last player who should have been coming onto it was me. Could we have come back from 2-0? It's speculation, of course, but we were an extremely fit team and there would have been the guts of half-an-hour still to play. I believe we could have – but you might have expected me to say that.

QUESTION FROM GLENDALYSTONSILS

Do you remember smashing a clearance out of play in 1968 and almost decapitating a young bhoy in the old enclosure in front of the stand? I'm still dizzy by the way!

Glad you survived and lived to tell the tale! Thankfully, I normally took my frustration out on rival goalkeepers.

QUESTIONS FROM GRANNY MACS BHOY

My question for Tommy is, 'If you had been born in another time and unable to play in the Lions era, which other Celtic era/ team would you now choose to play in and why?'

Honestly, can't think of one because I was just so happy to be associated with the Lisbon Lions. It might have been interesting to play in Big Billy's Centenary Double-winning side where Anton Rogan and Derek Whyte shared the left-back duties during the memorable 1987/88 season. And it would have been intriguing to have played in a Martin O'Neill team too. I wouldn't have minded having a go at Porto in Seville. The nearest I got was a seat in the stand. But, no, I will always be more than satisfied to be a Lion.

QUESTIONS FROM RIOSKORRIE

Bom dia, Tommy. You played in two of the greatest-ever Scottish teams in 1967 – the Lisbon Lions and the Wembley Wizards. Had the two been able to face each other, who'd have won and would you have managed to crack one past Faither in the Scotland goal?

Well, of course, Celtic would have won because it would have been 11 versus 7. Scotland would have been without me, Faither, Wispy and Bobby Lennox. Wouldn't have been fair. I'm sure I could have stuck a few into an empty net!

QUESTION FROM EDDIEINKIRKMICHAEL

If you hadn't converted to being a full-back, what kind of winger would you have made and do you think you would still have had a career as a pro footballer?

I started my career as an outside-right with Coltness United, would you believe? To be honest, I might still have had a career in the game, but I believe I would have been a pretty average winger. I would never have played in two European Cup Finals and won a barrowload of medals, that's for sure.

QUESTIONS FROM BADA BING

Tommy, thanks for the memories and the history. Martin O'Neill made a big effort to get the Lions back involved at Celtic Park on Matchdays. How was this appreciated by the Bhoys? And do you think previous custodians could and should have done more to honour the Lions' remarkable achievement?

Martin took the Lions for a dinner at an Italian restaurant on the south side of Glasgow just a week or so after joining the club. That was greatly appreciated and he came across as being a big fan of Celtic. I think the custodians, as you call them, have done their bit. They've got a club to run and a present to take care of and a future to plan for. No complaints on that score.

273

QUESTIONS FROM JOHNNY CLASH

Back in the 1990s, I used to play 5-a-sides regularly at the Pitz at Townhead. I saw you playing on the neighbouring pitch a few times, but you were usually in goal. Was this because (a) You were an exceptional goalkeeper with cat-like reactions, or (b) You were the last to get picked?

Yes, I played a couple of times at the Pitz just to get some rust out of my joints. I would like to think I was requested to play in goal because of my remarkable agility. And also to give the other team a chance to get a kick at the ball.

QUESTION FROM ONEMALLOY

Wonderful to have you on CQN, Tommy! You are my hero from my early days of following Celtic as well as an absolute Celtic legend. I look forward to reading your book. My question is, 'Who were your football heroes through your career?'

I played with most of my heroes (Bertie paid me a fiver to say that!) The first real hero I saw in the flesh was the late, great Tom Finney. Preston North End played a friendly against Motherwell at Fir Park. I was about eight or nine at the time and Tom Finney was their big star. He didn't disappoint. He thrilled me with his exciting runs and wonderful dribbling qualities. He was a fabulous entertainer and, as I was to discover later in life, a true gentleman.

QUESTION FROM THE GREEN MAN

Welcome Big Tommy...absolute legend! The first time I saw the Hoops, I was five years old and have never forgotten that experience. It will stay with me forever. My auld maw tells me I was struck dumb for hours afterwards, when I eventually spoke, the first words I said...Bobby Lennox...wow...The Lisbon Lions...true genius in abundance! Tommy, Love you Big Man! My question is, 'How good was the Buzz Bomb?'

Bobby Lennox was grease lightning. Once he got past a defender they were in serious trouble. There was just no catching Bobby. Wee Bertie used to say, 'See that Lennox – he'd chase paper on a windy day!' He was a wonderful goalscorer, too, and a great team-mate. In fact, I think his goal tally would have been greater if he hadn't been so fast! He used to get into positions so quickly that the referee and lineman must have thought he had to be offside. And we rarely got the benefit of the doubt in those days.

QUESTION FROM MICKBHOY 1888

Mr Gemmell, yet to meet you and you aren't my favourite player... Henrik was and still is! Anyway, my question is, 'If Joe McBride would have been fit would he have been in the starting line-up in Lisbon and, if so, who would have been left out?'

Impossible to answer that one, of course. I can't think of anyone who would have been left out. Joe played in Stevie Chalmer's' position as the spearhead of the attack, but, remember, Stevie played in every European Cup game that season. He was in the team at the start of the campaign when Joe was fit. And, of course, he did hit the winner against Inter Milan, didn't he?

QUESTION FROM FIN75

Mr Gemmell, as you and the Lions lifted the Big Cup, did it ever dawn you that you had started the downfall of our rivals – as they never could accept we had won it and they never could? All I can say is – fantastic work and very much appreciated.

Rangers were fairly far removed from anyone's thoughts around Lisbon time. We concentrated completely on Celtic. However, I think it merely underlines our feats when you look at the Rangers team in 1967. It was strong enough to get to the European Cup-Winners' Cup Final where they played Bayern Munich in Nuremberg only a week after our triumph over Inter Milan. They lost 1-0 in extra-time to a very good Bayern line-up. I didn't think they could ever have won the European Cup in my days because you had to be champions to play in the premier tournament back then. And, of course, the Scottish League title was the exclusive property of Celtic at the time.

QUESTION FROM LENNON N MC...MJALLBY

Tommy, did you or any of the other Lions get to meet any of the big musical groups of the time like The Beatles?

No, our paths never crossed. We met all the Scottish entertainers of the time, but I don't suppose you can compare the Alexander Brothers with John, Paul, George and Ringo, can you?

QUESTION FROM TEUCHTER AR LA

When the referee blew for half-time at Tynecastle, Big Tam kicked the ball up into the 'shed'. As the stewards and the Polis tried to retrieve it, the Celtic support sang, 'We've got the ba' E-I-Adio we've got the ba'. Throughout the second-half, the Ba' would make regular appearances, held high, much to the frustration or the stewards and the delight of the supporters. 'Yer no gettin' it back E-I Adio Yer no gettin' it back.' Another great memory. Anyone remember? My question for Big Tam is, how come yer brother Davie is better lookin' than you? Winchburgh CSC.

What can I say? Has everybody in Winchburgh got dark glasses and a white stick?

QUESTION FROM GER57

When Billy had to go out alone at Lisbon to lift the Big Cup, were you all a bit sad that you couldn't go with him or just relieved to be in the safety of the dressing room?

It would have been marvellous to have done a lap of honour, but there's no way we can blame the fans for their over-exuberance. By the time I got off the pitch and up the tunnel, Billy had already been handed the European Cup. I didn't even see the presentation. At the end of the day, we were all just delighted to have won and to have left our magnificent support with a memory to cherish.

QUESTION FROM TALLYBHOY

Tommy, what are your musical tastes? And can you tell us your favourite artists?

I like crooners and I'm a big fan of Frank Sinatra, Dean Martin and Perry Como. It's all nice and easy listening. Then I liked The Beatles and, to a lesser extent, the Rolling Stones.

QUESTIONS FROM A CEILER GONOF RUST

Given what's happened in Scottish football over the past three years and particularly around the corruption of RFC and the Scottish football authorities with regard to their handling of RFC, if you were playing during this era for Celtic do you think you would feel cheated? If so, why?

The Rangers situation is of their own making and it's entirely up to them to get themselves out of the mess. Obviously, there has been a lot of in-club fighting and, ultimately, that will not help actual football matters out on the pitch. Would I feel cheated? I'm assuming you mean missing out on Old Firm games. To tell the truth, these were never confrontations I looked forward to with any particular relish. They were always played in a hostile atmosphere and, although their taunts never actually bothered me too much, I was well aware I had relatives in the stand who took exception to them. They could take the gloss off yet another Celtic win.

QUESTION FROM SCULLYBHOY

First book (not just on football) that I ever bought was the BIG SHOT. I think it was in the early 70s when I bought it in a bookshop in Smithfield. Anyway, what I do clearly remember is the excitement of hurrying home to read it. Can you tell us something about this book and why you decided to write in in 1968 when you were still a young man?

Well, I was making my name in the game at the time and football autobiographies seemed to be springing up all over the place. Big Billy did one and so, too, did Ronnie Simpson. A journalist by the name of Ian Peebles discussed it with me and, as I've said elsewhere, I didn't see

277

the harm in going with it. Presumably, you read it inside an hour!

QUESTION FROM LIVIBHOY

Tommy, you were a friend of the late George Best. Would Jock Stein have got more playing years out of George than Manchester United did?

Yes, I would say so. Bestie was a smashing wee guy who liked the good life, but what a player. If there was any manager out there who could have got him to knuckle down my money would have been on Big Jock. Mind you, he had Wee Jinky to contend with at that time. Possibly, the combination of Bestie and Jinky might have driven Jock, a strict teetotaller, to drink! But I genuinely think Bestie could have flourished under Jock and maybe extended his career by a few years. It's so sad to think his career at Manchester United was all over by the time he was 28. He should have been at his peak.

QUESTION FROM JUDE 2005

Tommy, Willie Henderson said you crossed like a good winger. Did you enjoy that comment? Was it true?

That was very kind of my wee Rangers pal. Yes, I worked hard on being able to get in a good cross and, obviously, I picked up a hint or two while I was an outside-right with Coltness United. I never saw the point of racing 80 yards or so into a good wide position to simply hammer over a hopeful cross that could often hit the first defender. I liked to try to measure crosses and pick out a team-mate. If Willie had asked me nicely, I might have given him a few hints!

QUESTIONS FROM TBJ

Tommy, Jim Craig or Danny McGrain? And why?

Good question. Both were great defenders who would never be famous for their goalscoring. Cairney was an athlete, straight-forward and hard running. Danny was a bit more polished. Both had excellent timing in the tackle. Cairney is 6ft-plus and rarely dived in because as he would point out, 'I've got a long way to travel to get back up.' To a certain extent, they both had different strengths, but I wouldn't like to separate them. I rated both very, very highly.

QUESTIONS FROM HAMILTONTIM

Mr Gemmell, thank you. You represent the pinnacle of what Celtic achieved as a football team. It was never better before and it will never be bettered in the future. The faithful are forever in your debt. How often do you think about what you achieved for Celtic?

I think about it all the time. In fact, I'm never allowed to forget it. Everywhere I go, punters want to talk about those great Celtic days. Equally, I'm just as happy to talk to them about a golden era for the club. I'll never forget how those supporters embraced a young Tommy Gemmell back in the early sixties. They gave me wonderful encouragement right from the start. I'll always owe them for that. And, of course, it's nice to know you're not forgotten. Celtic fans, I salute you.

QUESTION FROM PALACIO67

Tommy, what do you think of this?

'Oh well you may have heard or even read somewhere,

That a Racing player was attacked, (From the Back...)

By Big Tam Gemmell, The gentle Giant,

The Glasgow Celtic's full-back.

Well I asked Big Tam who's as gentle as a Lamb,

Is there anything that he would like to say,

He said, I saw it on TV, and I know it looks like me,

But I swear it was Danny Kaye...'

Dannykayecsc

That Danny Kaye was forever getting me into trouble!

QUESTIONS FROM CELTIC MAC

Tommy, the answer to my question is probably in your earlier book, (you know the one from forty-five years back), but haven't got that to hand so here goes. I notice on CelticWiki that you played two league games and one Scottish Cup game in season 1962-63, (wee Jimmy played in the Final), can you remember those first games and were any of them at Celtic Park?

I made my debut in a 5-1 win over Aberdeen at Pittodrie on January 5 1963. I was delighted to kick off with a win because the Dons had beaten Celtic 2-1 at our place earlier in the season. Big John Hughes rattled in a hat-trick that day in one of his unstoppable performances. My next game was a 2-0 win over Falkirk at Brockville in the Scottish Cup three weeks later. Yogi scored again. And I was included in the line-up for 5-2 win over Queen of the South at Palmerston a couple of months afterwards. A player called Bobby Craig, who left us at the end of the season, notched up a trio that afternoon. Three away games, three wins. The start of something good!

QUESTIONS FROM ISTANBULCELT

Tommy, Hail! Hail! Who were the international players at the time of Lisbon that you thought could do a right good job for Celtic, if only they had been Scottish? Which other Celtic players do you wish you had the chance to play with from the last 30 years? Hail Hail to a real legend.

Honestly, I look at the Lisbon Lions and I wouldn't have changed a thing. Scottish players at Celtic? Denis Law could have played anywhere, but he always insisted if he ever signed for a Scottish club it would have been his hometown team Aberdeen. Also, you might look at Bobby Moore, England's immaculate World Cup-winning captain. He played in the same defensive role as John Clark, but would he have been as effective alongside Big Billy? Probably not. There were so many good players around at the time, but I wouldn't have changed a thing. As far as playing alongside Celts from the last 30 years, I have got to say I would have enjoyed being a team-mate of Henrik Larsson. There are others, of course, but Henrik was something special.

QUESTIONS FROM MNCELT

Here is my question for TG. Assuming you take a close interest in the current team, how do you think the players are feeling now with the league won and nothing else to play for, having lost in the Scottish Cup to Aberdeen and earlier in the season to Morton in the League Cup? How do they motivate themselves for the remainder of the games and, finally, how do you think Neil Lennon should approach the remainder of the season?

The players shouldn't need any motivating. They have a duty to themselves, the club and the support to go out and do their very best in every game. Yes, the league's in the bag and it's been a good effort. To go through the season unbeaten until Aberdeen in February was an excellent feat. Neil Lennon is probably already planning for the new season and another tilt at the Champions League. He may be tempted to play some of the younger players just to give them a run in the first team. The young Israeli midfielder Nir Biton might be one of the players to benefit from a run of games at this level.

MALORBHOY

Tommy, would I be correct in saying I saw you playing with Coltness United at Craighead Park, home of the Famous Blantyre Celtic in the early 60s, and also a wee red head from Uddingston was playing for the home team?

Correct! Well spotted, sir. Yes, I played at Blantyre Celtic's ground and Wee Jinky was in the opposing team. Thankfully, I wasn't a left-back in those days or I might have been tempted to give up the game after tussling with the Wee Man!

QUESTION FROM CHAIRBHOY

Hello, Mr Gemmell, it is great to see you contributing to CQN. I was privileged to meet you with Mr Murdoch several years ago. It was one of the proudest moments of my life. In 1967, as well as the

281

legendary game in Lisbon, you also played in a historic encounter at Wembley. My question is, that, although the 70s and 80s were probably more successful for the National team, do you think that the Scotland squad/team you played with in the late sixties was better?

Well, the Scotland team in 1967 was good enough to beat the world champions on their own ground. Does that answer your question? We had so many good players back then and could afford to leave out a winger of the quality of Willie Henderson to play Wee Jinky. Willie would walk into today's team. I believe we were superior and I mean that as no disrespect to Gordon Strachan's lads. There are a few who could walk down Sauchiehall Street and no-one would recognise them. That wouldn't have happened with the likes of Denis Law, Billy McNeill, Jim Baxter, Alan Gilzean, Billy Bremner etc.

QUESTION FROM B11OYS

It's great to see TG getting involved with CQN. My wee brother and I got our first-ever Celtic strips for Christmas in 1966. I was 7 and he was 5. I got to sew number 3 on my shorts and he got a number 7. Will never forget the excitement of the two of us running up to Springburn Park with our new boots and a new ball and our Celtic strips on (long sleeves-no adverts-no badge). I was Tommy Gemmell and he was wee Jinky. Great memories, indeed. Every shot I ever hit for years was followed by shouting, 'Gemmell!' Great to see Tommy is keeping better these days. All the best Big Man! My question for Tommy, 'What do you recall of Jinky from the Di Stefano Trophy when we beat Real 1-0 two weeks after Lisbon? Was that his finest game?'

Jinky was unbelievable that night. He tormented Real Madrid right from the start to the very end. The Spaniards just couldn't get the ball off him. He was incredible and simply ran the show. The Real fans had packed out the stadium to say farewell to their club legend Alfredo di Stefano and by the end of the night they were shouting 'Ole!' every time Jinky got the ball and sidestepped challenge after challenge. It wasn't all for show, either. I knocked the ball to Jinky deep in our own half and he took off before sliding a pass in front of Bobby Lennox who netted the winner. His finest game? Not too sure about that because there were just so many from which to choose. But it was right up there with the best of them, that's for sure.

QUESTION FROM UGH AYE

Hi Tommy. Who were some of the older players you trained with when you first arrived at Parkhead? Any stories on the real talents that really impressed you?

Dunky MacKay was right-back at the time and I have to say he was one of the best ball-playing full-backs I had ever seen. He was way ahead of his time. Dunky had been converted from the old right-half berth to play a more defensive role, but he was great getting forward. Subconciously, I may have picked up a hint or two from him. Jim Kennedy was the left-back, but the man known as The Pres was an out-and-out defender and concentrated completely on that side of his game. He rarely, if ever, crossed the halfway line. Old favourite Willie Fernie had just returned from Middlesbrough . He was about 32 at the time and was in the twilight of his career, but you could see he had been a class act. Mike Jackson was there, too, and I rated him very highly. Celtic sold him to St.Johnstone and no-one could ever work out why. Stevie Chalmers won't thank me for this, but he was a first team player at the time and there were two good wingers in Bobby Carroll and Alec Byrne. A lot of good and entertaining players, but we couldn't win anything of substance until Big Jock returned in 1965.

QUESTION FROM GEAROID 1998

Here is my Big Tam question. July 12th 2012 Sean Og's Gweedor Donegal. Big Tam, Wee Bertie and Charlie and the Bhoys. Has he ever been to a better or more drunken 'alternative' July 12th celebration?

What a great bunch of lads! Yes, I recall we shared a small sherry that evening! Wee Bertie used to lead me astray, you know. I was massively impressed by the guys I met and their obvious devotion to Celtic. It was a pleasure to spend time in their company.

NO QUESTION FROM GREENDREAMZ

As John Hartson says…you walk into Celtic Park and the Big Cup just stands there and looks at you. Celtic were first and Tommy Gemmell was a fundamental part of it all. He stands there in the sunshine with Mr Stein and the rest of the 'immortals' and will never know what it's like to stand in a cold shadow. His and their place in the history of world football are assured. They have given us the ultimate bragging rights for almost 50 years now. Thank you Tommy, truly.

Thank you, too, sir. I had a ball myself!

QUESTION FROM CHE598

What did Jock Stein have to say in the dressing room after the third match against Racing Club? Did they need to cheat to win the tie?

We were never allowed to play. If we had done so, we would have won the trophy and, rightly, been acclaimed as the best team in the world. They refused to allow us to get into our stride and stopped the game as often as possible. It was most frustrating, to say the least. Big Jock warned us before that game not to get drawn into a kicking match. However, they had the temperament to deal with that and we, being Scottish, hadn't. We have an entirely different mentality. What would the Racing players have done if we had started spitting on them? You would have needed the qualities of a saint to tolerate the treatment we got from them. Jock didn't say too much afterwards. He was left alone with his thoughts.

QUESTION FROM KINGLUBO

BIG TAM G! What a guy! There is only one word to describe him – brilliant! Going back a few years now, but following a Hibs game in Edinburgh, I was invited to a party and when in full swing who

turned up – you guessed it! Big TG! I'm sure, but may be wrong, but did TG not have a bash on the old piano that night? Great night had by all. Memories, eh!! Nostalgia isn't what it used to be!

I might have a go at the piano, but I don't remember it. Are you sure it wasn't that guy Danny Kaye?

QUESTION FROM POGMATHONYAHUN

Greetings Big Tam Gemmell from Germany from another Tam. A wee question you may answer or not and it concerns this iconic photograph.

Now, I know your fellow full-back Mr Craig pretty well as we worked together for a while. I believe you turned up for the photograph sporting a bit of a keeker. He says you refused to tell anybody how this came about and the last time I saw him, some time ago, this was still the case. So my question, Thomas, is: How did you get that black eye? Tommy, don't feel compelled to answer that question. I have met you a few times, but wouldn't expect you to remember me. I once met you at your insurance company office and if I remember correctly you worked with a lad I went to school with - big Jim Stewart. I have many great memories of you and the teams you played in, but an abiding memory is getting into Celtic Park (the-then 'Rangers' end) as this white blur hit the back of the net against Benfica. Take care and looking forward to reading the book.

Thank you, fellow-Tam. Okay, the mystery over the black eye can now be revealed. Actually, I received a dunt in the eye near the end of the Inter match. It didn't begin to actually turn black and blue until a day after the game. The picture in question was taken at Celtic Park only a few days after the Lisbon game. The keeker by then was quite visible. I hope that puts Cairney out of his misery!

QUESTION FROM CELTIC QUICK NEWS

Tommy, would you say that Jim Craig should have stuck to football? What was he like as a dentist as you were a patient of his once I believe?

As a footballer, Cairney was a good dentist and as a dentist, he was a good footballer! Yes, he did once work on a tooth of mine. He tried to put in a filling, but it was still giving me trouble. He had another go at it. I was still in a bit of pain. As he was about to have another go, a fully-qualified dentist had a look and said, 'That's an extraction.' I think he got more points from the Dental Hospital for a filling. I didn't go back!

QUESTION FROM E SNO

Mr Gemmell, I have a copy of Lion Heart (signed by yourself) and, though I never ever saw you play, I regard you as a hero, not just because of your role with our club, but because you stand as an example about what a west coast lad can go on to achieve in the world. My question, in light of the wonderful shenanigans and carousing which the Lions got up to (and which helps make the legend), is, 'Do you think that the side would have won more European Cups if the modern footballing culture requirements of

eating certain foods and avoiding the drink had been the practice then?' Thank you.

I don't think so. The Lisbon Lions had a drink after every game and it didn't do us much harm. However, and I think I am speaking for the entire team, I never had another drop of alcohol after a Wednesday. Thursday and Friday were days of complete abstinence and, by the time Saturday rolled round, we raring to go. The Lions were all good trainers and were so fit I reckon we could have coped with 120-minute games. We were completely focused, too. I really don't believe a change in our diet would have altered a thing.

QUESTION FROM MOUNTBLOW TIM

Welcome to CQN Tommy. I remember being at Kilbowie Park just after Clydebank built their new club house with the unbreakable windows. And you rattled a shot right into these windows. The ones behind the glass all ducked and spilt their beer all over the place. I never laughed so much in my life! Don't suppose you recall this happening?

Me? Hit a shot off target? Are you joking? No, funnily enough, I don't remember this occurrence. I'll have to take your word for it.

QUESTION FROM GERALD766

All Hail The Lions! Welcome, Tommy. I have had the pleasure of meeting you many times. Always the perfect 'spokesman' for the Lions! If I have to give credit to Martin O'Neill, for all the trophies he won for us, and I readily do, then the greatest of these was the re-instatement of the fabled 'Lisbon Lions', to their rightful place at Celtic Park! Following Martin's first Treble, I was party to an 'Evening With The Lions' in my home town of Lurgan. It was left to me to negotiate a 'fee' with two of these giants, only to be told, 'Well, nobody have ever paid us a fee before!' Looking back, did the Lions make enough money for what they achieved for Celtic?

We might have earned more, but a lot of the lads weren't in it for the financial rewards. We enjoyed a night out with the fans just as much they enjoyed spending time with us. It certainly wasn't a hardship mixing with the club's supporters. These guys meant a lot to us and if we could spread the feelgood factor around, then great. Everyone's a winner.

QUESTION FROM BACK TO BASICS – GLASS HALF FULL

Welcome, Tommy. I hope the book sells in the millions. The first football biography I ever read was 'The Big Shot' written by our esteemed guest back in 1968 when he was a mere 25 years old. I must have read it (cover to cover) at least 10 times over the years. It never fails to bring a smile to my face and a lump to my throat. I hope this new book is half as good. Which book of yours is the best?

Well, I really enjoyed putting this one together. I hope you agree there's a bit more humour about it and a few more anecdotes. For instance, I didn't talk about Bestie in the previous books, but got a chance to do so in this one. There's some other stuff about Wee Jinky I didn't dare publish while he was still around! (I know you're up there, Jinky, forgive me!). And performers such as Henrik Larsson, Lubomir Moravcik and others have come on the scene over that period of time and are worth commenting upon. So, all three books have their merits, but I believe 'All The Best' might just edge it.

QUESTION FROM ROCKET MAN

Question for Tommy: 'Would Jock's instructions change from game to game? If the opponents had a tricky winger would he ask you to mind that before you went bombing up the wing or was it just get forward, help the team and have a dig or a cross regardless of who you were playing? Also, did you feel you were a better outside-left than a left-back? If you had your own way would you have liked to have played in a more forward position?'

No, Jock never asked me to mark a specific winger. It didn't matter who it was, Jock expected me to push up the park and force the winger to mark me. That happened all the time. I can tell you a lot of them couldn't handle the defensive side of the game. I was perfectly happy playing full-back where I think my stamina and strength were better suited. I liked to charge forward and there were so many players around with the ability to play the right ball to allow me to have a bash at goal. Goodness knows how many Bobby Murdoch and Wee Bertie set up for me.

QUESTION FROM RALSTON ROW

Tommy, the only poster I had on my wall as a youngster was the one of you taken and distributed by Typhoo tea - an empty Celtic Park and my hero shot as he lined up a volley. What a player! What a shot! Do you remember this poster? How much did you get paid by Typhoo?

I think I got about two bob (10 pence in today's money)! I remember posing for that photograph and feeling a wee bit of a wally. It was obviously staged, but that's the way the Typhoo people wanted it and I had to give them their two bob's worth!

QUESTION FROM PRAECEPTA

My question for Tommy G. I am of the age where I had the pleasure of watching your entire career (and the Lions) at Celtic Park – unforgettable football – brilliant times! You were the Mhan for the penalties. I am hard pressed to remember your thunderbolts missing the target. The only one that comes to mind was one where you hit the ball so hard and it rebounded somewhere close to the centre-circle, No moans from the crowd – we were all dumbstruck by the distance it travelled. Did you ever take a penalty where you deliberately chipped it or put it away with a wee side-foot placement?

I missed one – I think it was against Kilmarnock – when I tried to place it low into the keeper's right hand corner. I missed by a couple of inches and that was the only time I recall failing to hit the target. I believe I missed three from 37 attempts which wasn't too bad a record. I once just about knocked Rangers keeper Norrie Martin into the net in a game at Parkhead. And something similar happened against Donald Mackay at Dundee United. I never chipped them. Mainly, I used to thunder them as hard as I could and hoped the keeper would get out of the way!

QUESTION FROM BURGHBHOY

Tommy, if I was to meet you by chance and offered you a drink would you buy me one back? The reason I ask is I'm a pal of your nephew Davie, we go to the games together on the Winchburgh CSC and I think that in the last 20 years I don't think he's as much as bought me a pint! Only joking BTW. My real question is, 'Did you ever score any tap-ins or were they all rip-roaring efforts?' I've seen videos of your most famous goals and wondered how long were the games held up for to replace the nets?

Most of my goals were from outside the box, but I do recall a close-in header against Rangers in a League Cup-tie at our place in 1969. Their keeper, Gerry Neef, missed a free-kick and I was at the back post to throw myself full-length to nod the ball home. That was a bit of a rarity. By the way, are you sure the bloke who doesn't buy his round is not my brother? Sounds like him!

QUESTION FROM PINTAGUINNESS

Tommy, when you returned to Glasgow after Helmut Haller smacked your boot with his backside, did Big Jock have anything to say?

No, Big Jock said very little. In fact, he didn't even mention the incident. The first time I realised he wasn't too happy was when he left me out of the team for the League Cup Final against St. Johnstone a few days later.

QUESTION FROM EUROCHAMPS67

Tommy G, would you swop places with Celtic's other Tommy G(raveson)? burdsandmillionsbutnaebigcupwinnersmedalCSC

I read recently that the Danish player had made millions in property deals back in his homeland. Good luck to him. I believe he is also married to a topless model. My wife Mary will probably read this, so my answer is, 'Of course, not!'

QUESTIONS FROM EXILED TIM

Apart from winning the Big Cup, what was your favourite game that you played in? And what was your favourite game watching Celtic?

Lisbon is obviously up there, but I keep getting back to that 1965 Scottish Cup win over Dunfermline. That was pivotal to all that followed. It really was a major breakthrough. I had just joined Celtic when they were due to play the famed Real Madrid, Di Stefano, Puskas et al, in a Charity Match at Parkhead. That was a tremendously exciting evening against a very special team. Celtic lost 3-1, but the fans refused to leave the ground until the players took a lap of honour!

QUESTION FROM GALLAGHER

Tommy, I remember well and would look forward to your Monday morning visits to The Twa Tams in Perth around 1976/77 when I believe you were in town doing the banking for the Commercial Hotel you owned in Errol. You enjoyed coming in for a small libation with Martin Sweeney, my late father George and Mary, my mother. I was the teenage scamp who invariably served the drinks. I loved hearing the craic and just being in your presence, great memories. I never quite forgave my parents, though, for not getting in touch with me when I was at Perth College. I came home one teatime to be told that Jinky had spent the afternoon in the Tams, I believe alongside your good self, holding court and on the lash! Do you remember these occasions? Looking forward to your book, Tommy HH and all the best to you and yours, cyber glass raised... Son of Tam.

Aye, Wee Jinky could get me into trouble, too! Yes, I enjoyed those days, they bring back so many happy memories of times spent with smashing people.

QUESTION FROM MIGHTY TIM

Mr Gemmell, in all the games you played in have you ever seen a goalie as scared as St.Etienne's when he faced you taking a penalty? You are a Legend!

Yes, I recall their keeper moving his arms and legs before I took that spot-kick. The goalies weren't allowed to move their feet in those days, they had to be planted on the goal-line, but they could move other parts of their body. We were 2-0 down on aggregate at the time and were drawing 0-0 with the half-time whistle about to blow when we were awarded that penalty-kick. It was absolutely crucial that I stuck it in the pokey. I battered it with everything I had and it went straight up, struck the underside of the crossbar and, thankfully, flew into the net. We scored three after the interval to win 4-2 on aggregate.

QUESTION FROM YOGIY

Hi, Tommy, my favourite Celtic player of all time. What an honour to know that you might read this question! In 1969 I had just got settled when Bertie nudged the ball back to you at a free-kick. I was right behind the shot as it went straight into the Benfica net, first of three in a sublime performance on a beautiful floodlit evening. My simple question is this, 'Were you born with this gift of a thunderous shot or did you work at it for hours on end?

I worked on it every day, as I've answered elsewhere. I always had a natural flair for going forward – that would have come from my days as an amateur outside-right – and I realised if I wasn't going to get my fair share of goals I would have to hit shots from long distance. We had enough born goalscorers in the team such as Joe McBride, John Hughes, Bobby Lennox, Stevie Chalmers and Willie Wallace. They didn't need me in there cluttering up the penalty box and getting in their way! So, I simply developed my shooting from distance and, happily, got a wee bit of success.

QUESTION FROM JUSTAFAN

Tommy, on Scottish referees – where some anti-Celtic?

You might have had some suspicions about a few of them, but, of course, you could never prove anything. I've already talked about Bobby Davidson, the referee from Airdrie. You should never speak ill of the dead, but some of his decision-making was impossible to fathom. There were some good ones, though. Tiny Wharton was fair and so, too, was Hugh Phillips, from Wishaw. So, they weren't all bad!

QUESTIONS FROM TWISTS N TURNS

Which referee was the most anti-Celtic and did you ever get the feeling any ref actually favoured the Hoops? Also which referee was on balance always fair?

See above! Tiny Wharton got most of the big games back then and I remember he sent off Jinky in New Year's Day match against Rangers at Ibrox. Even Perry Mason couldn't have got my wee pal off that charge. He had been taken a bit of stick, as usual, when, for no apparent reason, he flew at their inside-right, an Icelandic player by the name of Therolf Beck. Jinky just about separated his legs from his body. Tiny reached for his pocket when Jinky started to run towards the tunnel shouting back at the referee, 'Ach, put your pencil and notebook away, I know I'm going off!' True story.

QUESTIONS FROM TOOR A LOO

Both domestically and Europe, what did Big Jock and the team hope to achieve privately? By that I mean the behind closed door ambition and not the stories given to the Scottish media from 1965/66 onwards?

As I've answered in a previous question, Big Jock ordered us to win EVERY game. The only one where he was happy to take a draw was the goalless stalemate against Dukla Prague in the second leg of the European Cup. That was a one-off, though. Jock manipulated the media very well back then and would have been a great PR man if he hadn't been so successful as a football manager.

QUESTION FROM CELTIC QUICK NEWS

Willie Wallace reckoned that the Lions team was broken up too soon and that some of the guys who left could have stayed and assisted the Quality Street kids coming through. What is your opinion on this?

I agree with Wispy. I still believe too many of us were shown the door when we still had a lot to offer. Bertie and Stevie were in their thirties when they left, but others such as myself, Jim Craig, Bobby Murdoch, John Clark and Wee Jinky were hardly in our dotage. John Hughes, too. He was very much a member of the first team squad, but he was only 28 when he was sold to Crystal Palace. Wispy went at the same time. I don't think a single player who left Celtic at the time wanted to go. I know I didn't. But I got the idea Big Jock wanted to put together HIS team, a line-up he had put together. He had inherited 10 of the Lisbon Lions team, signing only Wispy. Maybe that's why he broke up that team so quickly.

QUESTION FROM GENE'S A BHOY'S NAME

My question for Tom. You won 18 caps, Billy got 29 and Jinky only 23. Was there a feeling in the dressing room that there was favouritism being shown elsewhere and that playing for Celtic was a disadvantage? And if so why?

Again, We've touched on this subject elsewhere. There was a lot of influence exerted by Rangers back then. The selectors picked the squad and they would often load it up with Ibrox players. Then the manager had to select the team from the squad presented to him. It was all very unusual, but that's the way it was in those unenlightened times, I'm afraid.

QUESTION FROM JOHANN MURDOCH

Welcome to CQN, Tommy. My question is, 'After a Rangers game - how difficult was it to get undressed with wee Willie Henderson in

your back pocket?'

I hope Wee Willie doesn't read this! He was a smashing wee guy and I enjoyed his company off the field, too, which will probably surprise a lot of people. After an Old Firm game, Willie, myself, Bertie, Wispy and Rangers' Ronnie McKinnon would meet up in Reid's Bar in Hope Street, Glasgow. They gave us a room upstairs away from the punters and we had a good wee natter about the game. It was all very civilized!

QUESTIONS FROM PARKHEADCUMSALFORD

Who were the opponents in your debut for the first team for Celtic? What season was it? I am trying to remember when I first saw you playing for the Hoops and can't remember when you took over from? Jim Kennedy or was it Willie O'Neill?

I've already stated my debut was a 5-1 win over Aberdeen at Pittodrie in January 1963. I took over from Jim Kennedy at left-back and they moved him into the left-half slot. Willie O'Neill was around at the time and, of course, played in the first four European Cup-ties in the 1966/67 season when I was in the right-back slot.

QUESTIONS FROM AULDHEID

I have three questions for Tommy. To pound up and down the flanks as you did must have required a certain level of fitness. How was that achieved and are modern-day full-backs as fit or fitter? Did you play in a game at Celtic Park v Dundee United when wee Jimmy sold the United such a dummy he ran off the park and the game slowed to a halt as all players - United and Celts laughed at him. If so, how do you remember it? Finally, who was it you booted in the haw maws in the World Championship Final in Montevideo and a two-part supplementary: Was he chosen at random and happened to be in the wrong place at the wrong time or had you painted a target on said sore area (metaphorically speaking, of course) beforehand and were delivering divine retribution as in 'God that must have hurt'?

It took sheer, hard work to reach a level of fitness where you can last an hour-and-a-half going up and down a wing. There are no short cuts to achieving the sort of stamina required to do that job properly. I'm not sure the current full-backs are fitter. The role has changed, though. Full-backs are expected to be ball-playing defenders. Gone are the days of the full-backs giving the ball welly just to clear their lines. The Wee Jinky incident should be true, but I have to admit I have no recollection of that happening. Nice story, though. And the Racing player was Norberto Raffo and, no, he wasn't selected at random. He had been annoying the hell out of us all day with his repertoire of dirty tricks. That was why I thought I would introduce him to my right boot!

QUESTIONS FROM CELTIC QUICK NEWS

Tommy, in the Lisbon season we were unstoppable – except against Dundee United who beat us home and away. What happened in these games and why where Dundee United able to beat us twice that season? Were they a good side?

Dundee United were a good side, if a little inconsistent. But when they rose to the occasion, they could be excellent. We've no excuses for the Tannadice defeat, but the loss at our place was a complete fluke. Maybe we took our eye off the ball. We were winning 2-1 with the game winding down and they managed to get upfield twice to stick the ball in our net. I don't think anyone at Celtic Park that night could believe what they had just witnessed – including the players or Big Jock.

QUESTION FROM MICK TT

Tommy, do you remember Wee Bert Padden, the former referee who passed away a few years ago? He was a right wee Celtic man, I knew him personally, a gentleman. Apparently, Bert sent off John Greig, Rangers, and Alex Ferguson, Falkirk, in the same match! He was a great and perceptive and brave referee!!! Bert was a lovely man and not that it matters, not an RC. He was a Mason, but Celtic to the core, I'm sure you will remember him as he was of that era. He was everything that our club epitomises, just a Celtic supporter.

Yes, I remember Bert Padden. The players were well aware he was a bit of a Celtic fan, but I don't recall him going out of his way to do us any favours. He did get on very well with Bobby Lennox as they were both from the Ayrshire area. Bobby was a Saltcoats lad and Bert was from Ardrossan. I thought he was a fair referee. I wish there were more like him around today!

QUESTION FROM HOOPY-DO

Tommy, for my 18th birthday I was given sparrows wings and a crow's backside. I had endless fun with those and still use them to this day. So what's the best present you have ever been given?

The gift of life is the best present I have ever received. No-one has ever thought to buy me sparrows wings or a crow's backside!

QUESTIONS FROM MACSPORRAN

Here is my question for Tommy. Denis Law makes reference to you in his own book largely around your comments about his tea-drinking capacity! I realise that there will be lots of players that you played alongside for Scotland, but who was your favourite and why? Is there anyone that you would have liked to play alongside, but didn't get the chance? (either for Scotland or Celtic). Looking forward to the book!

The Lawman would be up there among my favourites. He was an outstanding goalscorer, exceptionally brave and lightning quick. He was a helluva nice guy off the park, too. I would have loved to have played in the same side as Giacinto Facchetti, the Inter Milan left-back. I could play on the right. I thought he was a marvelous player and ahead of his time.

QUESTIONS FROM GORDON

Tommy, thanks for all the wonderful memories. Your goal against Benfica at Celtic Park is one of my all-time favourites! Another, a diving header no less, against Rangers (1872-2012) in the League Cup at Celtic Park is also highly cherished. With all the recent

297

headlines concerning Fraser Forster's clean sheet record, you, of course, have one of your own, don't you? 1969 – v Clyde (Scottish Cup) and v Airdrie in the League Cup. You took over in goal from Ronnie Simpson who had dislocated his shoulder on each occasion. You kept a clean sheet each time! Did you 'volunteer' or were there simply no other candidates for the job? 'All the best', Tommy!

I always fancied myself as a bit of a goalkeeper. I was our official stand-by if one of our keepers got injured. I would go into goal twice a week during training sessions and the players would spend about 10 minutes firing shots at me just to keep my eye in. As I recall, there weren't too many other volunteers for the job!

QUESTION FROM THE HONEST MISTAKE LOVES BEING FIRST

Tommy, how hard did you find the transition to civvy street, going from playing professional football at the highest level in front of crowds of tens of thousands to being part of that crowd yourself?

I can't lie, I found it extremely difficult to adapt to public life. I was a bit lost. Football had been my entire life and, suddenly, it was gone. I wasn't quite prepared for it. It took me awhile to get to grips with the real world. I got there eventually, thank goodness, but it was a massive step into the unknown.

QUESTION FROM MURDOCH McGRAIN LARSSON

Tommy, there have been a few comments about you scoring in two European Cup Finals. If my memory serves me right, you also scored in the World Club Championship in the away leg. Is this correct and how did this goal compare to the other two?

Yes, it's correct, but it doesn't really compare with the goals against Inter Milan Feyenoord. For a start, those two came from outside the box and the one against Racing Club came from the penalty spot. Mind you, I skelped that ball from 12 yards every bit as hard as I had the other two.

QUESTIONS FROM CELTIC QUICK NEWS

Tommy, you were in Seville in 2003 for the UEFA Cup Final. What did you make of the Celtic support at that Final and also what did the Lions think about the individual performance of Henrik Larsson that night?

Henrik was amazing, simply outstanding. I've said elsewhere that I didn't think Inter Milan keeper Sarti deserved to be on the losing team after his display against us in Lisbon. I could say the same about Henrik against Porto. He was inspirational, but, unfortunately, the breaks went against Celtic in Seville. By the way, I found out that evening what it must have been like for a Celtic fan in Lisbon. It was special even though the result went against us. The supporters were an absolute credit to themselves and the club.

QUESTION FROM JACKIE MAC

Tommy are you still in love with football?

Of course. Once that game gets a grip of you it never lets go. I don't get to as many games as I would like to these days, but when I can I'm there and supporting Celtic. Once a Celtic man, always a Celtic man!

QUESTIONS FROM SIXOCLOCKATTHECHAPEL

Tommy Gemmell. The very name oozes Celtic! All the best Big Mhan with the latest book – I'm sure it will be a big hit. Two questions for you. 'What took you so long getting on to Celtic Quick News?' And did Paul suggest that you include at least one chapter of the new book on Amortisation! Can you explain this to me, please? Thanks for all your heroic efforts in and for the Hoops. Legend!

I was brought up in the belief that it is always nice to be asked and when the CQN boys came on the scene I was only too happy to come on board. Funnily enough, Paul never mentioned anything about financial matters when we spoke. Wonder why!

QUESTION FROM CALTON TONGUES

Hail. HailTommy Gemmell! What are your thoughts on Bairds Bar being turned into a Carpet Shop and will you get a 67% discount? CarpetrightCSC.

I used to pop in for a quick pint with the owner, Tom Carberry. Wee Bertie used to frequent it, too, I believe. Willie O'Neill used to run the shop. Good pub and sorry to hear it had closed down. Not too sure about the 67% discount. Maybe I'll give it a try!

QUESTION FROM CAN I HAVE RASPBERRY ON THAT CHAMPIONS LEAGUE ICE CREAM

Tommy. I have been thinking all day about a question to ask you but was too young to remember about specific games or incidents. However, I have a question that I asked Bertie a couple of years ago. Tommy, what's it like to be a Lisbon Lion, simples?

It's wonderful to go down in history. People will always be able to look at the team and watch the game and see what we did that day. It was so nice to be part of it all.

QUESTION FROM CELTIC QUICK NEWS

Regarding the consequences of the World Championships battles with Racing. What do you think of this? 'There's no doubt as a result of this ill-fated competition Jock Stein was removed from the New Year Honours list. Stein had been expected to receive an honour for leading Celtic to a famous European Cup win in Lisbon over Internazionale in May 1967. But a letter sent by the Scottish Office to Prime Minister Harold Wilson in 1970 revealed how Stein's name was removed from the list. This only became known in 2007 under the freedom of information act. It read, 'When Glasgow Celtic became the first British club to win the European Cup in 1967, we failed to recognise this with an honour for Stein to whom, as manager, a great deal of the credit was due. His name was I understand removed from the New Year's Honours list

because of the unfortunate events in South America. The next year when Manchester United won the European Cup an immediate knighthood went to Matt Busby in the birthday list. Had we been able to move as quickly the previous year, Stein would have had his honour before the troubles in Argentina.'" Was this fair on Jock Stein?

Honestly, I don't think not getting a knighthood would have bothered Big Jock. If he was upset in any way, no-one detected at the club. He was a very matter-of-fact down-to-earth sort of guy. He was awarded the CBE, of course, but I don't recall him ever making a big thing of that. We'll never know if he felt let down, but my feeling is that it didn't really mean that much to him.

QUESTION FROM CELTICROLLERCOASTER

Tommy, what was your best European goal scored? Milan, Lisbon or another one?

I believe the one I got against Zurich – our first-ever European Cup goal – in the First Round tie at Parkhead was the best. It was goalless around the hour mark when I got forward, steadied myself and hit the perfect shot from long range into the roof of their net. Lisbon and Milan were special, but I think that was the best of the lot – even better than the belter against Benfica and that's saying something.

QUESTION FROM FRED C DODDS

The Jungle at its best...what was it like from the pitch?

Absolutely magic. What a feeling when those fans in there were in full voice and roaring you on. The reception they gave the team before a game and the encouragement throughout the 90 minutes were appreciated by every single player. They were a special lot in The Jungle.

QUESTIONS FROM 50 SHADES OF GREEN

Tommy, as a tough-tackling full-back, how do you feel about the introduction of the sin bin idea that has been spoken about recently? Do you think it would give referees too much or, should I say, even more influence on the outcome of a match? And, just for fun, which of the Lisbon Lions would have suffered the most had it been about in the sixties? Also, like to thank you for taking the time awhile ago to sign a book I was buying for my oldest son. He was too young to recognise you, but after I explained to him about you he was delighted! Cheers, Tommy.

Any introduction of the sin bin would put the refs under a microscope in an era where there appears to be TV cameras all over the place. I don't see it ever being implemented. It might just be a little too complicated to exercise and would certainly interrupt the flow of play. Wee Jinky might have had to sit out half a game each week!

QUESTIONS FROM FRITZSONG

Tommy, Celtic signed a player called Pat McMahon in 1969. He played pretty well and scored a few in his first ten games. Why did Jock Stein sell him? Indeed why did he sign him? I'd always been curious about McMahon because I found his brief but successful Celtic career more than a bit curious. From the scraps I gathered: he was from Croy, then a seminarian at the Gregorian in Rome. When he returned to Scotland he played Junior football before joining Celtic. After leaving Aston Villa he emigrated to Canada where he had some success as a folk singer. Do you remember him, Tommy? Also, why did he sell Willie Wallace, John Hughes and Tommy Gemmell? Mistakes?

Pat McMahon was actually Celtic's first signing after we won the European Cup, so he arrived two years before 1969. Big Jock signed him from Kilsyth Rangers and he was an old-fashioned inside-right with a lot of nice touches. We had heard he had trained as a priest. He was very quiet in the dressing room and chose to read a book rather than play cards with his team-mates when we were travelling to away games. On the field, he was a bit hot and cold and Big Jock hated inconsistency in any player. That's probably why he let him go to Aston Villa two years later. As for myself, Wispy and Yogi leaving the club, I've already had my say on that matter. I'll repeat, though – I think we were all offloaded far too early.

NO QUESTIONS FROM THE BOTTOM LINE IS

Tam, a real honour to address you, sir. You brought us so much pleasure over the years it's not really possible to thank you enough. Yes, I was one of those lucky enough to witness that great team from the very start. Hard act to follow? No-one could; no-one did. No-one will. Not got a question for you, but do have a great memory of you in Milan Airport after that game. It was chaotic. There was a flight controllers' strike and there was no info about flights so every time one landed there was a rush on to the tarmac to try and get on it. Some guys ended up in Rotterdam and some Dutch guys in Prestwick. Anyway, you appeared, striding through the concourse swinging an umbrella. Seriously. It wasn't even raining outside! Even the Dutch recognised you – you were pretty famous, Tam – and the clamour died down. You strode up to the automatic doors and pointed the brolly at the sensor like Steed off the Avengers. The doors parted. We all fell apart. The Dutch guys, too. You grinned and disappeared into the night. OK, we'd lost but, somehow it wasn't the end of the world. Thanks, Tommy.

Yes, I remember that. Haven't a clue where the brolly came from, though. It was bedlam in that airport and no-one knew what was going on. Needless to say, I was happy to get out of Milan and head for home. Not one of my most memorable trips.

QUESTIONS FROM KITALBA

Mr. Gemmell (Tommy), two questions. In various books it is recorded that certain players in the Lions era, and team, were not of the Catholic faith and were subject to 'Catholic' banter. For the record, did you ever perceive this banter to be threatening with a sectarian bias (in any way)? Secondly. I was lucky. I started

watching Celtic back in '63, I've always been of the mind that the players then were not as tough and hardy as the players in the 40s and 50s (although I based that on my dad's and his friends reports and memories) and the players of the modern era, let's say are a wee bit plasticine-ie compared to the players of your era. Would you agree with that? Also, playing in a team full of such talent and confidence and bravery, were there many, if any, training ground punch–ups? Also, the club always gave you a club blazer with crest, and grey trousers, were they really too tight back then to buy you an overcoat or a army surplus parka, after all, it was Baltic Glasgow not Corfu?

I talk about the 'religious banter', as you put it, in the book. Actually, there wasn't anything that was worth bothering too much about. As they say, humour is individual and what someone thinks is funny won't necessarily make someone else smile. Didn't see much of football in the 40s or 50s – what age do you think I am? – so can't really comment. One thing is certain, though, is that there is a lot more play-acting in today's game. We didn't have too many divers when I was playing. Training ground punch-ups? There might have been a bit of friction sometimes, but nothing to write home about. And I was quite happy with my blazer and flannels, thank you very much.

QUESTION FROM CELTIC QUICK NEWS

Tommy, what do you make of the criticisms that Ian Young made in his book on prior claims you made in an earlier biog? Where you made a fairly off-the-cuff remark that has been used as a totem by Rangers supporters to accuse Celtic of what they were always guilty of. Could you set the record straight on this?

Yes, things can get a bit exaggerated in this game and quotes bent out of shape. These things happen. I've made my feelings clear on this. Ian Young and I were Protestants at a predominantly Catholic club although it must be remembered that Celtic did always sign Protestants – Jock Stein, for a start. There were a few comments in the dressing room, but, upon reflection, I can look back and smile. It was probably just someone trying to be smart. One of my biggest pals at the club back then was Wee Jinky and I don't remember either of us ever talking about religion. Billy McNeill and Stevie Chalmers were big mates, too, and they were Catholics. We were Celtic players and we only ever discussed the club and our hopes for the future.

QUESTION FROM SEOC COLLA

TG, you seem to have been temperamentally suited to a successful material life in the public eye. if you hadn't been a top footballer, what alternate life would you have sought?

Good question. This will probably make the media people laugh, but I wouldn't have minded a career as a football writer. That would have been interesting, writing about the game rather than actually playing it. My co-author Alex Gordon has warned me I might have been expected to spend some time in pubs if I had chosen a profession in journalism. I would have given it a try! Actually, I was a time-served electrician at Ravenscraig, so, in all probability, I might have become a sparky if I hadn't make the grade at Celtic. Perish the thought!

QUESTION FROM CHARLES CAVANAGH

Tommy, do you remember playing at centre-forward in Kearney High School, New Jersey in the 1966 tour? I spoke to you about it in Jerez before the Seville game. Of course, you told me you played a stormer. Was Big Jock trying out ideas then? Also, did that trip help cement relationships in the team and pave the way for success in Lisbon?

I pestered Big Jock into playing my as the main striker against the Hamilton Select side and I scored a hat-trick as we won 11-0! I can only think I inspired the team to new heights in that match. Either that, or the Hamilton Select was made up of waiters from our hotel! No, it wasn't an experiment by the manager, it was just a little fun. I was more than happy to return to left-back. And I have no doubt that the trip did, indeed, cement friendships and relationships within the players. It was a masterstroke to put the tour together and we really got to know one another that little bit better. Yes, I'm sure that was the first step towards Lisbon.

NO QUESTIONS FROM WEERON

Just wanted to pass on the good wishes of all at the Ottawa Celtic Supporters Club, Tommy. We have great memories of your time here. Wishing you and yours all the very best. Can't wait to read the book. Hail, Hail, Ronnie.

Thanks for the kind wishes, Ronnie, and I hope you enjoy 'All The Best' as much as I did putting it together.

LAST WORD FROM MARRAKESH EXPRESS

All the best TG. You scored the most important goal in Celtic's history.

I'm feeling a lump in my throat after all this. I can only say a massive 'thank you' to one and all. It's been an absolute pleasure going through the emails. They've brought back so many fabulous memories. So, to Celtic supporters everywhere, let me sign off with this heartfelt message, 'All the best!'

YOGI BARE: THE JOHN HUGHES STORY

THE LIFE AND TIMES OF A CELTIC LEGEND

John Hughes, the original Yogi of sixties' fame, is undeniably a Celtic legend, his place in the club's proud heritage earned after eleven extraordinary years as a player in the green and white hoops.

This is the powerful, insightful and long-awaited autobiography of the player who can claim to be the seventh highest goalscorer in Celtic's history.

It's the explosive tale of a raw youngster coming into the first team at the start of what eventually became a golden era for the club. It's the remarkable chronicle of how life changed so dramatically for an individual who became a cult figure with the Celtic support.

Yogi pulls no punches as he talks about the secret Jock Stein kept from him. And the dreadful day he knew his Celtic career was over.

There's humour in his first meeting with Jimmy Johnstone and his enduring friendship with the controversial, colourful character who was voted the Greatest-Ever Celtic Player.

The Hoops icon tells of the game where he should have been sent off in an Old Firm flare-up after an 'ugly incident' with a Rangers player. And the unfortunate repercussions for the referee who didn't punish him.

He tells of being driven to drink because of the pressure of playing for Celtic and why he refused the lure of the lira to knock back a massive move to an Italian team, one of the biggest names in world football.

Yogi talks candidly about what it meant to play for Scotland and the personal insult that upset him. And he reveals what it felt like to play for another club after believing he would play all his days for his beloved Celtic.

Why did manager Jimmy McGrory not offer any advice after his breakthrough at Celtic as a seventeen year old? What was the real reason he didn't play in Lisbon? What happened when he was banished in the brawl of Montevideo? Why does he refuse to watch the 1970 European Cup Final? What does he think of Celtic today?

Yogi answers them all - and more. It's the unmissable life story of a true Celtic legend. Don't miss it!

PUBLISHED IN APRIL 2014 and available to order from www.celticquicknews.co.uk

WILLIE WALLACE – HEART OF A LION

THE LIFE AND TIMES OF LISBON LION WILLIAM WALLACE

With a foreword from Rod Stewart and a tribute from respected broadcaster Archie MacPherson, Heart of a Lion has two main sections. The first and most important is the autobiography of Celtic's "lost Lion" Willie Wallace. The second is a career review written by the leading online Celtic writer Brogan, Rogan, Trevino and Hogan who puts into context just how incredible a footballer Willie Wallace actually was.

After a hugely successful career in Scottish football, plus a cameo role in the English first division, Willie Wallace made a new life for his family in Australia.

In 2013 Willie and his wife Olive returned to Scotland to publish his biography on CQN Books. Willie reflected, "in my mind, I raised a glass in tribute to the many people who had helped me in my life which had begun in fairly humble circumstances in a small town just outside the Glasgow city boundaries."

From there we are invited to join Wille on a journey of a lifetime.

From Kirkintilloch to the life of a professional footballer criss-crossing Scotland and Europe as part of the all-conquering Celtic squad of the late 1960's, to the decision to make a post-retirement home under the warmAustralian sun.

Scotland has had two famous men named William Wallace. Heart of a Lion reveals the journey of Celtic's favourite Wallace who turns out to be no less colourful, courageous and loyal that that of his predecessor.

PUBLISHED IN MAY 2013 by CQN Books and available to order from www.celticquicknews.co.uk

SEVILLE – THE CELTIC MOVEMENT

WRITTEN BY JIM MCGINLEY AND CONTRIBUTORS AND FRIENDS OF CELTIC QUICK NEWS. EDITED BY DAVID FAULDS.

Seville – The Celtic Movement is the story of over 80,000 Celtic supporters who travelled to Seville in May 2003 for the UEFA Cup Final between Celtic and Porto. Many of these supporters didn't have match tickets and most didn't really care. They weren't going to support Celtic, rather they were going to BE Celtic. Over 50,000 supporters watched the final in various parks and bars in Seville.

Inside the Estadio Olimpico the Celtic support filled over 80% of the stadium and produced an amazing atmosphere roaring the team on in the intense, dry heat on this early summer evening in Spain's hottest city. This book is the collective tale of the Celtic support in Seville. It is packed full of supporters' stories and captures perfectly the very special relationship that exists between Celtic Football Club and her wonderful supporters.

With 64 pages of colour photography, supplied by the supporters, the book is just as colourful within the text as the heart warming stories, the sheer humour, some joy and some real sadness, not about the football mind you. If you want to read a book about the ninety minutes plus extra time then you should go elsewhere. This isn't book isn't about a football match. It is about a football support, a magical football club and a very special week in the lives of this huge support when they got together, had a party that was so big it made news all over the world. The say if there is going to be a show then the Glasgow Celtic will be there. In Seville in May 2003, the Glasgow Celtic were indeed there and what a party they had!

SEVILLE – THE CELTIC MOVEMENT was published in March 2014 by CQN Books. The book is available now to order from www.celticquicknews.co.uk and from Celtic stores and all good booksellers.